MORALITY, REFLECTION, AND IDEOLOGY

How FAR can our moral beliefs and practices survive the reflective understanding we have of them? This is the question posed by *Morality, Reflection, and Ideology*, thus initiating a discussion in which the concept of the moral or ethical and those of reflection and ideology appear together for the illumination of each. The intricate relations between these concepts are explored by eminent contributors from the UK and the US, including Bernard Williams. They demonstrate how this question arises in a variety of different areas of philosophy, from the work of a particular historical figure to the metaphysics of morals, and from moral psychology to ethical and political theory.

Morality, Reflection, and Ideology

Edited by
EDWARD HARCOURT

OXFORD
UNIVERSITY PRESS

OXFORD

UNIVERSITY PRESS

Great Clarendon Street, Oxford OX2 6DP

Oxford University Press is a department of the University of Oxford.
It furthers the University's objective of excellence in research, scholarship,
and education by publishing worldwide in

Oxford New York

Athens Auckland Bangkok Bogotá Buenos Aires Calcutta
Cape Town Chennai Dar es Salaam Delhi Florence Hong Kong Istanbul
Karachi Kuala Lumpur Madrid Melbourne Mexico City Mumbai
Nairobi Paris São Paulo Shanghai Singapore Taipei Tokyo Toronto Warsaw

with associated companies in Berlin Ibadan

Oxford is a registered trade mark of Oxford University Press
in the UK and certain other countries

Published in the United States
by Oxford University Press Inc., New York

British Library Cataloguing in Publication Data

Data available

Library of Congress Cataloging in Publication Data
Morality, reflection, and ideology / edited by Edward Harcourt.
p. cm.
Includes bibliographical references and index.
Contents: The Marxist critique of morality and the theory of ideology / Michael Rosen—
Ideology, projection, and cognition / A. W. Price—Is morality a ruling illusion? / Anthony
Skillen—Confidence and irony / Miranda Fricker—Morality, ideology, and reflection, or the
duck sits yet / Peter Railton—Naturalism and genealogy / Bernard Williams—Liberal
double-mindedness / John Kekes.
1. Ethics. 2. Ideology. I. Harcourt, Edward.
BJ1012. M6357 2000   170—dc21   00-056655
ISBN 0-19-825056-8

1 3 5 7 9 10 8 6 4 2

Typeset in Times
by Best-set Typesetter Ltd., Hong Kong
T.J. International Ltd
Padstow, Cornwall

ACKNOWLEDGEMENTS

This collection of papers overlaps, though it does not coincide, with the set of papers given at the Morality and Ideology conference held at Lady Margaret Hall, Oxford, in 1996. The conference could not have taken place without the generous assistance of the Mind Association, the British Academy, the Board of the Faculty of Literae Humaniores, Oxford University, and Lady Margaret Hall. Thanks are also due, for their help either with the conference or with the present volume, to at least the following: John Burrow, Roger Crisp, Jane Day, Elizabeth Frazer, Miranda Fricker, Brad Hooker, F. M. Kamm, Erin Kelly, Jonathan Lear, Sabina Lovibond, Lois McNay, Peter Momtchiloff, David Owen, Gillian Peele, Simon Price, Michael Rosen, and Mark Sacks. Special thanks, finally, to Bernard Williams, both for many helpful conversations and because it was in thinking about his work as much as anything else that the idea for this collection originated.

CONTENTS

NOTES ON THE CONTRIBUTORS

MIRANDA FRICKER is Lecturer in Philosophy and British Academy Postdoctoral Fellow at Heythrop College, University of London. She is co-editor, with Jennifer Hornsby, of *The Cambridge Companion to Feminism in Philosophy* (2000) and has published articles in epistemology and social philosophy. Her book *Epistemic Injustice* is forthcoming with Oxford University Press.

EDWARD HARCOURT is Lecturer in Philosophy at the University of Kent at Canterbury. He has published articles in ethics and philosophical logic, and on Wittgenstein.

JOHN KEKES is Professor of Philosophy and Public Policy at the State University of New York at Albany. His most recent books are *A Case for Conservatism* (1998) and *Against Liberalism* (1997).

A. W. PRICE is a Reader in Philosophy at Birkbeck College, London. He is the author of *Love and Friendship in Plato and Aristotle* (1989) and *Mental Conflict* (1995).

PETER RAILTON is Nelson Professor of Philosophy at the University of Michigan, Ann Arbor. His areas of specialization are ethics and the philosophy of science.

MICHAEL ROSEN is Fellow and Tutor in Philosophy at Lincoln College, Oxford. He has published extensively on topics in German philosophy as well as in political philosophy more generally. His most recent book is *On Voluntary Servitude: False Consciousness and the Theory of Ideology* (Cambridge: Polity Press, 1996).

ANTHONY SKILLEN is Reader in Philosophy at the University of Kent at Canterbury. Since his book *Ruling Illusions* in 1977 he has written on many issues in social and practical philosophy.

BERNARD WILLIAMS is Monroe Deutsch Professor of Philosophy at the University of California, Berkeley, and a Fellow of All Souls College, Oxford.

Introduction

Edward Harcourt

I

It is common enough to find ideology mentioned side by side with the aesthetic in theoretical discussions, from the more or less straightforwardly Marxist to more subtle recent elaborations.[1] So it is surprising, on the face of it, that the notions of ideology and of the moral or ethical are discussed together comparatively rarely, and in the mainstream of analytic moral philosophy (as far as I know) hardly at all,[2] and this despite the fact that analytic philosophy is often to be found working with an undifferentiated idea of 'value' designed to encompass aesthetic and ethical value alike. One reason for the anomaly may be that the concept of ideology has hitherto been at home mainly in social science, or in philosophical traditions other than the analytic,[3] while moral philosophy—some would say moral thought more generally, at least thought in which the moral figures under that description—can seem, no doubt for good enough reasons of history and culture, to

---

[1] In the first category, see e.g. John Berger, *Ways of Seeing* (London: BBC Books; Harmondsworth: Penguin, 1972); in the second, Terry Eagleton, *The Ideology of the Aesthetic* (Oxford: Blackwell, 1990).

[2] Though see Anthony Skillen, *Ruling Illusions* (Hassocks: Harvester Press, 1977; Aldershot: Gregg Revivals, 1993); K. Nielsen and S. Patten (eds.), *Marx and Morality, Canadian Journal of Philosophy*, suppl. vol. 7 (1981); Steven Lukes, 'Marxism, Morality and Justice', in G. H. R. Parkinson (ed.), *Marx and Marxisms* (Cambridge: Cambridge University Press, 1982); K. Nielsen, 'Marxism and the Moral Point of View', *American Philosophical Quarterly*, 24 (1987), 295–306; Alan Ryan, 'Justice, Exploitation, and the End of Morality', in J. D. G. Evans (ed.), *Moral Philosophy and Contemporary Problems* (Cambridge: Cambridge University Press, 1987); Allen Wood, 'Marx against Morality', in P. Singer (ed.), *A Companion to Ethics* (Oxford: Blackwell, 1991).

[3] This is not to say that the concept of ideology has not been investigated within analytic philosophy: see, notably, G. A. Cohen, *Karl Marx's Theory of History: A Defence* (Oxford: Oxford University Press, 1978); Jon Elster, *Making Sense of Marx* (Cambridge: Cambridge University Press, 1985); Raymond Geuss, *The Idea of a Critical Theory* (Cambridge: Cambridge University Press, 1981).

be a pursuit local to those parts of the English-speaking world
where the analytic tradition prevails. As to reflection, though it has
gained a wider currency in recent years chiefly through the work
of Bernard Williams,[4] in anything like a technical usage the term
has been more at home in the works of the Frankfurt School[5]
than in analytic moral philosophy. This collection of papers aims
to rectify this situation, and to initiate a discussion in which the
concept of the moral or ethical and those of reflection and ideology appear together for (it is to be hoped) the illumination of each.
This is not to claim, however, that all the issues addressed in this
collection are entirely new. For though it is comparatively rare, as
I have said, for analytic moral philosophy to mention ideology, or
reflection, these terms are well adapted to express what are in fact
already some of its central preoccupations. Once these preoccupations are so expressed, it should be possible to make connections
between them more easily visible, and thus to carry them forward
in new directions.

If there is an issue that unifies the preoccupations in question, it
is the issue of the reflective stability[6] of our moral beliefs and practices, though, as should become apparent in what follows, that issue
arises in different areas of moral philosophy in different ways.
The question which contributors to this collection were asked to
address, therefore, was this: how far can our moral beliefs and practices survive the reflective understanding we have of them? And
they were invited to approach this question with the concept of ideology in mind. 'Reflective understanding' was to be taken broadly:
certainly to encompass reflection on the metaphysics of morals, for
example, or on the nature of moral language; but also reflection on
morality which is itself moral, whether or not in the form of the
construction of an ethical theory; and reflection, whether from the
armchair or informed by empirical research, on the causes and
origins of moral thought. The concept of ideology, meanwhile, was
introduced, rather minimally, as mystification or motivated lack
of transparency. (I shall have more to say about it shortly.) Thus

---

[4] See notably Williams, *Ethics and the Limits of Philosophy* (London: Fontana,
1985), *passim*.
[5] For the concept of reflection and the Frankfurt School, see Geuss, *The Idea of
a Critical Theory*.
[6] I adapt the term 'reflective stability' from Williams, Ch. 6 in this volume,
Sect. 6.

to the extent that a moral belief or practice fails to survive when reflectively understood—to the extent, that is, that its survival requires that it not be understood, if not that it actually be *mis-understood*—the belief or practice would stand revealed as a piece of ideology.

The contributors have approached the above question from a variety of different directions, either focusing on the work of a particular historical figure (Rosen), or focusing chiefly on moral metaphysics (Price, Fricker), epistemology (Railton), or psychology (Skillen), or chiefly on the explanation of moral thought (Williams) or on the fundamentals of political theory (Kekes), and of course these directions of approach coincide in many places. Rather than baldly summarizing the papers which follow one after the other (and they in any case speak clearly enough for themselves), my aim in the rest of this Introduction is to sketch in a little more detail what I take to be the shape of the terrain they cover, introducing them along the way and indicating some of the areas where the contributors are in at least notional dialogue.

2

First, then, a word about the notion of ideology, which I hope will show why it is less out of place in analytic moral philosophy than its infrequent occurrence there might make one think. The notion is, familiarly enough, a contested one. As Miranda Fricker notes in Chapter 4 in this volume, some post-modernists reject it on the grounds that ideology-critique must invoke the norm of truth. Other objections to the notion have no quarrel with truth itself, but argue that deploying the notion of ideology is unlikely to lead us to it.[7] But even among those who agree that the notion of ideology is a serviceable one, there is disagreement as to what exactly it amounts to. There is disagreement, for example, about the sorts of *item* that can count as ideological: beliefs only, or desires and beliefs, or some broader category such as the 'social imaginary' which includes beliefs and desires but does not reduce to them?[8]

---

[7] For scepticism about the notion that has nothing to do with rejecting the norm of truth, see Elster, *Making Sense of Marx*, ch. 1.4 and ch. 8.

[8] For the social imaginary, see John B. Thompson, *Studies in the Theory of Ideology* (Cambridge: Polity Press, 1984), introd. and ch. 1.

There is disagreement also as to whether to describe an item as ideological is to describe it as false. Some, emphasizing Marx's association between ideology and illusion, have said it is, and if they are right, that will evidently have a bearing on the first topic of disagreement, assuming at any rate that of the items mentioned above only beliefs are truth-apt. But the association with illusion is just one of many sometimes conflicting strands in Marx's writing on ideology,[9] and in any case we have good reason to seek to develop the concept beyond Marx.

As I introduced it in the previous section, ideology is a relatively weak notion: a form of consciousness—to pick a term deliberately neutral between beliefs, desires, and the rest—counts as ideological in this weak sense if its survival requires that it not be understood by those whose consciousness it is. In a way this weak notion will do perfectly well for the purposes of this collection since, being weak, it is also inclusive. However, I would like to set alongside it two stronger ways in which ideology might be understood, not in order to argue for either one of them but because it will help to show how the notion connects with other current philosophical concerns, both ethical and epistemological.

Many writers who have turned away from the idea that ideology implies falsity have connected ideology with *explanation*: consciousness counts as ideological in virtue of its having a certain type of explanation.[10] The type of explanation in question, however, may be more or less narrowly defined. In G. A. Cohen's theory, consciousness is ideological if it both sustains domination and exists because it sustains it. Thus consciousness counts as ideological only if it has a certain type of functional explanation. This gives us a strong understanding of the notion of ideology, the strongest of the three I shall mention. But this understanding is open to question on more than one count.

First, there has been much discussion as to whether there are in fact any self-standing functional explanations, and even if there are, whether there are any in social science. Secondly, it seems plausi-

---

[9] On this point, see Michael Rosen, *On Voluntary Servitude* (Cambridge: Polity Press, 1996), 24–5, and, for Marx on religion and ideological illusion, ibid. 175–9.
[10] For this type of view, see e.g. Cohen, *Karl Marx's Theory of History*; Denise Meyerson, *False Consciousness* (Oxford: Oxford University Press, 1991); and Ch. 5 in this volume, by Peter Railton.

ble to claim—and it often is claimed—that belief in the divine right of kings is (or has historically been) part of the ideology of absolute monarchy. But it is on the face of it equally plausible to claim that belief in Rawls's Difference Principle is part of the ideology of Fabian social democracy, or that belief in an ideal of absolute equality of wealth is part of the ideology of an egalitarian state, even if those who have made such claims have preferred to speak more in terms of the genealogy of morals than of the critique of ideology.[11] But it will be harder to claim, especially perhaps in the last case, that the ideology sustains domination of one social group by another, and certainly harder to claim that it sustains domination by a social élite. Worries about functional explanation aside, then, these cases may point towards a notion of ideology on which consciousness counts as ideological only if it sustains certain social relations and exists because it sustains them, whether or not those social relations are relations of domination.

But pressure may also be put on Cohen's understanding of ideology from a different direction. To confine the discussion for simplicity's sake momentarily to beliefs, it is troubling to discover that beliefs which (in the appropriate context) seem to be well grounded turn out to owe their acceptance not to anything which in fact rationalizes them but merely (say) to the relative social positions of those who hold them. And because it *is* troubling to discover that, it is worth having a label for the kind of beliefs they are thus discovered to be. For some writers—Peter Railton in this collection among them—that label is precisely 'ideology':[12] omitting some necessary qualifications, consciousness counts as ideological on this account if what explains its existence does not also rationalize it so that, where the consciousness consists of beliefs, this will amount to the beliefs' being held for reasons incidental to their truth, if indeed they are true.[13]

The notion of ideology just explained falls in between the first, weak notion of ideology which I introduced and Cohen's notion. It is stronger than the first notion for the following reason: if a

---

[11] For Nietzsche as a critic of ideology, see e.g. Railton, Ch. 5, Sect. 1.

[12] For others, the relevant notion is rather false consciousness: see e.g. Rosen, *On Voluntary Servitude*, 262–70.

[13] Where the consciousness consists of something other than beliefs—again, if non-beliefs can count as ideological items—the notion of non-rationalizing explanation will need to be developed in a different direction, as Railton does in his paper for 'the attitude of valuing' (Sect. 5).

rational subject must suspend a belief if he comes to realize that he holds it merely for reasons incidental to its truth, then the belief is such that the believer must fail to understand why he has it if it is to survive, and thus counts as an ideological form of consciousness in the first, weakest sense. But there may be failures of understanding or of transparency which do not amount to ignorance of a non-rationalizing explanation: ignorance might be of a conflicting *rationalizing* explanation, and some examples appear below. At the same time it is weaker than Cohen's notion because the explanation of consciousness on this in-between notion, unlike Cohen's, need not be a functional explanation for the consciousness to count as ideological. Moreover, it is worth noting that on the strongest notion of ideology, the main reason for combating ideological forms of consciousness seems to be ethical: if one has reason to combat domination, that is an ethical reason, and a reason to combat domination will, on the strong notion, be a reason to combat ideology. On the in-between notion, however, what gives the notion of ideology its critical edge seems to have less to do with ethics than with general epistemology. For it has been said to be a rule of general epistemology that if a rational subject comes to believe that his acceptance of some proposition is for reasons that are incidental to its truth (beliefs based on veridical hallucinations being a favourite non-political example), the subject will suspend belief about it.[14]

3

Having done something towards locating ideology on a more general conceptual map, I want to turn to the relations between morality and the concepts both of reflection and of ideology, begin-

---

[14] See Michael Ayers, *Locke* (London: Routledge, 1991), i. 147–8: 'determinants of belief . . . dissociated from its propositional content cannot be acknowledged by us as believers. . . . In so far as we doubt that grounds wholly determine our belief, so far is our belief itself subjectively insecure.' (I am indebted for this reference to Ward Jones.) Compare Geuss's idea of ideologies as 'systems of beliefs and attitudes accepted by agents for reasons or motives which those agents *could* not acknowledge' (Geuss, *The Idea of a Critical Theory*, 20). Not every belief than falls victim to this rule counts as ideological, as the case of belief based on veridical hallucination shows. But what makes the difference will be to do with factors such as the content of the belief, presumably, rather than with the epistemology of the situation.

ning with some non-moral cases of the destructive effects of reflective understanding.

In Chapter 3 Anthony Price cites the case of first love: if it is part
of first love to think of the loved one as uniquely deserving of the
emotion, then first love cannot survive when understood, since to
understand it would be to come to see the accidental nature of its
object. For another case of a belief or practice's failing to survive
reflective understanding, consider the fate which religion, and in
particular the Christian religion, suffers under the kind of understanding of it recommended in various forms by Feuerbach, by
Marx, by Freud, and many others, that God is in some sense a projection of characteristics which in reality belong to human beings.
This understanding of religion may or may not be right. But
suppose one comes to believe that it is. If projectivism implies a
revision of the content of religious utterance, so what is believed
in is no more than what is projected, there is the problem that most
religious believers do not regard themselves as fit objects of
worship. And if projectivism doesn't imply any such revision,
religious observance involves the knowing avowal of what one
believes to be false. So having accepted the projectivist view of religion, it will require—to say the least—some mental agility to carry
on just as before. And much the same goes for the—possibly complementary—understanding of religion recommended by functionalist anthropologists, that the function of religion is not to relate
man to the divine but to express or promote social solidarity. This
is not to say that some people haven't tried to go on as before,
whether for the sake of some further end such as social solidarity,
or in order to rationalize a set of beliefs to which they find themselves inescapably attached. But it is hard to resist the thought
that when combined with a projectivist self-understanding, religious language and religious practice become what some critics of
religion thought they were even without the self-understanding,
that is, a kind of superstition.

So might moral thought, or some part of it, be vulnerable to
reflection in the way religion apparently is, on the projectivist or
functionalist understandings of it? To have introduced this question by way of the example of religion was no accident, since there
is at least one case where the vulnerability to reflection of religion
and of morality come into question in analogous and indeed historically connected ways. A common theme in nineteenth-century

social thought was the idea that public morality would be impossible to maintain without religious (in that context, Christian) belief.[15] For some, the problem was simply how to ensure the continued wide acceptance of what they themselves believed. Others, however, supported the institutional maintenance of a set of beliefs about which they were privately agnostic, merely as a means of preserving moral standards. A clear case, then, of—to borrow a phrase from Anthony Skillen's paper—a 'division between the rationale of the system and the reason for individuals' thought and action within the system',[16] and thus also a case where, were the rationale of the system to become transparent to all those living under it, the system might be unseated.

Now this division appears to have been, roughly, the state of affairs with regard to religion supported by Sidgwick. He insisted that morality could, thanks to moral philosophy, stand *among the educated* without the support of religion—indeed he conscientiously resigned his fellowship in Cambridge once he could no longer accept the Thirty-Nine Articles. But he recognized what he saw as 'the superiority of Christianity as compared with philosophy when we regard them both as addressing themselves to ordinary people, *individuals who compose "the masses"* '.[17] But of course this thought is precisely analogous to another for which Sidgwick is famous: that utilitarianism, though true, might need to remain an 'esoteric morality' on the grounds that utility is most likely to be maximized if the reasons for action of all but a minority of initiates remain the familiar jumble of moral ideas labelled 'common sense'.[18] But because parts of this 'common sense' morality require

[15] See J. B. Schneewind, *Sidgwick's Ethics and Victorian Moral Philosophy* (Oxford: Oxford University Press, 1977), 20.
[16] Skillen, Ch. 2 in this volume, p. 56.
[17] From Sidgwick's review of J. R. Seeley's *Ecce Homo*, quoted at Schneewind, *Sidgwick's Ethics and Victorian Moral Philosophy*, 35 (my italics). Seeley had argued that morality required the support of Christianity among the educated and uneducated alike.
[18] See Henry Sidgwick, *The Methods of Ethics*, 7th edn. (London: Macmillan, 1967), 489–90. The two thoughts are not merely analogous but one and the same if 'philosophy' is taken as utilitarian philosophy and 'religion' and 'common-sense morality' both boil down to the Ten Commandments. But they need not: it is possible, for example, to recommend religion on purely instrumental grounds without focusing on its moral content (but, for example, on the importance of public prayer). For a modern case where religion is recommended as a means to public moral improvement, see Patrick Devlin, *The Enforcement of Morals* (Oxford: Oxford University Press, 1965), 23: 'without the support of the churches the moral order . . . would collapse'.

that they be accepted as the most basic moral reasons there are, to recommend this view is to recommend that the ordinary person must misunderstand the basic rationale for his doing as he does, if his moral beliefs and practices are to be maintained.

Combining advocacy of common-sense morality, as Sidgwick did, with a moral theory according to which this morality is, in at least the weakest of our three senses, a form of ideology is obviously, like its religious analogue, a *possible* stance to take. But, as Bernard Williams has argued, there are just as obviously difficulties with it, and these difficulties are that much more acute where the distinction between utilitarianism and common-sense morality is embodied not in a division between initiated and uninitiated social groups but, as in, for example, R. M. Hare's work, in an intra-personal division between reflective and unreflective attitudes of mind.[19]

Such 'two-tier' versions of utilitarianism are an especially clear example of how uncomfortably a part of morality sits with a certain reflective understanding of it. The example has been a focus for recent moral philosophy, and the issues it raises are in some ways isomorphic with those raised, at the political level, by John Kekes in his contribution to this volume (Chapter 7). Attacking some influential liberal political theorists (e.g. Rawls, Dworkin, Nagel), Kekes argues that liberals are condemned to 'double-mindedness' because of a standing conflict between their political reasons and their personal reasons: agents will typically have personal 'forma-tive attitudes'—to work, family, sex, religion, death, and so on—which commit them to regarding certain other such attitudes as repugnant. But as liberals—so Kekes argues—they will also be committed to neutrality between all such attitudes, and to 'active toleration' of those they personally reject. Given the instability it is liberalism, in Kekes's view, that has to give way.[20] Moreover, the

---

[19] See R. M. Hare, 'Ethical Theory and Utilitarianism', in A. Sen and B. Williams (eds.), *Utilitarianism and Beyond* (Cambridge: Cambridge University Press; Paris: Éditions de la Maison des Sciences de l'Homme, 1982). For Williams's objections, see *Ethics and the Limits of Philosophy*, esp. 107–10, and 'The Point of View of the Universe: Sidgwick and the Ambitions of Ethics', in Williams, *Making Sense of Humanity* (Cambridge: Cambridge University Press, 1995), 164 ff. Williams's solu-tion is to reject utilitarianism, but another possibility (for all that has been said here) would be to reject common-sense morality. For present purposes, what is of inter-est is the difficulty of combining the two, albeit at different levels of thought.

[20] Though there are points of similarity here with Williams's attack on two-tier consequentialism, there are also differences. Williams, for example, sometimes seems to argue that it is psychologically *impossible* for a thoroughgoing utilitarian

liberal's double-mindedness flows, on Kekes's account, from what liberals regard as a moral requirement, since the liberals he has in his sights identify the level of political reasons with that of impartial reflection and the level of impartial reflection with the moral level. Kekes's critique of liberalism thus goes hand in hand with a critique of a certain conception of morality, and in consequence the similarity between the issues Kekes raises for the liberal and the issues which have been raised for the two-tier utilitarian may go beyond mere isomorphism.

However, recent moral philosophy also presses other putative examples of morality-as-ideology upon us. Those which follow are intended to give some idea of their variety.

4

One important such example comes from the area occupied by the various forms of meta-ethical projectivism. The version of projectivism which borrows most from the rhetoric of disenchantment characteristic of projectivist accounts of religion is Mackie's 'error theory',[21] discussed in this collection by both Price and Fricker. The feature of moral thought under attack in the error theory is an alleged mismatch between the meaning of ethical statements and the metaphysical lie of the land: ethical statements, according to Mackie, are such as to be made true or false by how things are in a certain sort of moral reality which, however, does not exist. And part of the argument for its non-existence relates to the *explanation* of moral belief. Beliefs about the physical world—at least (presumably) when they are at their best, i.e. when they are true—cannot be explained without appeal to that world. But moral beliefs—again (presumably) at their best, though there is a problem, granted the error theory, in saying what that actually amounts to—can be adequately explained by (say) evolutionary or psychological or cultural factors: in any case, without appeal to a

---

to have (non-utilitarian) attitudes deep enough to count as what Kekes calls 'formative', while Kekes on the other hand characterizes the liberal's state of mind not as impossible but as a state of self-division of frustration.

[21] See J. L. Mackie, *Ethics: Inventing Right and Wrong* (Harmondsworth: Penguin, 1977), esp. ch. 1, and also 'A Refutation of Morals', *Australasian Journal of Philosophy* 24 (1946), 77–90.

moral reality.[22] Mackie's reliance on an argument from explanation invites a reformulation of his position in terms of the notion of ideology. Mackie of course argues that ethical statements are false,[23] while on most of the accounts of ideology canvassed above it was not essential to a form of consciousness' counting as ideological that its contents be false. Moreover, it might be objected that it is part of the concept of ideology that no form of consciousness can be proved to be ideological a priori, but whereas Marx was engaged in social science, Mackie's meta-ethics is an a priori inquiry. So any resemblance between moral thought, on the error theorist's account, and (say) religion on a Marxian account, can only be superficial. The error theorist's reply should presumably be that it is indeed an a priori claim that if beliefs (at their best) about some sector of reality can be explained without appeal to any such sector, then there is no such sector. But the claim that moral beliefs can be fully explained without appeal to moral reality is an (admittedly high-level) *empirical* claim: unless philosophers had at least *some* idea of what such explanations look like, and some confidence that they will succeed, they would have no business making the claim. Moral thought, therefore, for the error theorist, is a global form of ideology.

It is one of the oddities of Mackie's theory that he does not regard it as even potentially revisionary. For if his theory is true,

[22] The crucial section of Mackie's work in this connection is perhaps *Ethics*, ch. 1, sect. 10, 'Patterns of Objectification': 'objectification', for Mackie, labels a family of processes capable of empirical investigation and which, when investigated, would supply an explanation of moral belief to rival any explanation invoking a supposed moral reality. Mackie of course is not alone in invoking explanation as a touchstone in discussions about moral reality, or the possibility of moral knowledge: Blackburn, Harman, and Williams all invoke the notion in one way or another to the disadvantage of ethical thought as compared to scientific thought, while Wiggins and in this volume, Railton agree that explanation is the right test but argue that ethical thought need not be disadvantaged by it. See Simon Blackburn, 'Realism, Quasi, or Queasy?', in J. Haldane and C. Wright (eds.), *Reality, Representation and Projection* (New York: Oxford University Press, 1993); Gilbert Harman, *The Nature of Morality* (Oxford: Oxford University Press, 1977), ch. 1; Williams, *Ethics and the Limits of Philosophy*, ch. 8; David Wiggins, *Needs, Values, Truth*, 2nd edn. (Oxford: Blackwell, 1991), postscript, sects. 3-4. Of these at least Williams, Blackburn, and Wiggins are interested not only in the comparison of ethics with science, but in the possible impact which awareness of the result of the comparison might have on ethics.

[23] A more sympathetic reading of Mackie would perhaps say that all ethical statements imply a false statement, or that their meaning is such that in virtue of one component of it something false is said.

ethics seems to be a case, like religion, where reflective understanding ought to have a dramatic effect on belief and practice, at
least if a rational person cannot hold on to beliefs which he or she
has come to think of as explained by factors incidental to their
truth. Fricker in Chapter 4 takes seriously the idea that accepting
Mackie's theory *could* have a destabilizing effect on moral thought
and offers a characterization of what that effect might be. It is not,
she says, 'practical instability' but rather 'the destruction of authenticity: the onset of a sense of alienation from our own concepts and
attitudes'[24]—a state of mind comparable, perhaps, to the way one
might feel about religious beliefs or habits of observance which one
sees oneself as stuck with because of one's psychological make-up,
though one rationally concurs with arguments for their ground-
lessness. In Fricker's presentation, Rorty offers his 'ironism'[25]—
which echoes both Sidgwick on religion and two-tier utilitarianism
in its combination of public commitment with private convictions
that subvert or undermine it—as a way of going on once the error
theory has been taken to heart. But if that *is* what ironism is meant
to be, ethical thought is (as Fricker says) not much better for
depending on a psychological movement in and out of awareness
of the metaphysical truth of the matter than it would be for depending on naïve error.

There is a question, however, as to whether Rorty's ironism and
Mackie's error theory connect in quite this way. For Rorty—and
not only for Rorty[26]—the destabilizing thought *par excellence* is a
thought of contingency, the historical or cultural contingency of
having fetched up with one set of ethical attitudes rather than
another. But if Mackie is preoccupied by contingency at all, the
contingency must surely be the contingency that we think in ethical
terms simply as such, and the thought of *that* contingency would
still have been available even if ethical attitudes had been culturally and historically invariant. Correspondingly, if that thought is to
be destabilizing, its destabilizing effect would (it seems) have to be
more global than simply inducing the sceptical worry as to whether
the ethical attitudes we have, as opposed to some other ones, are

[24] Fricker, Ch. 4, introduction.
[25] See Richard Rorty, *Contingency, Irony, and Solidarity* (Cambridge: Cambridge
University Press, 1989).
[26] Compare Williams, Ch. 6, in this volume, on the unsettling effects of genealogical inquiry (Sect. 6).

the right ones. As befits a theory which says that ethical thought *simply as such* involves error, the destabilizing effect would seem to have to be comparable to that of projectivism about religion: just as the latter seems to require us to abandon religious belief, taking the error theory to heart would seem to require us to abandon ethical thought altogether.

But while we can see exactly what it would mean to give up religious belief, it is not clear what it would mean to give up ethical thought. One idea, suggested by the rhetoric of disenchantment, is that it would be to come to see the world without those evaluative properties which, as projectivism teaches, are merely our projections onto it; to see the world, that is, as evaluatively blank. Something like this idea seems to be what Julia Kristeva has in mind in her work on depression, 'an exceptionality', as she calls it, 'that reveals the true nature of being'.[27] On Kristeva's view, we experience in depression the world without those values which, in the normal course of psychological development, we discover (or feel as if we are discovering) in it. However, the world's appearing to us to be meaningless, or without value, is surely still a way for the world to look from *within* ethical thought, akin more to experiencing a grey silent world than to experiencing a world without any secondary qualities. So the possibility Kristeva envisages, though it may be a true description of depressive experience, is not the possibility which taking the error theorist's lesson to heart would appear to call for.

5

If there isn't any such thing as giving up ethical thought, it would certainly explain why Mackie doesn't expect acceptance of his error theory to have any practical impact. But where does this leave the idea that Mackie's error theory is a species of ideology-critique, aimed at ethical thought simply as such? One route to take is obviously that the very inconceivability of giving up ethical thought simply as such shows the misguidedness of any purported ideology-critique of it. This conclusion converges with a line of thought pressed in this volume by Price. Adducing Wittgensteinian and

---

[27] Julia Kristeva, *Black Sun* (New York: Columbia University Press, 1989), 8.

Davidsonian considerations about meaning, Price argues that the meaning of ethical statements is given exhaustively by the way we use them, in particular by the grounds we give for and against them. So once the grounds for an ethical statement are fulfilled, the claim is true: the meaning conferred upon it by its use leaves no further room for it also, as it were in some 'higher' sense and as the error theory requires, to be false. This may imply there is something amiss with debates about moral reality altogether. But in any case Price takes it to show—and here his conclusion is in agreement with Skillen's in Chapter 2 in this volume—that though parts of our ethical thought may be ideological, the whole thing can't be.

But perhaps we should also think more carefully about the alleged rule of general epistemology I mentioned earlier, that a rational subject cannot maintain a belief of which he has come to think that his having it is explained only by factors incidental to its truth. For the apparent impossibility of abandoning ethical thought simply as such ought to call to mind philosophical accounts according to which there are categories of belief beyond the ethical such that a rational subject can come to think this of them *without* being disposed to give them up, or to lose confidence in them even minimally. If we follow Hume, belief in external existence would fall into this category, and if we follow Wittgenstein, modal beliefs and (following the Wittgenstein of *On Certainty*, at least) 'framework beliefs' with no special restriction as to subject-matter.[28]

One might of course accept the epistemological rule and, in conjunction with the inescapability of beliefs of some or all of these kinds, take it as showing the limits of naturalistic (where this implies non-rationalizing) belief-explanation in one or more of the relevant areas.[29] Or, armed once again with the idea that the naturalistic 'placing' of some area of discourse—the phrase is Simon Blackburn's—means the non-rationalizing explanation of it, and taking such an explanation—say of a projectivist sort—to be available, the inescapability of the beliefs might lead one to reject the rule. But even if certain types of belief are impervious to aware-

---

[28] On Hume, Wittgenstein, and naturalism, see P. F. Strawson, *Skepticism and Naturalism: Some Varieties* (London: Methuen, 1987).

[29] As Blackburn does, apparently, in the case of modal but not of moral thought: see 'Morals and Modals', in Blackburn, *Essays in Quasi-Realism* (Oxford: Oxford University Press, 1993), 72.

ness of non-rationalizing explanations of them, there is no getting away from the fact that there are other types—here again beliefs based on veridical hallucinations are an obvious example—which are not. So it would be an interesting task to show why the epistemological rule should hold good for some cases but not for others, and which those cases are.

But the assumption that naturalistic explanation in ethics—even naturalistic explanation which invokes some notion of projection—must be non-rationalizing is controversial, and treated sceptically by Price, who indicates the possibility of an alternative account invoking the idea of 'correspondence'.[30] And that assumption in turn is closely connected to an assumption which Williams attacks in his contribution to this collection, 'Naturalism and Genealogy' (Chapter 6), that a respectable naturalistic explanation of humans' capacity to 'live in an ethical system' must explain it in terms familiar from our understanding of non-human species. Williams identifies this assumption as common on the one hand to Blackburn's projectivism and to sociobiology (according to which such an explanation is possible) and, on the other, to those who see explaining the human in terms of the non-human as impossible and hence dismiss the possibility of naturalistic explanation in ethics at all. Against the assumption, Williams invokes the 'ethological platitude' that the way in which a given drive expresses itself in a species depends on that species' way of life, so even the drives we have in common with other species are influenced by culture in their expression. Consequently, what the naturalistic explanation of ethical life in fact requires is that that part of human psychology necessary for it be explained by appeal to other parts of human psychology, though as far as possible parts that are themselves prior to the ethical. As a result such an explanation may in part be a historical or quasi-historical enterprise with Nietzschean genealogical investigation a case in point.

This cluster of issues concerning naturalism and explanation shows that the concept of ideology—which, on the in-between account set out in Section 2, relies on the epistemological rule—is not only an instrument with which to probe ethical thought: there is much to learn about each by thinking about the other.

[30] For the notion of correspondence, see e.g. Richard Wollheim, 'Correspondence, Projective Properties, and Expression in the Arts', in Wollheim, *The Mind and its Depths* (Cambridge, Mass.: Harvard University Press, 1993).

6

A more obvious ethical application, or family of applications, of the notion of ideology perhaps than any so far mentioned is in an area of thought in which first-order ethics joins hands with social science. A central example, where the critique is coeval with the notion of ideology itself, is Marx's critique of *Moralität*, and he had the ethics of Kant in particular in mind here, the 'whitewashing spokesman of the German burghers'.[31] But contrary to the claims of some 'scientific' Marxists and, in a sense, of Railton in this volume (Chapter 5), this is not a critique of ethical thought as such but, Rosen argues (Chapter 1), of a particular construction of it which makes the concepts of rights and duties central and assumes a conflict between duty and inclination.[32] *Moralität* counted as ideological in Marx's eyes because to identify the concepts of rights and obligation with the whole of ethics is falsely to universalize a mode of thought in fact suited only to a transitory state of society characterized by 'egoism' and 'separation' and in which the bourgeoisie, preoccupied with property and contract, dominate ethical discourse. Of course it is questionable whether *Moralität*, or at any rate the whole of it, is as much the creature of a particular state of society as Marx makes out: Rosen, for example, argues that simply getting rid of 'egoistic' desires would not obviate the need for a concept of justice, since non-selfish desires, of a kind that might be presumed to be present even in a society more nearly utopian than the bourgeois version, can also conflict. Be that as it may, the object of Marx's critique connects him not only with Nietzsche's genealogical investigations but with some more recent analytic philosophy which does not make explicit play with the concept of ideology, for example Anscombe's attack on a 'law conception of ethics' and Williams's critique of the 'morality system'.[33]

[31] See Rosen, Ch. 1 in this volume, Sect. 4.

[32] Compare Railton, Ch. 5, Sect. 7: 'One . . . has to look outside mainstream philosophy—to Marx or Nietzsche, say—to find attitudes more openly dismissive of the core of conventional morality.' Though most if not all contributors to this volume agree that *parts* of ethical thought survive ideology-critique, the parts of ethical thought which survive it in Railton's view are perhaps closest to those which fall victim to it in Marx's.

[33] See G. E. M. Anscombe, 'Modern Moral Philosophy', in Anscombe, *Ethics, Religion and Politics: Collected Philosophical Papers*, iii (Oxford: Blackwell, 1981), 30, and Williams, *Ethics and the Limits of Philosophy*, 174.

Examples of ideology-critique are easily multiplied: critique of norms of intelligence testing, for example, on the grounds that they claim to be universal but conceal a class or gender bias; critique of the idea that fox-hunting is an occasion for the display of courage; or critique of the supposed virtue of gentlemanliness (see Rosen's paper). In all these cases, unlike the error theory's apparently global application of the notion of ideology, a large part of ethical thought is supposed intact for the critique to be launched. But the cases are otherwise diverse (and there is more diversity than I have space to catalogue here). In the first case the critique is launched in the name of an ethical ideal, namely fairness or equality, but the object of critique does not belong to ethical thought. In the second and third cases, the critique invokes an ethical ideal—animal rights, or non-violence, in one case, fairness or freedom from oppression (say) in the other—and its object of critique belongs to ethical thought. But whereas in the second case all that is under attack is a specific application of a concept— courage—whose respectability is not in question, in the third case the aim of the critique is to withdraw a concept from circulation altogether.

These examples should be taken as an indication of the many varieties of ideology-critique rather than as an indication of anything in particular that either falls victim to it or survives it. Both Railton and Fricker, however, are optimistic that a good deal of first-order ethics—be it concepts, or particular attitudes, or whatever—will survive it, and the vindicatory explanation[34] of ethical thought, or at least of parts of it, is a concern of both their papers in this collection. For Fricker, what fills the place of Mackie's 'queer' ethical properties is the authority of a collective ethical practice in which, borrowing a term from Williams, there is 'confidence';[35] and it is this authority which provides a vindicatory explanation of the externalizing moral phenomenology Mackie accuses of error. However, while collective authority might vindicate the *phenomenology* of ethical experience—that is, show how something experienced as coming from outside ourselves really does so—to take collective authority as simultaneously vindicating the *content* of the demands thus experienced as external is, unless some

---

[34] For the phrase, see Wiggins, *Needs, Values, Truth*, 354.
[35] The term is from Williams, *Ethics and the Limits of Philosophy*, 170.

more is said, to risk making what Skillen in his paper calls the leap from 'the illusory autonomy of the moral' to 'the real heteronomy of the social'.[36] Fricker makes it clear that she understands confidence to be a partly normative notion, and pursues the question—if we can sheer off the normative dimension of the notion momentarily in order to pose it—how we are to discriminate between warranted and unwarranted states of ethical confidence.

To answer this question is a central ambition also of Peter Railton's paper. After critically assessing the normative authority of reflection itself—for it does not go without saying that reflection is epistemically beneficial—Railton argues that the relevant 'reflection test'—the test such that if moral beliefs pass it, they are non-ideological, and so vindicated—is whether one's moral beliefs are explained (solely) by non-epistemic interests. The reflection test shows how we can have a notion of ethical warrant which is independent of any idea of 'correspondence to moral reality': for Railton, this is (roughly) stability in the light of certain kinds of new information, including information about the sources of familiar beliefs. And while such new information can destroy knowledge—thus partially confirming a well-known and controversial thesis of Williams's expounded elsewhere[37]—further new knowledge could reinstate it. So no ethical knowledge is *essentially* local. Railton's model therefore favours the idea of a set of ethical beliefs and other attitudes on which rational persons will converge, and thus, in contrast to Mackie, Williams, and others, points towards an analogy between ethical and scientific thought.

7

It may be that the ideology-critique of first-order ethics need not be carried on in the light of any systematic conception of what ethics would look like once the critique is over—if it ever could be over. None the less, it is interesting to note how far the business of ideology-critique in the above examples appears also to be the business (or part of the business) of an enterprise carried on in

---

[36] See Skillen, Ch. 2, p. 53. In the passage in question, Skillen's target is a discussion of Williams's on guilt and shame rather than anything that connects directly with the error theory.
[37] *Ethics and the Limits of Philosophy*, 148.

what is often regarded as a quite different department of thought, namely ethical theory. The parallel between the two types of activity is also visible in relation to spontaneous ethical reactions—pleasure, for example, or disgust or indignation. These reactions may seem to be ethically fundamental—as Mill put it, 'the supposed corollaries seem to have a more binding force than the original theorem; the superstructure seems to stand better without, than with, what is represented as its foundation'[38]—but the search for principles from which they follow is the special business of ethical theory. Moreover, they may also seem to come out of nowhere, in the sense that there seems to be no behind-the-scenes from which they emerge into consciousness. But a look backstage reveals any amount of psychological, cultural, and historical clobber, and bringing it into the open is the province of social scientific or psychological explanation, and therefore also of the critique of ideology. Both ethical theory and ideology-critique, then, will have a tendency to put us on our guard *vis-à-vis* the more spontaneous manifestations of the ethical life[39] and so, in their effects if not their methods, the two types of activity are closely related.

Perhaps this closeness should be neither surprising nor disturbing: for Railton at least, what is left standing of morality after being submitted to the reflection test is, as it were, a framework which awaits completion by the construction of whatever proves to be the right variety of ethical theory. But if the results of an ideally exhaustive ideological critique of morality and those of ethical theory construction converge, it does not go without saying that the results must be unequivocally beneficial. For our finding value in the world, or even seeming to find it, may rely in part on our bearing the untheorized relation to it expressed by spontaneous ethical reactions and our pre-theoretical reasons for them, a relation which reflection threatens to disrupt. Nor does it go without saying, in any case, that the end-product of ethical theory construction and the end-product of ideology-critique—again, if it can be said even ideally to have an end—must coincide. On a more sceptical view, the progressive integration of the ethically immediate into ethical

---

[38] J. S. Mill, *Utilitarianism*, ed. M. Warnock (Glasgow: Collins/Fontana, 1978).

[39] Cp. e.g. the editors' introd. to E. Frazer, J. Hornsby, and S. Lovibond (eds.), *Ethics: A Feminist Reader* (Oxford: Blackwell, 1992), 18, which emphasizes 'the political value of a sceptical attitude towards what is experienced, pretheoretically, as *pleasure*'.

theory allegedly characteristic of modern societies[40] would appear not as progress towards greater ethical knowledge but as the mere effect of social change, and ethical theory itself (perhaps especially utilitarian ethical theory) as the ideology of (in Adorno's phrase) the 'administered society': like Marx's *Moralität*, a prospective casualty rather than a survivor of ideology-critique.

These are issues that I cannot hope to resolve here. Evidently, however, the relations between morality, reflection, and ideology are intricate, with many avenues open for investigation. With that, I shall leave the next word, though surely not the last, to the contributors.

---

[40] The allegation is Williams's: see e.g. *Ethics and the Limits of Philosophy*, 163. For an objection in relation to thick concepts, see Fricker, Ch. 4 in this volume, Sect. 2.1.

I

The Marxist Critique of Morality and the Theory of Ideology

Michael Rosen

The question whether Marx's theory has a moral or ethical dimension is one of the most controversial of all issues of Marx interpretation. The difficulty is easily seen. On the one hand, Marx has a number of uncompromisingly negative things to say about morality. Moreover, after 1845 at least, he affirms that his own theory is not a utopian or ethical one but 'real positive science'. Yet, on the other hand, much of the language that he uses to describe capitalism is plainly condemnatory (for instance, that it is antagonistic, oppressive, and exploitative). Does this not represent an inconsistency on Marx's part? Is he not moralizing and rejecting morality at the same time?

This paper will present a line of interpretation according to which Marx is not inconsistent. The interpretation depends on a contrast between certain doctrines typical of moral philosophy (which, it will be argued, Marx rejects) and the rejection of ethical values as such (to which, it will be argued, he is not thereby committed). Marx's antipathy to morality and moral theory as he found it in his own day is to be explained, I shall argue, by the role that morality plays, in his view, in helping to sustain the existing social order, as ideology.

It is only fair to say, however, that my interpretation involves a very considerable amount of reconstruction and projection from the very sparse evidence that we have of Marx's views on ethics. His extreme hostility to certain kinds of ethical value is well documented, but the reasons behind that hostility are much less explicit. Moreover, it is clear that Marx's views on ethics underwent considerable changes in the course of his intellectual career. To illustrate this, let us consider two quotations taken from opposite ends of that career. Marx writes in the 'Introduction to *A Contribution to the Critique of Hegel's Philosophy of Right*' (written in 1843) as follows: 'The critique of religion ends in the doctrine that man is the supreme being for man; thus it ends in the categorical imperative to overthrow all conditions in which man is a debased, enslaved, neglected, contemptible being.'[1] By the time of the *Critique of the Gotha Programme* (1875), however, Marx calls it a 'crime' to 'pervert' the party's 'realistic outlook' with 'ideological nonsense about right and other trash so common among the democrats and French socialists'.[2] It is tempting to see this change of attitude as a move on Marx's part from an initial endorsement of a distinctive ethical position to a subsequent rejection of ethical attitudes as such. In my view, however, this is mistaken. On the contrary, there is, in fact, a considerable degree of continuity between Marx's earlier and later attitudes towards morality; as I shall argue, Marx's mature rejection of received forms of morality is made from a position that is not ethically neutral and which has its basis in some of Marx's very earliest intellectual positions.

Before turning to Marx's explicit views, one further point should be made. When discussing Marx's attitude towards morality, it is important to bear in mind that three different things may be at stake. (1) There is, first, his attitude towards the moral principles and ethical beliefs actually at work in a particular society—its 'ethical life', if one will. (2) Secondly, there is his attitude towards the content of the moral doctrines advocated by moral philosophers within that society (which may or may not correspond directly to its ethical life). (3) Thirdly, there is his view not just of the content of moral doctrines but of their status (that is, roughly, his meta-ethical views). Most of Marx's pronouncements concern the first and the second topics and he has practically nothing to say on the third subject—as is, in fact, hardly surprising. It is one of the mature Marx's most distinctive positions that the issues characteristic of 'pure' philosophy—and that includes, surely, general questions of ontology and epistemology—are not so much problems to

---

[1] K. Marx, 'Towards a Critique of the Hegelian Philosophy of Right: Introduction', in Marx, *Critique of Hegel's 'Philosophy of Right'*, ed. J. O'Malley (Cambridge: Cambridge University Press, 1970), 137.

[2] K. Marx, *Critique of the Gotha Programme*, in K. Marx and F. Engels, *Selected Works*, iii (Moscow: Progress Publishers, 1970), 19.

be solved as symptoms of a malaise: the detachment of ideas from life.[3]

1. *Hegel on* Moralität *and* Sittlichkeit

It is helpful to start, as Marx's own views on morality certainly did, by looking at Hegel's critique of Kant. Marx endorses Hegel's claim that morality, as embodied in Kant's moral philosophy, is, as they both put it, 'abstract'. What did they mean by this? Hegel expresses his criticisms of Kant's view of ethics at many places in his writings, but his treatment of Kant in paragraphs 133–5 of the *Philosophy of Right* is particularly clear and helpful on this point. Hegel starts this discussion by taking up and partly endorsing Kant's idea of moral action as acting on the principle of 'duty for duty's sake': 'In doing my duty, I am by myself and free. To have emphasized this meaning of duty has constituted the merit of Kant's moral philosophy and its loftiness of outlook.'[4]

Thus Hegel agrees with Kant that we act in accordance with moral rationality only if we act from the motive of duty (rather than from contingent, personal ends). Nevertheless, he goes on to ask, what is to determine what our duty is? It is this question, Hegel famously charges, that Kant fails to answer satisfactorily and this, in his view, nullifies the chief virtue of Kant's position—its endorsement of the idea of autonomy and moral rationality: 'This is the same question as was put to Jesus when someone wished to learn from him what he should do to inherit eternal life. Good as a universal is abstract and cannot be accomplished so long as it remains abstract. To be accomplished it must acquire in addition the character of particularity.'[5]

In consequence, Kant's ethical theory remains, Hegel argues, at the level of the 'merely moral standpoint' (*der bloss moralische*

---

[3] 'The philosophers would only have to dissolve their language into the ordinary language, from which it is abstracted, to recognize it as the distorted language of the actual world, and realize that neither thoughts nor language in themselves form a realm of their own, that they are only *manifestations* of actual life' (K. Marx and F. Engels, *The German Ideology*, trans. W. Lough, ed. and abridged C. J. Arthur (London: Lawrence & Wishart, 1970), 118).

[4] G. W. F. Hegel, *The Philosophy of Right*, trans. T. M. Knox (Oxford: Oxford University Press, 1967), para. 133, addition.

[5] Ibid. para. 134, addition.

Standpunkt). In consequence, it amounts to no more than an 'empty formalism':

> we must notice here that [Kant's] point of view is defective in lacking all articulation. The proposition: 'Act as if the maxim of your action could be laid down as a universal principle', would be admirable if we already had determinate principles of conduct. That is to say, to demand of a principle that it shall be able to serve in addition as a determinant of universal legislation is to presuppose that it already possesses a content.[6]

Kantian morality is thus alleged by Hegel to be abstract in the sense that, while its principles may perhaps function as a test upon proposed actions, they do not determine the content of the particular action to be performed: they fail to make the transition from the universal to the particular, or, to put it in less Hegelian terms, they provide a necessary condition for determining whether an action is morally acceptable but not a sufficient one. If Kantian moral philosophy appears to have specific ethical content, then that can only be, Hegel claims, because that content has been surreptitiously imported from the existing institutions or codes of behaviour of the society in question: 'of course, material may be brought in from outside and particular duties may be arrived at accordingly, but if the definition of duty is taken to be the absence of contradiction, formal correspondence with itself—which is nothing but abstract indeterminacy stabilized—then no transition is possible to the specification of particular duties'.[7]

Hegel's own response to these difficulties flows from his contrast between morality (*Moralität*) and ethical life (*Sittlichkeit*). The alternative to abstract morality of the kind represented by Kant, in Hegel's view, is for the formal principles of morality to be given content thanks to the institutionalized ethical life represented by *Sittlichkeit*. *Sittlichkeit* thus resolves the indeterminacy inherent in the formal principles of *Moralität* in a way which is, he claims, itself rational. It can do this because, Hegel believes, customs and social institutions are themselves products of reason—reason as embodied in the logic of historical development. In other words, institutions are more than just a 'tie-breaker' when the requirements of reason no longer serve to specify a particular action as right or wrong; they are themselves, in some historical sense, bearers of

---

[6] G. W. F. Hegel, *The Philosophy of Right*, para. 135, addition.
[7] Ibid. para. 135.

rationality. Earlier societies were characterized by a conflict between individual morality and institutionalized ethical life, but it is
a mark of the fact that reason has completed its historical development, in Hegel's view, that modern society embodies the principles of *Moralität* within an institutionalized form of ethical life that
is itself rational.

2. *Marx on* Moralität *and* Sittlichkeit

When Marx himself first deals with the issue of morality at any
length it is in the context of a discussion of Hegel's *Philosophy
of Right*. This work, the *Critique of Hegel's 'Philosophy of Right'*,
written in 1843, remained unpublished during Marx's lifetime
(unlike the introduction written for it, which he published sepa-
rately) and so must be treated with some caution. Nevertheless,
it does, in my view, give a clear picture of Marx's earliest views
on morality. Marx's starting-point is to endorse Hegel's criticism
of the 'abstractness' and 'formalism' of principles of *Moralität*,
taken on their own. There is, he claims, a parallel between the
abstractness of *Moralität* and the abstractness of the notion of
private, individual rights.[8] Yet Marx challenges the account that
Hegel gives of how *Moralität* and *Sittlichkeit* are to be reconciled.
He disputes Hegel's claim that the *Sittlichkeit* of the modern
state effectively counteracts the separation between *Moralität* and
Sittlichkeit. On the contrary, the deficiency of the modern state lies
in the fact that it is simply the public expression of the abstractness
of private life:

Hegel develops private rights and morals as such abstractions, from which
it does not follow, for him, that the state or ethical life (*Sittlichkeit*) of which
they are presuppositions can be nothing but the society (the social life) of
these illusions; rather, he concludes that they are subordinate aspects of
this ethical life. But what are private rights except the rights of these subjects of the state, and what is morality except their morality?[9]

---

[8] 'Hegel calls private rights the rights of abstract personality, or abstract rights.
And indeed they have to be developed as the abstraction, and thus the illusory
rights, of abstract personality, just as the moral doctrine (*die Moral*) developed by
Hegel is the illusory existence of abstract subjectivity' (K. Marx, *Critique of Hegel's
'Philosophy of Right'*, ed. J. O'Malley (Cambridge: Cambridge University Press,
1970), 108).   [9] Ibid.

Although this passage is somewhat ambiguous, I take it that Marx is making two rather different points. First of all, he is objecting to Hegel's account of the role played by the state (in the narrow sense of the organs of law and government). Hegel, according to Marx, presents the state as morally neutral and infers from this that it is subordinate to the *Sittlichkeit* of society in general. Marx, on the other hand, claims that this apparent neutrality is illusory. It is in its very distance from morality—its own 'abstractness'—that the contemporary state shows itself to be representative of the 'abstract' realm of private right: the state, says Marx, is 'nothing but the society (the social life)' of these 'illusory' private rights. Thus Hegel has, Marx says, albeit unconsciously, performed a great service, for in his account of the state 'he has done nothing but develop the morality of the modern state and modern private rights'.[10]

Marx's second point concerns Hegel's view of the place of *Sittlichkeit* within state and society taken as a whole. As we have seen, for Hegel, *Sittlichkeit* supplements, but does not replace, *Moralität* by overcoming *Moralität*'s indeterminacy. Yet Marx's objection is that in the modern state *Sittlichkeit* in fact fails to play this role: instead of *Moralität* being a 'subordinate aspect' of *Sittlichkeit*, it is *Sittlichkeit*, rather, which is determined by the abstract character of *Moralität*. This second criticism could itself be taken in two different ways. We could understand Marx as pointing to a particular deficiency of the modern social system. Under this system, we could understand him as saying, *Moralität* is not subordinate to *Sittlichkeit* but vice versa; but in another form of state and society (or, perhaps, in society which had gone beyond the state) things would be different, and *Sittlichkeit* would indeed be such as to give *Moralität* a rational content. The objection to this interpretation is that it is not open to Marx to resolve the opposition between *Moralität* and *Sittlichkeit* in this manner because he cannot possibly accept the Hegelian premiss on which it rests: that *Sittlichkeit* is itself a product of reason—a doctrine quite at odds with Marx's professed commitment to historical materialism. Thus we are led to a second interpretation. On this view, Marx is critical of *any* separation between *Moralität* and *Sittlichkeit* whatsoever. In which

---

[10] 'What did that prove except that the separation of the present-day state from morals is moral, that morals are non-political and that the state is not moral?' (ibid.).

case, Marx would seem to require not just that we should go beyond the supposed abstractness of formal moral principles but, in some sense, that we should go beyond morality as such.

3. Marx's Objections to Rights

The nature of Marx's objections to morality is clarified further in the comments on the *Declaration of the Rights of Man* (1791) and the *Declaration of the Rights of Man and of the Citizen* (1793) to be found in his article 'On the Jewish Question' (written, again, in 1843). Marx there takes issue with the idea of the rights of man in general: 'the so-called *rights of man*, as distinct from the *rights of the citizen*, are quite simply the rights of the *member of civil society*, i.e. of egoistic man, of man separated from other men and from the community'.[11]

Marx's objection here resembles those already raised in the *Critique of Hegel's 'Philosophy of Right'*. The rights that are institutionalized in the political sphere do not counter the isolation of individuals from one another that is characteristic of their economic life ('civil society'); on the contrary, the conception of rights at stake simply mirrors the egoistic and individualistic structure of civil society, Marx asserts. Marx makes similar points when it comes to the discussion of specific rights such as the right to liberty. He quotes the two declarations' definitions of the right to liberty as follows: ' "Liberty is the power which belongs to man to do anything that does not harm the rights of others", or according to the Declaration of the Rights of Man of 1791: "Liberty consists in being able to do anything which does not harm others." '[12]

Marx's comments on these definitions again focus on the claim that such rights presuppose the 'egoism' of the individuals whose freedom is being guaranteed:

Liberty is therefore the right to do and perform everything which does not harm others. The limits within which each individual can move *without* harming others are determined by law, just as the boundary between two fields is determined by a stake. The liberty we are here dealing with is that of man as an isolated monad who is withdrawn into himself . . . [The] right

---

[11] K. Marx, 'On the Jewish Question', in Marx, *Early Writings* ed. L. Colletti (Harmondsworth: Penguin, 1975), 229. [12] Ibid.

of man to freedom is not based on the association of man with man but rather on the separation of man from man. It is the *right* of this separation, the *right* of the restricted individual, restricted to himself.[13]

I shall return to these criticisms below, but, for the present, it is significant to note the distance that Marx has covered from the original, Hegelian criticism of Kantian *Moralität*. For Hegel, the objection to the idea of acting from duty was simply that the content of such duties remained indeterminate. For Marx, on the one hand, the target is much broader: the criticism of abstract morality does not just apply to the Kantian categorical imperative but, apparently, to rights-based moral theory in general. Moreover, Marx's objection is not just to the failure of the categorical imperative to determine the content of moral principles, but something rather different: he objects to the 'egoism' and 'separation' that are, he claims, presupposed by the notion of rights.

4. *The Origins of Abstract Morality*

For Hegel, the separation between *Sittlichkeit* and *Moralität* and their subsequent reconciliation are both stages in the self-development of *Geist*—Hegel's word for the collective intellect in which we all, according to him, participate. Now Marx, as we have seen, agrees with (and, indeed, reinforces) Hegel's criticism of the abstractness of *Moralität*. But what he obviously cannot do is endorse Hegel's idealist account of how this abstract form of moral life has come about. This is not an issue that Marx addresses in the *Critique of Hegel's 'Philosophy of Right'*, but in *The German Ideology* (written in 1845–6 but again not published) he gives an account of the genesis of ideas in society that includes an account of the origin of abstract morality. Instead of seeing the development of ideas in the context of a series of stages in the self-development of *Geist*, Marx tries to explain them in relation to the stages of the division of labour in society.

The account of the production of ideas in *The German Ideology* starts from the claim that thought (including moral thought) is always constrained by the conditions and circumstances under which it is produced:

---

[13] K. Marx, 'On the Jewish Question', in Marx, *Early Writings* ed. L. Colletti (Harmondsworth: Penguin, 1975).

The production of ideas, of conceptions, of consciousness, is at first directly interwoven with the material activity and the material intercourse of men, the language of real life. Conceiving, thinking, the mental intercourse of men, appear at this stage as the direct efflux of their material behaviour. The same applies to mental production as expressed in the language of politics, laws, morality, religion, metaphysics, etc. of a people.[14]

At this initial stage of social development, then, the connection between the lives led by individuals and the ideas to which they adhere was, according to Marx, immediately clear and intelligible. Yet that is now no longer the case, he believes. On the contrary, politics, law, morality, religion, and metaphysics have turned into apparently independent bodies of thought with their own internal history and dynamics. The reason, Marx claims, is that, in the course of the division of labour, mental and manual labour have become separated from one another:

Division of labour only becomes truly such from the moment when a division of material and mental labour appears. (The first form of ideologists, *priests*, is concurrent.) From this moment onwards consciousness *can* really flatter itself that it is something other than consciousness of existing practice, that it *really* represents something without representing something real; from now on consciousness is in a position to emancipate itself from the world and to proceed to the formation of 'pure' theory, theology, philosophy, ethics, etc.[15]

The separation between mental and manual labour, Marx maintains, explains the formal, abstract character of moral ideas, but it does not lead to the formation of autonomous ideas in fact; the ideologists who produce ideas are still part of the ruling class whose interests their ideas represent. In this way the division of labour offers an explanation as to why such ideas should be accepted by those, the dominated classes, whose interests they go against. They are accepted because they are *apparently* disinterested. The ideologist, on this view, is like a bribed referee: able to influence the outcome of a game all the more effectively for the fact that he is falsely believed to be impartial. The ideologist is not engaged in deception, however. On the contrary. According to Marx, ideologists are *sincere*—and, because they sincerely believe in the independence and objective validity of their own ideas, they are able to persuade others to accept them as such all the more effectively. Here, however, is the problem. How are we to suppose it to be true that the ideologists should both be constrained so that they produce ideas in the interests of the ruling class of which they are, appearances to the contrary, a part and that they (and those who accept the ideas from them) remain sincerely unaware of the nature of this connection? Why do they *think* that they are independent when in fact they are not? And, if they are not independent, how do their shared class interests with the rest of the ruling class assert themselves?

In any case, it is clear why Marx should be so hostile to morality: like any supposedly 'pure' theory, morality represents a deceptive abstraction from the particular circumstances and material interests that it serves. The move to detach ideas that are the products of material interests from the interests that they represent is epitomized, for Marx, in Kant:

We find again in Kant the characteristic form which liberalism, based on real class interests, assumed in Germany. Neither he, nor the German burghers, whose whitewashing spokesman he was, noticed that these theoretical ideas of the bourgeoisie had as their basis material interests and a *will* that was conditioned and determined by the material relations of production. Kant, therefore, separated this theoretical expression from the interests it expressed; he made the materially motivated determinations of the will of the French bourgeois into *pure* self-determinations of 'free will', of the will in and for itself, of the human will, and so converted it into purely ideological determinations and moral postualates.[16]

For Marx at this stage 'moral postulates' are, by their very nature, *ideological*.

5. *Marx's Attitude towards* Moralität

Having surveyed these relatively explicit comments of Marx's on the nature of morality, we can now offer a reconstruction of his position. I shall present it, for the sake of clarity, in the form of seven theses:

(1) Marx endorses Hegel's claim that Kantian *Moralität* is abstract, in the sense of failing to determine a specific content for ethical action.

[16] Marx and Engels, *The German Ideology*, 99.

(2) Nevertheless, it is important that *Moralität* appears to be universal and disinterested. This is not simply a failure of perception on the part of moral philosophers but is, according to Marx, a product of the fact that moral ideas are themselves products of a certain stage within the division of labour.

(3) In actual fact, however, moral content is given to moral principles from a source external to those principles themselves: the institutions that happen to exist in the society at the time. Thus, while *Moralität* may appear to be universal and timeless, its actual content—its application in practice—is particular and relative to the society in question.

(4) Although *Moralität* appears to be disinterested, it (and the further content that determines its application in practice) is, in fact, the product of interests, whose role is ideologically concealed.

(5) There is a further sense in which *Moralität* is 'abstract', for Marx, and that is that it issues in principles or imperatives that remain at the level of mere injunctions. Thus moral theory falls under the strictures that Marx applies to philosophy in general: 'the weapons of criticism', as he puts it, 'cannot replace the criticism of weapons'.[17]

(6) *Moralität* is a 'false' or defective moral theory, for the reasons given. But, although it is 'abstract' in the sense of failing to give content to the action that is supposed to fall under its aegis, it is, in another sense, a reflection of actually existing society. If there is a defect, Marx believes, it lies in the 'abstraction' of ethical life in society which *Moralität* faithfully reflects.

(7) Thus Marx's meta-ethical position seems to be what we might, for want of a better phrase, call 'institutional realism'. Given Marx's strictures on the ideological nature of supposedly 'pure' ethics, we must attribute to him the belief that values, or value-beliefs, do not represent a realm of independently real items. Realism of that kind would be characteristic of ideological thought, in Marx's view. On the other hand, ethical values *do* embody the values implicit in the life

---

[17] Marx, 'Towards a Critique of the Hegelian Philosophy of Right: Introduction', 137.

of their community and, in that sense, they reflect a reality
independent of themselves.

6. *The Alternative to* Moralität

But what is Marx's alternative to *Moralität*? To answer this
question let me start by addressing what is surely a nagging uneasi-
ness about the plausibility of his position. The problem is clear:
if the criticism of moral theory is to extend as widely as Marx
appears to suppose, his target must be some general feature of
morality, not just the particular difficulties that follow from the
Kantian attempt to derive content from the general idea of moral
rationality.

It is clear that Marx, from the time of the Paris Manuscripts, sees
social progress as characterized by a form of community in which
(as he and Engels put it in the *Communist Manifesto*) 'the free
development of each is the condition for the free development of
all'. Marx's ethical ideal is one of solidarity in which all advance
together. In other words, Marx assumes that the good for individuals is complementary: in advancing my good I advance yours and
in advancing your good you advance mine.[18] As I understand him,
Marx believes that the idea of the complementarity of the good
stands opposed to most, if not all, of the central family of moral
concepts for the following reasons.

Speaking roughly, we may think of rights as permitting individuals to act in certain ways, in given circumstances, should they wish
to do so, and to be able to claim correlative duties on the part of

---

[18] Marx makes this view particularly clear in his 1844 discussion of James Mill.
He writes: 'Let us suppose that we had produced as human beings. In that event
each of us would have *doubly affirmed* himself and his neighbour in his production.
(1) In my *production* I would have objectified the *specific character* of my *individu-
ality* and for that reason I would have enjoyed the *expression* of my own individual
life during my activity and also, in contemplating the object, I would experience an
individual pleasure . . . (2) In your use or enjoyment of my product I would have
the *immediate* satisfaction and knowledge that in my labour I have gratified a *human*
need, i.e. that I had objectified *human nature* and hence had procured an object corresponding to the needs of another *human being* . . . In the individual expression of
my own life I would have brought about the immediate expression of your life, and
so in my individual activity I would have directly *confirmed* and *realized* my authentic nature, my *human*, *communal* nature' 'Excerpts from James Mill's *Elements
of Political Economy*', in Marx, *Early Writings*, ed. L. Collett: (Harmondsworth:
Penguin, 1975), 277–8.

others. A duty, correspondingly, would require individuals to act in some way, whether they wished to or not. Liberty, as Marx understands it, is the ability of the individual to act as he or she happens to wish subject to certain limits (the ability of others to do likewise). Justice (if we do not think of it simply as a matter of rights and duties) can be thought of similarly as consisting of principles on which benefits and burdens are distributed in cases where interests conflict.

Put like this, these values do indeed have an important structural element in common. They all, in different ways, can be thought to provide a framework which regulates and limits the self-seeking behaviour of individuals. They are values that assume a conflict between (to put it in Kantian terms) 'duty' and 'inclination'. And it is precisely this that Marx objects to. Just as Marx supposes that the categories of bourgeois economics eternalize the forms of bourgeois economic life, so, he believes, the treatment of ethics in terms of rights and similar values eternalizes a situation in which the good of each individual is independent and so can only be advanced at the expense of others.

It is in this context, in my view, that we should understand Marx's criticisms that moral concepts such as rights (including the right to liberty) presuppose a situation of 'egoism' and 'separation'. As they stand, however, such criticisms are hardly persuasive. Hume, in the *Enquiry concerning the Principles of Morals*, identifies it as a necessary condition for the 'cautious, jealous virtue of justice' to have application that 'benevolence' must not be so extensive 'that every man has the utmost tenderness for every man, and feels no more concern for his own interest than for that of his fellows'.[19] There is surely little doubt that this condition will be fulfilled in any society that we can reasonably envisage.[20] For there to be some kind of a conflict between duty and inclination it is by no means necessary for people to be wholly or even primarily egoistic; it is sufficient that there should be times when duty and inclination are not coincident, and even people who are very ready to acknowledge

---

[19] David Hume, *Enquiry concerning the Principles of Morals* (1977), ed. L. A. Selby-Bigge (Oxford: Oxford University Press, 1986), 184–5.

[20] Concerning the first point, Robert Nozick has an excellent example. It does not seem unreasonable to desire—other things being equal—to have the whole of the Harvard Library at one's individual disposal. Surely, he argues, there will always be some degree of scarcity in that sense.

the claims made upon them by others are hardly likely to be free of such conflicts.

Marx's idea of the complementarity of the good, it should be noted, makes no such unreasonable assumptions about human nature. On the contrary, the claim that shared endeavours can bring benefits to the participants over and above the benefits flowing to them directly from the outcome itself, in my view, records a truth about the nature of human social life that is as important as it is obvious. But, on the other hand, nor is this fact sufficient to transcend the opposition between duty and inclination. The fact that our goods are mutually reinforcing does not remove the potential for a conflict of interests. Although the positive 'externalities' envisaged by Marx may have the effect of overcoming the problem of the Prisoners' Dilemma by giving each participant in a joint enterprise a further incentive to co-operate, it does not remove the fact that the good for me is still different from the good for you and may be valued differently by the two of us. And indeed, even if that were not the case and Hume's supposition that every individual were 'a second self to another'[21] were true, this would not be sufficient to transcend the question of justice, for, as Rawls has pointed out, questions of distribution still arise even here: there is still a question of how best to distribute potential welfare, even assuming that we are all selflessly impartial in our attitude towards who should receive it.

In the light of this, we must, I think reinterpret (and perhaps reduce in strength) Marx's claim that morality (conceived as a set of duties that override what one might otherwise do) is necessarily connected to 'egoism' and 'individualism' in such a way that opposition to egoism and individualism requires the transcendence of morality. One way of doing so would be to take Marx's claim as being simply that morality *promotes* egoism and individualism and that, therefore, to transcend morality would at least help to diminish the latter. It might seem that this claim is hardly difficult for Marx to establish. If it is true that capitalism promotes egoism and selfishness and it is true that morality promotes capitalism, then the claim obviously follows. On the other hand, even if it is true that the morality characteristic of capitalism does indeed promote capitalism, it does not follow that all morality must promote egoism

---

[21] Hume, *Enquiry concerning the Principles of Morals*, 185.

and selfishness. Why should there not be a socialist morality which promotes not egoism and selfishness but altruism and solidarity? The idea that the pursuit of justice is opposed to altruism and solidarity has seemed plausible to many, of course—and not just on the left. But it should not be accepted without question. After all, if we were to think of the principles of justice as establishing a kind of moral minimum—a baseline or guarantee—then it certainly seems plausible to think that someone who was sure of getting his or her due would be more, not less, inclined to be benevolent and public-spirited.[22]

But, that said, two aspects of Marx's position still, in my opinion, deserve to be taken very seriously. The first is that we have no right to treat justice as the sole virtue of social institutions.[23] Marx would disagree utterly with Kant's remark that the problem of government could be solved by 'a nation of devils, provided that they have understanding': in his view, the character of the individuals composing a society and the quality of the interactions that take place between them have overriding importance, and institutions—economic ones, above all, of course—should be such as to develop these aspects of social life, so far as is possible.

It is also true, I believe, that conventional approaches to the study of welfare and distributive justice underestimate the interdependence of individuals' well-being. By treating the allocation of benefits and burdens as if it were a matter of dividing a 'cake' of material (or quasi-material) goods whilst minimizing the disutility of expended effort, the abstraction characteristic of conventional theories of justice seriously understates the degree to which welfare has a social dimension. It is a truth too little recognized in contemporary discussion that one society may in the strictest sense be better off than another, despite having a smaller bundle of goods at its disposal, if the welfare accruing to its members from their participation in a satisfyingly co-operative common life is greater than in a more ruthless and unfeeling form of collective existence. We have no right to assume that, because bundles of goods are

---

[22] A point made very well by Jeremy Waldron in his paper 'When Justice Replaces Affection: The Need for Rights', in Waldron, *Liberal Rights* (Cambridge: Cambridge University Press, 1993).

[23] Or to assume that it is so related to the other virtues that once that virtue obtains in a society so, too, will all other significant virtues.

(relatively) easy to measure and social well-being almost impossible, the former matters more than the latter.

Thus Marx's reluctance to use the conventional language of rights and justice to condemn capitalism is intelligible, if not entirely persuasive. It is not that Marx thinks that exploitation, expropriation, oppression, slavery, misery (a few of the terms he applies to the capitalist system) are morally acceptable or that he believes that the language of ethical condemnation is epistemologically suspect.[24] He is, however, reluctant to use language that would suggest that these are forms of injustice for which 'justice' (in the sense of giving 'each their due') is the final and sufficient remedy. The best understanding of Marx's view of morality, in my view, lies in appreciating that, for him, socialism and communism represent a form of social existence that is ethically superior to capitalism, one mark of whose superiority consists in the fact that it has gone beyond morality.

APPENDIX
Allen Wood on Marxism and Morality

Marx's views on morality have, in recent years, generated a surprisingly extensive debate in the Anglo-American philosophical community. The most vigorous and original participant in that debate (to a large extent, in fact, its initiator) has been the American philosopher Allen Wood. Many of the views presented in this paper come close, so far as I can judge, to Wood's, although the angle of approach is, of course, somewhat different. But our views do not, in fact, coincide completely and I would like to take up two points of disagreement. I want to take issue with two of Wood's claims: first, that Marx distinguishes between moral and non-moral goods and that, whilst rejecting the former, he endorses the latter. The second is that Marx believes that capitalism is just.

I have argued that Marx's critique of morality is focused on *Moralität*, and that, although he envisages the scope of the latter more broadly than just formal, Kantian ethics, *Moralität* is not to

---

[24] What *is* suspect, for Marx, is an attitude towards politics that believes that ethically desirable changes can be brought about by appeals to ethical principles and disinterestedly held values.

be understood so broadly as to force Marx to reject all ethical values whatsoever. Thus it might seem that I am attributing a similar distinction to Marx as Wood does in the distinction that he makes between moral and non-moral goods. I do not believe that this is so, however, for the way that Wood draws the distinction is as follows:

We all know the difference between valuing or doing something because conscience or the 'moral law' tells us we 'ought' to, and valuing or doing something because it satisfies our needs, our wants or our conception of what is good for us (or for someone else whose welfare we want to promote—desires for nonmoral goods are not necessarily selfish desires). This difference roughly marks off 'moral' from 'nonmoral' goods and evils as I mean to use those terms here. Moral goods include such things as virtue, right, justice, the fulfillment of duty, and the possession of morally meritorious qualities. Nonmoral goods, on the other hand, include such things as pleasure and happiness, things which we would regard as desirable even if no moral credit accrued from pursuing or possessing them.[25]

On the most natural reading of this passage, what Wood has in mind is quite clear. Non-moral good is 'good' in an agent-relative or functional sense—a sense of the word that can be accepted by the ethical egoist or moral sceptic. It is the sense in which a sharp knife is good for a murderer, just as it is for a brain surgeon, the sense in which to say of something that it is good carries no automatic force of impersonal, ethical commendation. Read in this way, my disagreement with Wood is clear. It seems me that when Marx commends (for instance) pleasure, freedom, self-affirmation, and community, or when he condemns (for instance) slavery, oppression, theft, and alienation, he is doing so in a straightforwardly ethical way: the thing in question is being commended (or condemned) not (just) because it is good (or bad) *for* some individual or group but because it is good (or bad) as such.

But it is only fair to say that there appears to be a backstream to the meaning that Wood gives to the idea of non-moral goods that somewhat muddies the distinction. He writes in a footnote to the passage quoted above:

Moral and nonmoral goods, though different in kind, may not be unrelated. It is arguable that qualities we esteem as morally good (such as

[25] A. Wood, *Karl Marx* (London: Routledge & Kegan Paul, 1981), 126–7.

benevolence, courage and self-control) are also nonmorally good for us to have. On the other hand, some moral theorists (such as utilitarians) believe that what is morally good is determined by what is conducive to the greatest nonmoral good.[26]

The last sentence just quoted seems to me to be of some importance. Depending on how we read it, it seems to me that either Wood and I (also) have a disagreement about how to understand utilitarianism or he is using the idea of a non-moral good in a highly idiosyncratic way. As I read Mill (and if Mill is not a utilitarian, who is?) he believes that the pursuit of happiness supplies the supreme principle for the regulation and evaluation of conduct because happiness is good as such. Thus my happiness is good for me not just because it happens to be mine but, more importantly, because happiness is impersonally good in a way in which, by contrast, the murderer's sharp knife is not. Now either Wood disagrees with my reading of utilitarianism (and thinks that the goodness of happiness for the utilitarian is in each case agent-relative) or he is using the notion of the non-morally good to include both the impersonally good and the good which is agent-relative (despite the fact that the examples of the non-moral good that he gives all appear to fall into the latter category).

This issue matters, for the structure that Wood attributes to the utilitarian—believing that conduct should be regulated by being directed towards a good end—is clearly not confined to utilitarianism. Aristotelianism, for example, seems to have a similarly teleological structure. If Wood were to think that the Aristotelian *summum bonum* were a non-moral good, then—his misleading use of terminology apart—I would have little about which to disagree with him. For it seems to me that a kind of consequentialism is the most appropriate ethical position to ascribe to Marx. If utilitarianism is (as Sen and Williams have suggested) 'welfarist consequentialism', it seems to me that the best label for Marx's view is 'developmentalist consequentialism', having regard to the fact that the goodness of the development in question is to be assessed objectively, with regard to some externally given conception of the human good, not subjectively, as in the forms of utilitarianism with which we are familiar.

The second claim of Wood's with which I wish to take issue is an

---

[26] A. Wood, *Karl Marx* (London: Routledge & Kegan Paul, 1981), 254.

equally striking one. In Wood's view, Marx believes that capitalism is just. The reason, he believes, is that, for Marx, the condition for an institution or practice being just is that it 'harmonizes with and performs a function relative to' a given mode of production.[27] In support of this interpretation Wood cites the following passage:

The justice of transactions which go on between agents of production rests on the fact that these transactions arise out of the production relations as their natural consequences. The juristic forms in which these economic transactions appear as voluntary actions of the participants, as expressions of their common will or as contracts that may be enforced by the state against a single party, cannot, being mere forms, determine this content. They only express it. This content is just whenever it corresponds to the mode of production, is adequate to it. It is unjust whenever it contradicts it.[28]

This passage certainly seems to offer very strong support for Wood's reading. It can be pointed out, of course, that the passage is from *Das Kapital*, volume iii (which was left in draft form by Marx and only revised for publication by Engels), but, given how far any interpretation of Marx's views on ethics must rely on recon-structions using writings not published by Marx himself, that seems a rather weak objection. Another point to be made is that the word *Recht* in German can mean indifferently 'law' and 'right'. The words for 'just' and 'unjust'—*Gerecht* and *Ungerecht*—thus signify that something is in conformity with law or otherwise. So it is very hard to signal in German (or, at least, in the German of Marx's day) a thought that is, by contrast, easily expressed in English: namely, that something may be in conformity with the law (legitimate) without being in conformity with justice; in German, one would have to say (apparently absurdly) that an action was *gerecht* but *ungerecht*. But again this point is quite weak. At best, it explains why it should be that Marx should have slipped into making the claim that existing institutions are just; it does not seriously call into question the idea that he thinks so.

But it must also be said that Wood's striking passage can be matched against another that seems to point equally clearly in the opposite direction. G. A. Cohen in his review of Wood[29] draws

---

[27] Ibid. 131.
[28] *Das Kapital*, iii (New York, 1967), quoted in K. Marx, Wood, *Karl Marx*, 130–1.   [29] *Mind*, 92 (1983), 440–5.

attention to a passage in the first volume of *Das Kapital* in which
Marx comments on the relationship between capitalists and
workers as follows:

Even if the [capitalist class] uses a portion of that tribute [annually exacted
from the working class by the capitalist class] to purchase the additional
labour-power at its full price, so that equivalent is exchanged for equivalent, the whole thing still remains the age-old activity of the conqueror,
who buys commodities from the conquered with the money he has stolen
from them.[30]

To which passage Cohen offers the following powerful comment:

Now since, as Wood will agree, Marx did not think that by capitalist criteria the capitalist steals, and since he did think he steals, he must have meant
that he steals in some appropriately non-relativist sense. And since to steal
is, in general, wrongly to take what rightly belongs to another, to steal is
to commit an injustice and a system which is 'based on theft' is based on
injustice.[31]

Granted that Marx believes that the capitalist steals in a non-
relativist sense, only two possibilities seem open. Either, Cohen to
the contrary, Marx does not believe that theft is unjust or else there
is a serious discrepancy in his beliefs: he believes that capitalism is
unjust, but he also believes (falsely) that he does not believe that
capitalism is unjust. In favour of the former interpretation is the
point made about the notion of *Recht* made earlier: if *gerecht*, for
Marx, means only 'in conformity with the established laws', it is
clear how a practice could be 'theft' (and hence to be condemned
in an impersonal, non-relative way) whilst at the same time being
gerecht.

Against both Wood and Cohen, however, I would like to offer a
different interpretation according to which Marx can consistently
both believe that principles of justice are products of, and are
limited by, given modes of production and, at the same time, believe
that capitalism is unjust. To present my interpretation, let me turn
to the critical remarks made by Marx against the programme of the
German Social-Democratic Party—the *Critique of the Gotha Programme*. The discussion to which I wish to draw attention concerns
the initial stage of a future communist society, not, as he puts it, 'as

---

[30] K. Marx, *Capital*, i (Harmondsworth: Penguin, 1977), 728.
[31] Review of Wood, *Karl Marx*, 443.

it has *developed* on its own foundations, but, on the contrary, just as it *emerges* from capitalist society'.[32] This stage of society will, Marx asserts, still bear 'the birth marks of the old society from whose womb it emerges'[33] and, for this reason, its principle of distribution will not be the same as in a higher stage of communist society:

Accordingly, the individual producer receives back from society—after the deductions have been made—exactly what he gives to it . . . He receives a certificate from society that he has furnished such and such an amount of labour (after deducting his labour for the common funds), and with this certificate he draws from the social stock of means of consumption as much as costs the same amount of labour. The same amount of labour which he has given to society in one form he receives back in another.[34]

Marx notes that in this respect the economic relations of (the initial stage of) communism in fact resemble those of commodity production, to the extent that both embody the principle of the exchange of equal values.[35] The basis for this exchange is, of course, very different for, under the communist system, no one has anything to offer in exchange except his or her labour. Nevertheless, Marx notes, the transaction is still one involving 'equal right'. It is the comment that he makes next, however, that is, in my view, particularly significant: 'Hence *equal right* here is still in principle— *bourgeois right*, although principle and practice are no longer at loggerheads, while the exchange of equivalents in commodity exchange only exists *on the average* and not in the individual case.'[36]

What Marx is saying in this passage, if I read him right, is that bourgeois right is indeed (as Wood's passage from volume iii indicates) a product of and limited by a particular mode of production. But from the fact that that standard is produced by a particular society it does not follow that the society itself automatically meets the standard in question. On the contrary, Marx seems to be saying, quite plainly, just the opposite: that bourgeois right is a standard which capitalist society itself fails to meet (in which 'principle and practice are . . . at loggerheads'). In other words, capitalism is a society with a contradiction at its heart: which fails to meet the standards that it sets for itself. The initial phase of communist

---

[32] Marx, 'Critique of the Gotha Programme', iii. 17.
[33] Ibid. [34] Ibid. iii. 17–18. [35] Ibid. iii. 18. [36] Ibid.

society redeems the standard of bourgeois right and is, in that sense, just in a way that capitalism is not. Nevertheless, this conception of justice is tainted: 'In spite of this advance, this *equal right* is still constantly stigmatized by a bourgeois limitation.'[37]

There are important reasons, in my view, why Marx is reluctant to condemn capitalism as unjust, but the fact that he thought it was just is not one of them. Perhaps a slightly strained analogy might help to understand Marx's dilemma. Let us take, as an example, the ideal of 'gentlemanliness' as it was found in Great Britain up till the Second World War, understanding thereby (amongst other things) certain standards of reticence, courtesy, and unwillingness to resort to force. Now concede, at least for the sake of argument, that this ideal was the product of a set of institutions and social practices that involved steep class divisions, fiercely (if informally) enforced systems of social exclusion, and a highly unequal distribution of power between the sexes. Let us concede too that some of these institutions and practices led to behaviour (for instance, contemptuous and violent treatment of wives by husbands) that stood in flagrant contradiction to the accepted code of gentlemanly behaviour. Would one then want to condemn such behaviour as 'ungentlemanly'? I think that the most natural answer would be both yes and no. Yes, to the extent that the behaviour produced by the institution violates that institution's own moral code; no, to the extent that that moral code itself appears to be limited and tainted. If I am right, then Marx's reluctance to condemn capitalism as unjust in case he might be thought thereby to be endorsing the bourgeois ideal of justice has similar grounds.

In further support of this interpretation, let me quote a passage from volume i of *Das Kapital*. According to Marx, 'the wage-form . . . extinguishes every trace of the division of the working-day into necessary labour and surplus-labour. All labour appears as paid labour.'[38] This illusion (as Marx considers it to be) is of the very greatest significance. He goes on:

We may therefore understand the decisive importance of the transformation of the value and price of labour-power into the form of wages, or into the value and price of labour itself. All the notions of justice (*Rechtsvorstellungen*) held by both worker and capitalist, all the mystifications of the capitalist mode of production, all capitalism's illusions about freedom

---

[37] Marx, 'Critique of the Gotha Programme'.   [38] Marx, *Capital*, i. 680.

(*Freiheitsillusionen*), all the apologetic tricks of vulgar economics, have as their basis the form of appearance discussed above, which makes the actual relation invisible, and indeed presents to the eye the precise opposite of that relation.[39]

On the basis of this passage, in my view, it is clear that Marx believes that both workers and capitalists believe, necessarily, that capitalism is just; that, for the same reason, they suffer from (unspecified) 'mystifications'; that they believe, necessarily but also *falsely*, that capitalism embodies the value of freedom (they are subject to *Freiheitsillusionen*). It is hardly plausible in this context to think that Marx thinks that (unlike their belief that capitalism is free) the citizens' belief that capitalism is just is *true*. The interpretation argued for shows how it can be possible both that Marx should believe that capitalism is unjust (and that he believes that he so believes) and, at the same time, that he believes that the standard that makes capitalism unjust suffers from limitations as a result of the mode of production of which it is a product, limitations which make justice unsuitable to function as a trans-historical standard by which the ethical worth of societies may finally be assessed.[40]

[39] Ibid.
[40] I am grateful to G. A. Cohen, Edward Harcourt, and Jonathan Wolff for helpful comments on an earlier version of this paper.

Is Morality a Ruling Illusion?

Anthony Skillen

What elasticity, what historical initiative, what a capacity for sacrifice in these Parisians! After six months of hunger and ruin, caused rather by internal treachery than by the external enemy, they rise, beneath Prussian bayonets . . . History has no example of a like greatness. If they are defeated, only their 'good nature' will be to blame. They should have marched on Versailles . . . The right moment was missed because of conscientious scruples . . . the present rising in Paris—even if it is crushed by the wolves, swine and vile curs of the old society—is the most glorious deed of our Party since the June insurrection in Paris. Compare these Parisians, storming heaven, with the slaves to heaven of the German-Prussian Holy Roman Empire, with its posthumous masquerades reeking of the barracks, the Church, cabbage-junkerdom and above all, the philistine. . . . But acceleration and delay (in world history) are very dependent on . . . 'accidents', which include the 'accident' of the character of those who at first stand at the head of the movement. . . . The struggle of the working class against the capitalist class and its state has entered upon a new phase with the struggle in Paris. Whatever the immediate results may be, a new point of departure of world-historic importance has been gained.[1]

Here is 'ordinary-language' Marx: characterizing and assessing the now doomed Communard struggle. In saluting its greatness, Marx speaks of deeds as heroic as their cherished ends were noble, and denounces the agents of its defeat in appropriately antithetical terms. Yet this, as I would call it, ethical account is tucked, some

[1] K. Marx, Letter to Dr Kugelmann (Apr. 1871), in K. Marx, *The Civil War in France* (New York: International Publishers, 1940), 85–6.

would say obtrusively, between a picture of moral scruple fettering the Communards' campaign on the one hand and on the other a broadly utilitarian accountancy of the whole event in terms of its predicted long-term consequences. In this last respect, the inspiring potential of the Paris Commune enters a 'world-historic' balance sheet. There it lies alongside, for example, the modernizations through which the British 'crimes' in India were 'the unconscious tool of history'.[2] Layering of this sort—economic analysis ('mode of production', 'surplus value', and so on), ethical characterization ('alienating', 'degrading', 'oppressive', 'mutilating'), and anti-ideological puncturing ('slaves to heaven', 'morality, religion, metaphysics', 'superstitious worship of the state')—pervades Marx's writing.

The Communards were massacred and the European world made safe by the bourgeois state for capital's hegemony. Marx thought this respite for the powers-that-be but temporary, but he also thought the regime of capital itself a necessary evil, a condition through its coercive creativity of the development of the human-technological powers essential to a globally harmonious flourishing. Sceptical of labour's even organized power decisively to ameliorate its life under capital's system, he inclined to see organized struggle as prefiguring 'the brotherhood of man' and as a perhaps multi-generational education, a preparation for human self-rule, for the communist association of producers. Such, with its idea of human potential coming to fruit and flower, was Marx's historical materialist humanism. Without such a vision the whole thing signifies next to nothing; without a causal story of 'determinations' it is pie-in-the-sky. Now, primary among the determinations, both of stasis and of change, was the 'dull compulsion of economic life', the sheer necessity established by the capitalist class's control over the means of production, for the mass of its subjects, on pain of penury or starvation, daily to take their labour-power to market. The state entrenched this discipline, with its civil and criminal laws enshrining and policing the rights of property and the conditions of its legitimate exchange. As articulated by Political Economy, the structure was self-winding, with individuals forced and induced to act and interact from self-interest in such a way as to maintain and

---

[2] 'The British Rule in India' (1853), in K. Marx, *Political Writings*, ii, ed. D. Fernbach (Harmondsworth: Penguin, 1973): tough on crime, tender on the consequences of crime.

advance it. There may have been mutually offsetting local gains within it, but there was (as there is) 'no alternative'.

Ideologies represent orders of society as inevitable or as the best possible order, given the nature of things. In *The Communist Manifesto* Marx and Engels seem to have thought the capitalist system so transparently transitional that the workers' movements would see through it and, through their necessary self-organization, discover the power to smash it. There was no need to educate, let alone to preach morality to those who were not only combining and resisting out of self-interest, but were, through that struggle, discovering a new interest, that of human association itself. Thus did Marx come to think his youthful battles with 'the German Ideology' of largely biographical interest compared with the project of ruthlessly organizing to build the Party and proving the evolutionary mortality of capital through the inevitable decline of the rate of profit. Yet just because he so misjudged the durability of bad things and the fragility of good ones, his debunking critique of ideologies remains central to our self-understanding in a world that remains Marx's nightmare of barbarism.

Though his weapons were those of the intellectual and many of his targets fellow members of that class, it is, at least from a Marxian perspective, wrong to see ideology predominantly in terms of the productions of such ideologues or even of the function their works play in reinforcing regimes through rationalizing them. Sages, prophets, and intellectuals work up into doctrines, albeit to return them with interest to the soil that nourished them, discourses, vocabularies, modes of understanding, outlooks, that are already present in everyday social practice. That is a condition both of the production of these discourses and of their reception as intelligible reflective accounts of any way of life. When, therefore, as philosophers we look at Bentham, Kant, Hegel, or for that matter Marx or Nietzsche, it is idealistic to think of them as cultural constitutors whose ideas were embodied in social practice. Rather, to the extent that they are ideologues, they articulate explicitly ideas already implicit in the world of which they make their sense. Kant and Bentham, for example, were in many ways antithetical, but shared a view of the natural teleology and menace of desire or inclination. Both presented the subject as naturally isolated, naturally selfish, and naturally short-sighted—as a domain to be ruled over, a beast to be tamed. In the eyes of both, morality was opposite to and complementary with Political Economy's self-interest. Morality, in the absence of direct surveillance and tangible sanctions, is what ensures that the rules of market exchange, whether of worker and capitalist or among bourgeois owners, hold sway. Thus in both we find a debasing ideology of natural desire on the one hand and an aggrandizingly sublimated account of that which regulates desire on the other.[3] Thus do their philosophies interweave with bourgeois ideology's 'construction of the self', mirroring common sense and ramifying its hegemony. Thus does each legitimize what survives of the Church's gift to capitalism in the form of the notion of the sinfulness of man and the certain fear of everlasting life. And thus does each survive a thousand refutations. What else could we expect in a world where life teaches us daily both that we must look after ourselves and at the same time that this protégé is so worthless?

I argued in *Ruling Illusions*[4] that an authoritarian and reductive model of human life dominated and philosophically legitimized actually existing institutions of state, law, education, punishment, work, and, pervasively, morality. Attacking these interlocking ideologies, I claimed a Marxian inheritance. Marx was said to laugh whenever the name of Morality was invoked, while retaining, as we have seen, a rich, uneccentric, and sometimes deep ethical vocabulary. I argued that Marx was consistent here and, moreover, broadly right: not only is Morality—with its abstract laws to be obeyed, for duty's sake, by equally abstract individual moral subjects—in Marx's view an 'illusion'. It is an oppressive illusion, to be rejected by the parties both of Reality and of Humanity. Marx, in the main, had a quite specific conception of morality, not a generic one embracing the norms and values of all societies. For him, morality was a historically determinate ideological institution consisting of internalized commandments functioning to mystify and discipline people in accordance with the oppressive needs of class society. To describe an institution as ideological is to describe it as the expression of a restrictive perspective and as occlusive of actualities and possibilities liable, but for it, to be discerned

---

[3] I criticize this abstractive reductionist ideology in 'The Ethical Neutrality of Science and the Method of Abstraction: The Case of Political Economy', *Philosophical Forum*, 11 (1980), 215–33.

[4] (Hassocks: Harvester Press, 1977; Aldershot: Gregg Revivals, 1993). See esp. ch. 4.

and acted on. The concept of ideology is at once epistemic and ethical in so far as it implies concealment and thwarting, and sociological in so far as it implies determinations, functions, and mechanisms. In the spirit of this understanding, I argued along the following lines:

> Our society divides people up and presents this atomisation as the human condition; it pits them into competition with each other and calls this human nature; it demands the suppression of impulses and calls these humanity's enemy. . . . If the State is God's march on earth, Morality is his parade on the spirit. In the absence of positive cooperative ties and positive motives to work and create, the capitalist system requires 'specialist' forces of control, armed men and harsh consciences, bullies, to make us do what money alone cannot bribe us to do.[5]

Formulating a more positive account of morality, I wrote:

> To talk of morality in [a] 'non-moralistic' way, it seems to me, would be to talk in terms, not of a higher power, an authoritative voice, controlling our inclinations, but rather of the relation among our activities (dispositions, impulses, feelings, passions, values) as they are formed and expressed in our ways of life. . . . And 'socialist' restraint would be the preponderance of communal, productive, loving and communicative activities and motives over invidiously divisive (including moralistic) activities and motives.[6]

Moralism sets up rules, requirements, and duties as that which controls, inhibits, or overrides desires, inclinations, and affections. The non-moralistic philosophy I am advancing prefers to talk of morality as forms of, cultivations of, such passions or inclinations.

Something similar, I think, is implicit in Philippa Foot's 'Morality as a System of Hypothetical Imperatives'.[7] By her account, the moral 'volunteer' acts well out of intelligent care for the good of others, for truth, liberty, and for a life open and in good faith with his neighbours. No need here for a 'categorical imperative'. Lay people and philosophers alike adhere to the 'moral conscript' notion of the 'categorical imperative' thanks to the standard form of moral inculcation: 'moral rules are often enforced' . . . 'relative stringency of our moral teaching' . . . 'must do' . . . 'have to do' . . . 'the non-hypothetical moral "ought" by which society is apt to voice its demands' . . . Such 'psychological conditions of the learn-

---

[5] Hassocks: Harvester Press, 157.   [6] Ibid. 168–9.
[7] *Philosophical Review*, 81 (1972), 305–16.

ing of moral behaviour' explain for Foot the feelings of inescapability accompanying the 'magic' 'illusion' of a peculiar bindingness in the moral 'ought'. What I am inclined to say, agreeing that obligation is not by itself reason-giving, is that her critical account is more than a 'clarification' of moral thought: it is foundational to the defence of a clear-eyed moral life against an obscurantist and authoritarian one that rules in everyday language and practice in the name of 'Morality'. But Foot obscures this insight by the analogies through which she advances the Hypothetical against the Categorical imperative interpretation of moral reasons: etiquette, law, and club rules. For these suggest, contrary to the force of her examples of true virtue, that the moral imperative has the general, implicit form: 'If you are conscientious (if you want to act according to moral rules), do this'; which leaves unexamined what it is to obey moral rules, or to disobey them—what this 'system of morality' amounts to, whether for conscripts or for voluntary recruits. But alongside this institutional, quasi-legal account, Foot offers us a picture of suffering, need, tyranny, and injustice as being in their distinctive ways themselves reasons for response and action in so far as appropriately situated people care about such things. Such caring constitutes their individual or collective (Foot instances the defence of Leningrad) 'moral' character—their virtues.[8]

I find other fellow travellers. More recently, Bernard Williams, in *Ethics and the Limits of Philosophy*, has targeted as a 'particular development of the ethical' the 'Peculiar Institution' of 'Morality'.[9] It is, he says, something we would be better off without. As a way of clarifying my own thinking of where this consensus leaves us, I want to attend to some of the things Williams says here and in his *Shame and Necessity*.[10] There is not very much in the critique of 'the morality system' and of the meanly imperialistic spirit that Williams takes as its core that I would want to dispute; in particular I think Williams is right to see the philosophical illusions of the freely willing moral subject helping to underpin the moralistic stand's empirical and practical isolation of the blamed individual

---

[8] Whether, with Foot, Lawrence Blum (e.g. in *Moral Perception and Particularity* (Cambridge: Cambridge University Press, 1994)), and others, we call the rich territory threatened by the 'Kantian' defoliant a 'moral' field is a matter of judgement; a judgement I exercised in demarcating 'big-M Morality' from its humbler kin, also referred to as 'the ethical'.

[9] (London: Fontana, 1985), 6, and ch. 10, *passim*.

[10] (Berkeley: University of California Press, 1993).

as a sort of ultimate originator of sin. And he is right too to see a decolonized future for notions of obligation and responsibility, independent of moralistic mythology, 'as merely one kind of ethical consideration among others.'[11] But I have two worries with Williams's outlook which will serve to introduce larger issues.

The first has to do with moral blame. Williams denies that moral considerations are necessarily reasons for a person to do things. Moral blame, he says, is a piece of 'machinery' which involves the 'fiction' that the individual is necessarily susceptible to moral reasons, ascribing moral reasons to its target in such a way that 'this may help him to be such a person'. Thus, despite its dangers, it is a 'positive achievement' of the 'blame system' that it fosters 'recruitment into the deliberative community', the community who share ethical dispositions. But what constitutes this 'recruitment'? Anything more than the disposition to avoid (these people's) blame? For what reasons? Now, as a critic of moralistic blaming and as one who looks forward to our disembarking from the moral guilt-trip in general, Williams himself adumbrates such questions. But whereas an Old Left Footian like me might grant that a condemnatory attack on somebody just might have the consequence that they came to see the error of their ways independently of the attack—'How didn't I see that?'—Williams wants to see this part of the 'ethical system' demoted to a 'pragmatic blame' surrounded by other 'practices of encouragement and discouragement, acceptance and rejection, which work on desire and character to shape them into the requirements and possibilities of ethical life'.[12] What eludes me here is a sense of such social processes as anything other than 'recruitment', socialization into particular 'deliberative communities' on pain of rejection, blame, and exclusion. Minus moral metaphysics, I am not clear that we have really left behind the discourse of requirements and permissions.

The second worry has to do with Guilt, Victims, Enforcers. In *Shame and Necessity* Williams devotes a seminal endnote to 'Mechanisms of Shame and Guilt', giving a naturalistic social-psychological account of them as involving distinct 'internalised figures'. (I take it that this rooting is intended not merely to trace origins, but to characterize the nature of these sentiments.) Whereas shame internalizes the 'watcher or witness', guilt inter-

---

[11] *Ethics and the Limits of Philosophy*, 182.   [12] Ibid. 194.

nalizes the 'victim or enforcer'. My worry is over this account of guilt. First, since Williams says that the explicandum must not be implicit in the elements of the explicans, and since he says that guilt's 'primitive' form is fear at the victim's anger, he is going to be in some, though negotiable, difficulty over the subject's recognition of the object as 'angry' without presupposing too much. Anger surely is a response to perceived guilt in some sense of 'guilt', so one might have to see whether something more primitive, perhaps retaliation, might serve Williams's purpose better. But secondly, and more importantly, Williams runs victim and enforcer together. As I take it that guilt as constructed by the morality system is or involves rule-transgression, I find this hard to understand. Surely it is not 'primitively' the case that these two roles are, let alone have to be, identical; for surely the aggression in guilt as constructed by the morality system is internalized, broadly speaking, from the primitive enforcer of transgressed requirements. Retaliation implies power, and the victim, who may not even be hostile, may, if hostile, be unthreatening. Sorrow towards someone one has wronged seems to me something that the punitive recriminations of the Morality System get in the way of by focusing attention on the self—imagine the victim ignored as the parent turns on the offending child: 'Say sorry!' Thus I do not agree with Williams's claim, contrasting guilt with the 'narcissism' of shame,[13] that 'the victims and their feelings' are at the core of the guilt system. That connection is contingent on the presence of victims in the content of the prohibitions and sanctions. Still less, since it is the victim's hostile feelings, not their sufferings, that Williams highlights, do I see why focusing fearful attention on such feelings should be seen as 'an inherent virtue of guilt as opposed to shame'.[14]

Williams looks forward to the erosion of the Peculiar Institution of Morality: its machinery carries too much untenable baggage and wreaks too much damage to wider concerns, ethical and otherwise. It might be thought that emancipation from it would leave us with a better chance of clear-eyed ethical vision. But Williams is inclined to think an undimmed, perhaps even enlightened, capacity to be in touch with ethical realities an illusion: 'ethical thought has no chance of being everything that it seems'.[15] One such false

---

[13] *Shame and Necessity*, 222.   [14] Ibid.
[15] *Ethics and the Limits of Philosophy*, 135, 199.

appearance, as I understand Williams, is that of the possibility of full-blooded ethical truth. This appearance is undermined not only by the fact of disagreement within as well as among societies but by the fact that were such disagreements to dissolve and the world to converge in what Williams has more recently called 'one homogeneous ethical language',[16] this would not be because people's ethical outlooks had come to be guided by how things ethically are. Disagreements do not entail failure in any party, for any reason, to appreciate a truth that is there independently to be agreed upon; their existence will be best, if not sufficiently, explained sociologically, maybe by cultural imperialism—unlike purely sociological accounts of scientific disagreement which are hopelessly deaf to the way scientific inquiry is responsive to reality. Within the territory constituted by an ethical outlook, there will be a range of 'thick' concepts, picking out kinds of situation, disposition, and so on that are sufficiently stable and have sufficiently salient features in terms of that value-outlook to merit a label. But 'the question of what your repertoire of thick concepts is reveals your own or your society's attitude'.[17] Nothing 'in the situation' can 'recruit' people into using such concepts for, being a 'cultural' function, their being employed is determined not by the situation but by attitudes to situations.

Williams gives the example of boys who torture a cat for fun, saying that if an observer uses the concept 'cruel' at all, she will have to think that this is cruel. But the thought that this is cruel, as I understand Williams's view, no more has to be taken on board by the boys than an old-fashioned bystander's criticism of a bare-footed girl as 'immodest' would have to be taken on board by her—if she doesn't use that concept. The boys simply may not be disposed to view their actions in this light. Having such a concept, then, is having 'a disposition that expresses itself in categorising the world in those terms',[18] and gaining or losing a concept is a matter of disposition, hence not of discovery. So, for Williams, as I understand him, it is not the case that, getting away from a narrowly 'moralistic' understanding of, say, cruelty or bullying, we might be able to move towards a richer, sociologically and psychologically

---

[16] See Bernard Williams, 'Truth in Ethics', *Ratio*, 8 (1995), 240.
[17] Ibid. 237.   [18] Ibid. 238.

sophisticated understanding of such truly bad things; the ethical in general is as much a social construct as its metaphysically deformed subspecies, the moral. Thus, though there may be no independently describable interests disguised behind its posturings, of the sort which Williams takes to nourish the metaphysical claims of the morality system, ethical life will be 'ideological' at least in the epistemic sense that any basis in the transcultural nature of things will be illusory. There are, on Williams's account, cultural realities, but no ethical realities in so far as these would be more than facts of valuings. Or at least their existence is strongly doubted. However, it is one thing to say that only some ethical values can survive the transparency of reflective scrutiny, but if it is also conceded that the value of reflective scrutiny, as part of modern liberalism, is itself a cultural option, we are left with a darkness at enlightenment's noon.

It seems to me that some of the preoccupations of *Shame and Necessity* might be partly explained in terms of their complementarity with what I'll risk calling the subjectivist and cultural relativist drift that I've tried to catch in the above account of Williams's views. For the 'mechanisms' of guilt and shame depicted throughout *Shame and Necessity*'s terrific and restorative account of Homer and the Greek tragedians and analysed in the endnote are sociological or social-psychological mechanisms *par excellence*, with their internalizations of Significant Others and their implication that character formation progresses with such internalizations. Such mechanisms are compatible with just about any substantial content. A view of ethical learning, therefore, which was thus confined would be one of a learning to admire and obey what is laid down by the terms of any given society. This confinement, I suggest, remains despite Williams's successful rescuing of the ethical culture of shame from the reductive alienizings of the anthropologists. Lacking determination by their targets, ethical responses emerge on this account as socially constructed; and what is at the subject's end 'internalization' is at the other end 'recruitment', 'instilling'— the socialization process we keep hearing about from our students of sociology. Dumping the illusory autonomy of the moral, we seem to have jumped into the real heteronomy of the social, hanging by our bootstraps at the mercy of conventional prestige and its conditionings. Thus, of *The Iliad*, Williams says: 'The opinions of Nestor carried weight, and those of Thersites did not.'[19] But poor old Thersites, ugly nobody as he is, is heroically right in his attack on Agamemnon's vainglory. Thersites says:

> What are you panting after now? Your shelters packed
> with the lion's share of bronze, plenty of women too,
> crowding your lodges. Best of the lot, the beauties
> we hand you first whenever we take some stronghold.
> Or still more gold you're wanting?[20]

And what a paradigm of shaming is the toadying Odysseus' bullying reaction, like that of some playground henchman, to Thersites' pacifist protest![21]

My question is this: if we let shame supplant guilt, what exactly do we gain in the critique of oppressive and deceitful institutions and the struggle for an ethical life capable through its transparency of winning our 'unprejudiced assent', the dampened but undoused liberal aspiration of Williams's postscript to *Ethics and the Limits of Philosophy*? As Williams himself suggests, honour and shame presuppose not just an authoritative identity-conferring and -confirming 'honours system' but the formatively habitual face-to-face visibility of communal ethical life. Maybe these could have their electronic surrogates, but that is scarcely the direction of transparency we, with Williams, are after.

I have suggested that Williams is left with no more than recruitment machinery partly by his scepticism about the possibility of ethical knowledge that transcends the inwardness of a given way of life. This seems to imply that an objectivist would offer a different account of moral education: of what they will see as practical processes of coming to recognize, say, bullying, cruelty, exploitativeness, or servility for what they are—of judgements and responses best explained (even when not rationalized as such) as caring awarenesses of what is the case rather than simply as internalizations of socially accredited valorizations. I am inclined to go that way and to contrast good moral education through experience and reflection with moralistic and other forms of conditioning inculcation.

But although relativism is a sufficient condition of assimilating

---

[19] *Shame and Necessity*, 82.
[20] Homer, *The Iliad*, trans. R. Fagles (Harmondsworth: Penguin, 1992), ii. 263.
[21] Ibid. ii. 218–324.

education to conditioning, it is not a necessary one. For some non-relativists are content to think of the unreflective masses acquiring true opinion by what amounts to social conditioning: the compelling force of external socialization mechanisms is often assumed to be acceptable by naturalistic philosophers of an objectivist cast too. (See, for an ancestor, Hume's objectivistic defence of feminine modesty and the modes he thought appropriate for its inculcation in the 'ductile' minds of girls.) Rationalists for whom the existence of moral reasons is independent of individuals' or even cultures' grasp or disposition and for whom moral thought is the bloodless computation of a rational fish sometimes leave me mystified on behalf of the person-in-the-street, whose best hope is to have been so socialized as unreflectively to accord with norms elaborated over her head. How, socially, interpersonally, do such people see the normatively desirable getting 'internalized' as the formation of motivating desire? How is 'co-ordination' achieved? What instils 'mutually beneficent attitudes'? Kant himself wanted the educator to rely on the pupil's fear of his contemptuous tongue. Are we not left with a Benthamite split between the educated officers and the trained troopers, notoriously illustrated by Sidgwick's doctrine that Utility would be best served by its doctrines being the object of general revulsion? Peter Railton, who proposes a rich eudaimonistic objectivism, says something along those lines: 'My sort of naturalist reduces moral properties to complex social-psychological phenomena; not to extra-human Nature. At least since Durkheim there has been a naturalistic way of understanding how social phenomena may bring into individuals a notion of obligatoriness that will present itself to them as objective and independent of their personal inclinations.'[22] But this is a shaky hitching-post; it makes it hard, in my view, to develop a conception of moral education as something tying content to mode of becoming aware of content, in which the explanation of judgements vindicates them. Durkheim's model of moral education is basically one in which an official ideology, what Talcott Parsons was to call the 'central value system', is imposed through the orchestrated double whammy of guilt and shame. Whether such an ideology would accord with Railton's

---

[22] See Railton, 'Reply to David Wiggins', in J. Haldane and C. Wright (eds.), *Reality, Representation and Projection* (New York: Oxford University Press, 1993), 235.

'content' criteria of the moral is a contingent matter. Durkheim says, for example:

> It is through the practice of school discipline that we can inculcate the spirit of discipline in the child. . . . The principal form of punishment has always consisted in putting the guilty on the index, ostracising him, making a void around him and separating him from decent people.[23]
>
> If we renounce the option of calling upon a divine power, then we must seek another which can play the same role . . . This power is of course society. . . . For, in effect society stands in relation to its members as a god stands to his followers.[24]

Psychologically, I see Durkheim as offering as a model of moral education what amounts to something dangerously like the sort of school bullying that produces identification with the aggressor. But the main point I am making is this: relativists may see cultures as internally vindicated structures of conventionally constituted meaning; 'ideologies' on this picture would just be regimes of understanding. Some non-relativists, on the contrary, see cultural structures as open to criticism or theoretical vindication in terms of functional coherence and utility. In either case there is a tendency to see them, in effect, as ideologies in at least the sense of a way of thinking, feeling, and seeing things, whose explanation at the individual level makes only derivative reference to the things such mindsets are, apparently, focused on. There is, that is, a division between the rationale of the system and the reason for individuals' thought and action within the system. There is a tendency, then, not to see the ethical in terms of modes of being alive or dead, perceptive or blind, to situations, but as conventional modes of framing or defining situations in such a way that they are constituted as requiring this or that of us.

But consider the time in *Huckleberry Finn*, chapter 16, when the narrator's conscience fails to get him to hand over the 'nigger' slave to be returned to Miss Watson, his owner. All the moral arguments voiced in Huck's internal soliloquy line up against protecting Jim: the Guilt Mechanism, the Shame Mechanism, even the God Mechanism. All conspire to define Huck as a conspirator in criminal outrage. But, try as he does, Huck cannot live up to the com-

---

[23] E. Durkheim, *Moral Education* (Glencoe, Ill.: Free Press, 1961), 149, 175.
[24] E. Durkheim, 'The Teaching of Morality in Schools', *Journal of Moral Education*, 24 (1995), 30–1.

mands his conscience is shouting at him. Brilliantly he deceives the slave-hunters, judging himself to be a spunkless backslider. In his discussion of it,[25] Jonathan Bennett says that this is a case where all the reasons are on the wrong side, being defeated by 'unreasoned moral pulls'.[26] But this is surely not right; Huck's saving Jim is intelligible, is best explained, as a response to a grasped situation: that 'nigger' is his human companion, Jim. Emotional intelligence, nourished by the experiences Huck has been through with Jim, carries the day against the System. Had his generous mind not been darkened by ideology, Huck would have seen that there was nothing else to do than what, for at least some of the very best of reasons, he does do. Being good-natured and knowing more about life than he thinks, Huck can see more clearly, roundly, and subtly than, for example, Tom Sawyer, even though Huckleberry nearly always defers to Sawyer's judgement.

Williams rescues Homer, for all humankind, from the exoticizing archaeologists. But there is an aspect of Homer's 'humanity' that seems to me to get sidelined in the status-focused emphasis on shame-identity and in the tendency to write off anything that smacks of Christianity. I am thinking about themes of human pity and inhuman pitilessness, of Hector's more than hospitable kindness towards Helen of Troy, of his reaction to the infant Astyanax's fright at the sight of him in his helmet, of the winning boxer's gracious concern for the vanquished in the funeral games for Patroclus, and of the climactic shaft of the light of compassion between Achilles and old Priam. Throughout his portrayal of the mayhem, pitiably used for the gods' sport, Homer reminds us that each member of the to-be-devastated masses has, not just a status but a life, home, and loved ones, all soon to be lost. Here we are talking about a kind of recognition that is not expressed in a citizenly nod among the members of a Hegelian community of mutual regard. Plato thought Homer shamefully, 'womanishly', indulgent in pity. Can't we say that something was missing from Plato's sensibility, something of which his Guardians' orphanage was symptomatic? I complained earlier about the central place Williams ascribes to the victim in the morality system's version of guilt. I think victims and our capacity to respond to them belong somewhere else, more

[25] 'The Conscience of Huckleberry Finn', *Philosophy*, 49 (1974), 123–34; repr. in P. Singer (ed.), *Ethics* (Oxford: Oxford University Press, 1994). [26] Ibid. 299.

fundamental and more directly connected with our response to them than as the sources of retaliatory threat.

At one point in *Ethics and the Limits of Philosophy* Williams talks about 'the basic issue of what people should be able to rely on', and that sounds pretty fundamental and unrelativist: 'People must rely as far as possible on not being killed or used as a resource, and on having some space and objects and relations with other people they can count as their own. It also serves their interests if, to some extent at least, they can count on not being lied to.'[27] 'To some extent at least': what modesty with the truth! Williams then says that 'one way, perhaps the only way' in which these basic interests can be served is 'by some kind of ethical life' and again that 'one way' of achieving this is by 'instilling certain motivations'. Again, 'one way', one way, of securing these non-maleficent reliabilities is by constituting and instilling them as obligations with virtually absolute priority corresponding to basic rights. Perhaps an alternative might be for the interested parties' mutual interests to be protected by the police. But if that was all there was to it, as Williams himself says, you wouldn't have an ethical life here: 'certainly, if there is to be ethical life, these ends have to be served by it and within it'. But not only is ethical life in fact a condition of such minimum goods; we would get off to the wrong start if we wheeled in obligations and rights as our primary constitutive and protective 'mechanism' for securing reliabilities in this area.

If rights and obligations, permissions and requirements, are to have a character other than that of social demands and allowances, they must express and guide something that is in a different and more vulgar register. I think we are here on ground which needs to be understood in terms of basic or common humanity—of care, nurture, trust in and uptake of each others' responses, compassion, love, fair-mindedness, acknowledgement of the other in gesture, speech, and action—of patterns and structures of attention and failures of attention. This was the warmest wisdom of the eighteenth century, best articulated perhaps in Henry Fielding's novels. And Plato and Aristotle are deviant, as maybe a lot of the philosophers were, certainly Bentham and the elder Mill, in their extrusion or ignoring of these foundationally and seminally virtuous

---

[27] *Ethics and the Limits of Philosophy*, 185.

sentiments and dispositions—and of their destructive and ugly opposites.

Much of this reductive extrusion is achieved by an amnesic rhetoric that insults our passions and inclinations by representing them as psychic ephemera: inherently capricious and contingent bubbles on the stream of consciousness; alternatively, as wantons waylaying our unguarded selves. Such sabbatarian imagery, blind and deaf to the richness and depth of the working value-vocabulary of everyday life, belongs to the ideological ensemble that constitutes moralism's vision of its redemptively policing role.[28] But if we think of 'culture' generally in the imperative mood and correlatively of acculturation as a process of subjection rather than of structuring nurture—cultivation—we imagine we are only kept together by interest corrected by duty. That is why the term 'humanity', which points beyond and beneath our stature as 'rational beings', is invoked here, not as an essentialist slogan so much as a reminder of a family neglected by theory.

Certainly humane virtues (whose warm guise is taken on in the affected cheerfulness of even the most duty-bound acts) have their consequential utilities: they serve interests. But they entail responses in which others are more than a set of rivals whose rights oblige us to police our own usurping inclinations. That prohibition-fenced, 'bourgeois' model of life was of course one of the reasons why Marx was so hyperbolically hostile to the claims of 'rights' discourse and averse to recognizing its back-up functions. Thoughtlessly, he seems to have imagined a time beyond scarcity when interests would not seriously conflict. That said, however, it is not through recruitment and control mechanisms that the reliabilities of ethical life exist; rather, its taken-for-granted reliabilities are conditions of the elaboration, for good or ill, of such mechanisms. Not all virtues are artificial virtues.

I am attempting to question the adequacy of what I will call the Durkheimian model of socialization and of moral education, and at the same time to suggest that the concept of humanity brings with it a notion of naturally appropriate understanding responses to individuals, which are social and communicative without being

---

[28] Those seeking a more appreciative and realistic account of mind's feeling should go back to Alexander Shand's *The Foundations of Character, Being a Study of the Tendencies of the Emotions and Sentiments* (London: Macmillan, 1920).

the activity of 'Society' or 'the Community'. Cultures build on this and also articulate it so that there are many ways of being human. Cultural practices do represent themselves as ways of being human: as appropriate to the specific and individual nature of its members. Putatively, children everywhere are brought up, not just under. But not all cultural practices constitute equibrilliant contributions to life's rich tapestry; some but not all are sustainable only through ideological illusion. We recognize what it is to find criticism or defence, of our own and others' practices and responses, more or less understandable, sound, or wise. I am thinking of racist hatred and contempt, of child slavery and prostitution, of the ritual mutilation of girls' genitals and also of the dumping of elderly people into drugged isolation, young people into what is called 'care', and the banging up of the criminally convicted in institutions that make them worse people. These things hardly bear thinking about or looking, clear-eyed, at. If they are looked at, they need special stories to render them tolerable within an otherwise humane mind. It is a modern nervousness that, behind the ideology of cultural relativism, stills the voice of, or blocks the ears to, criticism. Valued qualities tend to flourish in structured syndromes and to need to be understood as part of situated patterns; some goods come at a price of other goods risked, damaged, or forgone. But that pluralist truth does not entail that any more or less coherent pattern is as good as another.

A child's shin is painfully bruised. This is a bad thing. It turns out that he is a newcomer, picked on because of his unusual accent. In a more complex but no more extraordinary or suspicious way, this is a bad thing too. Maybe the best explanation is in terms of the individual bully, maybe in terms of fairly stable patterns of such treatment. Ethical features of situations—summarized in terms of bullying, cruelty, cowardice, destructiveness, callousness, meanness —seem to be a part of everyday causal stories, and to play that part even under more sophisticated ethical descriptions. This consequentiality and importance for human harm and good perhaps distinguishes ethical attributes from those that Hume talks about that, in artworks, are the objects of aesthetic 'taste'. For there, the 'beauties fitted by nature to excite agreeable sentiments' exist only to be appreciated. They are created to excite and to be, given human responsiveness across 'nations and ages', the best explanation—as against prejudice, provincialism, partiality, and other candidates—of the sound judge's thereby sound appreciation. In aesthetics as in ethics, though, a term like 'ideology' is the wrong one to drive a wedge between the universally loved beauty of a flower and the properties that might be of interest to a molecular biologist. Rather, I want to say, ideologies are the sort of thing that get in the way of aesthetic and ethical judgement. Hume's 'Of the Standard of Taste', despite its circularities, is a brilliant reminder of the epistemic gutsiness of ethical language and of the appropriateness of quite ordinary terms like 'seeing' in such contexts. Hume's attributes of judgement—delicacy, vigour, disinterest, and so on—are isomorphic with the attributes of the works they track. We talk about blindness, blocking, distraction, lack of focus, in both agents and onlookers of aesthetic and ethical situations. The snob and the prig, inattentive as they are in their concern for supremacy in attention, have had their blindness to the obvious mocked throughout the ages.

Since it is not a nihilism, a Marxian outlook seems to me to presuppose some such humanist naturalism.[29] Otherwise we are left with a pan-ideological scepticism often accompanied by some arbitrary notion of 'commitment'. Stunting, distorting, and fragmenting divisions, penetrating to the heart of domestic life, Marx traced predominantly to the social mode of production, to whose reproduction he saw ideologies as functional. His 'historicism', his own 'illusions of progress' as Georges Sorel put it, disposed him to miss the contemporary trees for the future wood. But this longsightedness, which brought with it an obsession with attacking what he thought of as a sentimental nostalgia for the present, was consistent with an ethically rich and passionate grasp of that present. The eighteenth-century or even Dickensian notion of humanity that I have been advancing as a multi-piled foundation of ethical life and ethical consciousness might seem a long way from a historical materialist vision. But Marx's perception of capitalism's meanly malign neglect for its participants, its victims if you like, is not only continuous with but dependent on the more rudimentary sense of humanity and inhumanity. For the sense of violation of an infant, or an elderly man or woman, is under the aspect of maturational potentialities, possibilities, and powers

---

[29] I discuss this in 'Workers' Interests and the Proletarian Ethic: Conflicting Strains in Marxian Thought', in K. Nielsen and S. Patten (eds.), *Marx and Morality*, *Canadian Journal of Philosophy*, suppl. vol. 7 (1981), 155–70.

thwarted, damaged, or destroyed. Marx's account of capitalism's havoc is, at a macro level, akin to a story of the depredations of a vicious children's home: in each case we have a picture of limitation and of damage, of survival and natural resistance. In each case we have a picture of 'alienation', the twisting into a destructive chain of that whose nature is to be a creative communication. In each case too we have a sort of epistemic privileging of those without privilege, as those best if still precariously placed unreflectively to grasp the ethical reality of their oppression. And, although, certainly in the abstract, it makes little sense to think there is a determinate answer to the question what would be the best realization of such possibilities, within our ignorances and disagreements we have some that we would, truly, rank lower, and some that we would reject.

An endnote on moralism today. Surely, as Williams says, this peculiar institution, grimly memorable from my childhood but not, I expect, from that of my children or their friends, is in a state of erosion. It rested on a sanctified consensus among the Church, the Patriarchal Family, the Authoritarian School, and the Sovereign State, all of whose legitimacy is in eclipse. Teenage girls' magazines left brazenly about the house today give advice on masturbatory techniques and discuss the pros and cons of affairs with 'bad boys': something has got to the superego. But it seems to me that today we have a sort of backlash that goes beyond the pathetic yearnings for hellfire and brimstone heard among the battering classes. What we have, in the aftermath of a deliberate subversion of the ethos of public service and care is a spreading para-moralism of 'individual accountability'. Thereby, individuals, no longer relied on to police themselves through the moralistic conscience, let alone to be committed to their common work, are induced to supervise themselves in explicit tune to the demands of monitoring and auditing, a sort of openly heteronomous time-and-motion discipline. This increased institutionalization of mistrust seems to me to be backed by an ideology as suspicious of human nature as Original Sin in its heyday. Without the theology, we are being brought to see ourselves and our fellows, intimate or stranger, as weak if not depraved creatures, and to project this anxiety on to excluded and menacing categories for whom the prisons will never be big enough. Meanwhile, the economic world, its class power, and its global wheel of fortune and temptation is experienced as a struggle-free zone of no-alternative. Flexible and adaptable to the administrative rigidities of capital, we are brought laceratingly to criticize ourselves while the engine of our misery, as if an astronomical force, careers on. Where are those Communards?[30]

[30] Thanks to Richard Norman, Lawrence Blum, and Edward Harcourt for their efforts on behalf of clarity.

3

Ideology, Projection, and Cognition

A. W. Price

1. Ideology and Disenchantment

I start from an exchange in Thomas Hardy's *The Woodlanders*.[1] The doctor Edred Fitzpiers is talking with Giles Winterborne, implicitly about Grace Melbury, loved by one of the two and quasi-loved (as Simon Blackburn might say) by the other. Fitzpiers is speaking:

'Human love is a subjective thing . . . it is joy accompanied by an idea which we project against any suitable object in the line of our vision, just as the rainbow iris is projected against an oak, ash, or elm tree indifferently. So that if any other young lady had appeared instead of the one who did appear, I should have felt just the same interest in her, and have quoted precisely the same lines from Shelley about her, as about this one I saw. Such miserable creatures of circumstance are we all!'

'Well, it is what we call being in love down in these parts, whether or not,' said Winterborne.

'You are right enough if you admit that I am in love with something in my own head, and no thing-in-itself outside it at all.'

Fitzpiers is a dilettante of the heart as also of the head.[2] He will marry Grace Melbury, make love to Suke Damson, and be the lover of Mrs Charmond. He is the fox to Winterborne's hedgehog: Giles

---

[1] (1887), ch. 16, *The Wessex Novels*, 17 vols. (London: Macmillan, 1903), vii. 146.

[2] 'In the course of a year his mind was accustomed to pass in a grand solar sweep throughout the zodiac of the intellectual heaven. Sometimes it was in the Ram, sometimes in the Bull; one month he would be immersed in alchemy, another in poesy; one month in the Twins of astrology and astronomy; then in the Crab of German literature and metaphysics' (ibid. ch. 17, 154).

will lay down his life in order to save Grace from getting wet. They
form the pair of opposites so fertile of fiction.

I adduce the passage for two reasons: it explicitly introduces the
concept of *projection* (of which, as we shall see, the autodidact
Hardy has a better understanding than two of our current professional colleagues); and it can fuel reflection upon our present topic
of *ideology*. A way of thinking that is ideological cannot survive a
reflective understanding, and so suffers from a failure of transparency; engagement in it involves either pretence or delusion.[3]
Precisely in this sense, it is plausible to suppose that the experience
at least of first love is ideological in denying its true origins, as
Fitzpiers sketches them; for it cannot accept that its object is accidental, and its magic self-ignited. Perhaps it also tends to import,
as if to fortify the denial, a mythical aetiology. One might be spelled
out as follows. The first-time lover finds the loved one unique in a
way that makes his love as inevitable as a purely cognitive response
to a undeniable fact.[4] What puzzles him is not 'Why am I in love
with her?' but 'Why isn't everyone in love with her?' He believes
that he is the only man with sight in a country of the blind, who
alone perceives a substance that, spreading from the loved one
to her surroundings, is as it were the proper sensible of love (as
colours are the proper objects of sight). It is thus that Proust's
Marcel describes his love for Gilberte, the little girl of the Champs
Elysées:

I could scarcely imagine that that strange substance which dwelt in
Gilberte, and shone in her parents and her home, leaving me indifferent
to everything else, could be liberated, could migrate into another being.[5]

To detect this substance in and around her he needed a special
erotic sense:

For perceiving in everything that surrounded Gilberte an unknown quality
analogous in the world of the emotions to what in that of colours may be
infra-red, may parents were devoid of that supplementary and temporary
sense with which love had endowed me.[6]

---

[3] I derive this formulation from Edward Harcourt.
[4] Since this character is so fantastical, I may be permitted to speak of him as 'him',
in the manner of politically correct Aristotelians who revert to 'he' when talking of
the vices.
[5] *A la recherche du temps perdu*, 4 vols. (Paris: Bibliothèque de la Pléiade, 1987–9),
i. 568.   [6] Ibid. i. 408.

On this view, the first-time lover is an erotic intuitionist who assumes the existence in a particular person of an individually identifying erogenous quality accessible to a special sense. This intuitionism may be more familiar to us, without the particularism, from J. L. Mackie's error theory of morality.[7] Within a diagnosis of an illusion it seems to me more plausible of the first-time lover, whose inexperience and isolation may well import fantasy, than of the common moralizer. Since her practices are not idiosyncratic and so demand no explanation or defence, she has no reason to rest them upon any fanciful metaphysics or epistemology. If first love is delusive in the manner that Proust imagines, it invites correction precisely through Mackie's two lines of argument, the Argument from Queerness, and the Argument from Relativity. As the lover lives through later experience, he cannot but detect the delusion. Looking around, he will find that others find others unique; living a little longer, he will fall out of love, or fall in love with another. (He is unlikely to resort instead to an erotic pluralism that concedes as many special substances and senses as there are objects of love. This would be the least adjustment, but neither a minimal nor a credible one.)

Proust's reading of the mentality of first love is perhaps no less inventive than perceptive. (Of course, it may be intended as metaphor; if so, it withdraws into the safety of indeterminacy.) And it may be that, whereas the true cause of love that first love denies is broadly the same for everyone, though receptive of variations and relatable very variably, each lover spins his own story, if he is so minded, about a fictive cause.[8] Yet let us grant, vaguely enough, that any experience of first love is delusive to some degree. Let us further grant that the delusion is detectable by the lover himself. What will come of its detection? I ask this question of first love

---

[7] 'Ordinary moral judgements include a claim to objectivity, an assumption that there are objective values in just the sense in which I am concerned to deny this . . . If there were objective values, they would be entities or qualities or relations of a very strange sort, utterly different from anything else in the universe. Correspondingly, if we were aware of them, it would have to be by some special faculty of moral perception or intuition, utterly different from our ordinary ways of knowing everything else' (*Ethics: Inventing Right and Wrong* (Harmondsworth: Penguin, 1977), 35, 38).

[8] I recall, at the age of 16, being attracted by an aetiology rather Platonist than Aristotelian that spoke, in effect, not of immanent qualities but of transcendent forms. An implicit Platonism is natural to adolescence, and I wouldn't say that I didn't believe it. It came in handy when I was trying, years later, to get inside Plato.

precisely because it here hardly prompts or permits a general answer. To the extent that first love is unlike all later loves (including later love for the same person), disillusion surely makes a difference. A philosopher might argue that it must make—at least, ought to make—*all* the difference. Proust again supplies a text. Marcel is reflecting on his later feelings for Albertine:

Was it my hesitation between the different girls of the little band that left me later on a sort of intermittent and very brief liberty not to love her? From having strayed among all her friends before it finally turned to her, my love kept now and then between itself and the image of Albertine a certain 'play' that allowed it, like ill-adjusted lighting, to come to rest on others before returning to attach itself to her; the connection between the pain that I felt in my heart and the memory of Albertine did not seem to me necessary, I might perhaps have been able to coordinate it with the image of another person. Which allowed me, in a momentary flash, to make the reality vanish, not only the external reality as in my love for Gilberte (which I had recognized to be an inner state in which I drew from myself alone the particular quality of the person I loved), but even the reality that was internal and purely subjective.[9]

This may suggest that first love perishes of an understanding that has only to be developed and maintained to be fatal to love *tout court*. Fitzpiers's condition ('I am in love with something in my own head, and no thing-in-itself outside it at all') could be a passing predicament on the way towards a total emancipation. However, Marcel, though given to reflection, describes his disenchantment as 'intermittent and very brief'. Gilberte was his first love, but his last and greatest love is Albertine (as Albert was Proust's): his sufferings prove it. Winterborne is being wise and not naïve when he insists that Fitzpiers's consciously 'subjective' love is yet 'what we call being in love down in these parts'. Fitzpiers is fickle and unjealous, but not unfeeling. He can assure Grace towards the end, truly or not untruly, 'I can tell you honestly that I love you better than all of them put together.'[10] If he is a quasi-lover, that may go to show (as with quasi-realism in relation to realism) that quasi-love apes love all too indistinguishably. How could one hope to generalize here about how modes of thinking and feeling may change? Suppose that every love attempts to re-enact first love (as even first

---

[9] *A la recherche du temps perdu*, ii. 202 (slightly abbreviated).
[10] *The Woodlanders*, ch. 46, 434.

love, Freudians say, tries to re-enact primal love for the mother). Then lovers are always trying to recapture, like thrushes, the first fine careless rapture. Some may salvage from the illusions of inno- cence what infatuated thoughts they can. Experience may change others into ironists *à la* Nagel who see and say different, even con- tradictory, things from different points of view.[11] Others may detach their feelings and practices from evaluations within any perspec- tive. And different objects of love are likely to inspire in the same lover rather different adaptations.

As Sir Bernard Williams has complained of Hellenistic ethics,[12] philosophers like to exaggerate the effects of philosophy. Whatever edifying if marginal role it may at times have played within a pagan society, we have to accept that its part in a culture variably Chris- tian and secular is to be life-enhancing but not transforming. Where it is persuasive and imperfectly conservative, minor accommoda- tion may be made within receptive and adaptive minds. Where it is radical, it may more likely be relegated to an upper gallery of the spirit, some lofty space apart, perhaps to be retrieved in extremity, as by the victims of the French revolution who found solace in Stoicism.[13] Sir Peter Strawson has famously argued that it is an intellectualist illusion to suppose that a discovery that determinism was true (if such is conceivable) could make any real difference to our reactive attitudes and practices.[14] Of determinism in the abstract, if it could be abstractly established, he was surely right. And it would miss his distinctive point to grant this only by reason of a compatibilist conception of free will entailing that the dis- covery really was immaterial—though the intellectually flexible might well then resort to such a conception. Of specific instances of things determined it is harder to speak generally. Suppose that the genome project sheds more light on the genesis of moral char- acter than we have any ground to expect. Suppose, *per impossibile*, that it identified a specific gene for housebreaking (impossibly, since the practice is parasitic upon the institution of house-

[11] See Thomas Nagel, 'The Absurd' (1971), in Nagel, *Mortal Questions* (Cambridge: Cambridge University Press, 1979).

[12] 'Do Not Disturb', review of Martha Nussbaum, *The Therapy of Desire*, *London Review of Books*, 16/20 (20 Oct. 1994), 25–6.

[13] See Dorinda Outram, *The Body and the French Revolution: Sex, Class and Political Culture* (New Haven: Yale University Press, 1989), chs. 5–6; ch. 7, pp. 116–17.

[14] 'Freedom and Resentment' (1962), in Strawson, *Freedom and Resentment and Other Essays* (London: Methuen, 1974).

occupancy). Surely that would make more difference to our attitudes towards housebreakers than none at all. Yet one should be
at a loss to generalize over all reactive subjects (some of whom
might only be confirmed in their belief that housebreakers are 'a
bad lot'), or over all such cases (either of housebreaking, or of other
identifiably determined deviations). And perhaps we know intellectuals well enough to predict that they would vary unaccountably
between admitting an excuse, taking local advantage of a general
compatibilism, and coming up with something new. If historians
ever achieve a broad understanding of what came of unmasking
some ideology at some period within some society, they must do so
retrospectively, and sensitively to contingency and circumstance.[15]
Pretending to predict the proper or probable effects of disenchantment is trying to write history in advance, for even propriety
is relative to the existing alternatives; and attempts to anticipate
history are sure to fail the test of time.

2. *Projection and Correspondence*

I have started by mooting a marginal instance of ideology because
I shall not end by conceding a central one. I do not believe that
ethics, or even morality, is inherently ideological. This is not because
I see no point in talk of projection; on the contrary. But it must
make a difference how it is meant.

One naturally turns to Simon Blackburn. Yet his promotion of
projection from a notion to an 'ism' tantalizes the understanding.
In his book *Spreading the Word* he introduced the notion of
projection as follows: 'Suppose that we say we *project* an attitude
or habit or other commitment which is not descriptive on to the
world when we speak or think as though there were a property
of things which our sayings describe, which we can reason about,
be wrong about, and so on.'[16] This is rather a schema than a definition, and for two reasons. First, the phrase 'attitude or habit or other
commitment' is a place-filler. Secondly, the phrase 'property of
things' is clearly a term of art that needs a gloss, or series of glosses,

---

[15] Charles Williams credibly ascribed the decline in churchgoing in our time less
to disenchantment than to the pervasion of the motor-car.

[16] *Spreading the Word: Groundings in the Philosophy of Language* (Oxford:
Clarendon Press, 1984), 170–1.

to convey in what privileged sense, or senses, there may exist no 'property' to be ascribed by certain intelligible predications. Quasi-realism then made its appearance as a defensive supplement:

Quasi-realism is the enterprise of explaining why our discourse has the shape it does, in particular by way of treating evaluative predicates like others, if projectivism is true. It thus seeks to explain, and justify, the realistic-seeming nature of our talk of evaluations—the way we think we can be wrong about them, that there is a truth to be found, and so on.[17]

Here the unclarity continues: after it has been said that we project in treating evaluative predicates as equally property-connoting as others, it is now supposed that the fact that we treat them so is an apparent objection to projectivism that quasi-realism has to answer. A year later Blackburn reiterated the same conception of projection: 'We have sentiments and other reactions caused by natural features of things, and we "gild or stain" the world by describing it as if it contained features answering to these sentiments.'[18] He then anticipated the success of his programme ('According to me, quasi-realism is almost entirely successful')[19] as follows:

Protected by quasi-realism, my projectivist says the things that sound so realist to begin with—that there are real obligations and values, and that many of them are independent of us, for example. It is *not* the position that he says these for public consumption but denies them in his heart, so to speak. He affirms *all that could ever properly be meant* by saying that there are real obligations . . . It is just that the explanation of why there are obligations and the rest is not quite that of untutored common sense. It deserves to be called anti-realist because it avoids the view that when we moralize we respond to, and describe, an independent aspect of reality.[20]

Again, there are local difficulties. How can the quasi-realist only 'almost entirely' succeed if he affirms *all* that the realist can 'properly' mean? In what sense are many obligations and values 'independent of us' when morality answers to no 'independent

---

[17] *Spreading the Word: Groundings in the Philosophy of Language* (Oxford: Clarendon Press, 1984), 180.
[18] 'Errors and the Phenomenology of Value' (1985), in Blackburn, *Essays in Quasi-Realism* (Oxford: Oxford University Press, 1993), 152.
[19] Ibid.   [20] Ibid. 157.

aspect of reality'?[21] Why should 'untutored common sense' be supposed to offer any 'explanation of why there are obligations' (whatever that means) at all? More gravely, it is now clear that the quasi-realist aims to justify our 'realist-seeming' talk by making out that, in the only proper senses it can bear, it is literal and correct. This is doubly problematic. The success of quasi-realism requires that realism be both statable (so that it can be aped), and unstatable (since it can be aped perfectly).[22] And what becomes of the idea that projecting is speaking 'as though' or 'as if' describing (or ascribing?) a privileged property? Two years later, Blackburn explicitly deprecated the phrase 'as if' as suggesting an error theory, not mentioning that the phrase was his.[23] Projectivism now assumed a grammatical guise: 'We "project" when we use the ordinary propositional expressions of our commitments, saying that there is this causal relation, that natural law, this other obligation.'[24] This tells us when we are projecting, but not what it is to project. The term survives as the echo of a claim no longer voiced. A philosophy of 'as if' makes way for an as-if philosophy.[25]

In his review of *Essays in Quasi-Realism* Allan Gibbard offered another objection, and a way out:

I myself find Blackburn's 'projection' metaphor misleading: when I find an act of cruelty horrific, do I 'project' my feeling of horror onto the act? Not in the sense in which, say, I 'project' my hostility onto a person if my own hostility to him makes me groundlessly experience him as hostile. The quality I'm attributing to the act that horrifies me isn't feeling horror, but being horrific—not, I hope, a quality of my own mind . . . An alternative term that we share—'expressivism'—may be better.[26]

---

[21] See Ronald Dworkin, 'Objectivity and Truth: You'd Better Believe It', *Philosophy and Public Affairs*, 25 (1996), 110–12.

[22] See Crispin Wright, review of Simon Blackburn, *Spreading the Word*, *Mind*, 94 (1985), 319.

[23] 'Morals and Modals' (1987), in Blackburn, *Essays in Quasi-Realism*, 55–7.

[24] Ibid. 56.

[25] For a fuller complaint of vacuity, see my review of *Essays in Quasi-Realism*, *Utilitas*, 7 (1995), 172–5.

[26] *Mind*, 105 (1996), 332. Blackburn now half accepts this suggestion, though on the different and curious ground that the title 'projectivism' can 'make it sound as if projecting attitudes involves some kind of mistake' (*Ruling Passions: A Theory of Practical Reasoning* (Oxford: Clarendon Press, 1998), 77). It is unclear why it should be the title 'projectivism', and not 'the metaphor of projection' itself (as he had already called it in 'Errors and the Phenomenology of Value', 158), that misleads. But perhaps he intends to be deprecating both.

As we have seen, Blackburn had drawn on the famous paragraph
in Hume which, without actually using the term 'project', ascribes
to taste the power of 'gilding or staining all natural objects with the
colours, borrowed from internal sentiment'.[27] Gibbard has in mind
things like this in Freud: 'The proposition "I hate him" becomes
transformed by *projection* into another one: "*He hates* (persecutes)
me", which will justify me in hating him.'[28] Clearly the Hume is
metaphor, while the Freud is imperfectly à propos.[29] And yet the
notion of projection has deeper roots, though one can be well-read
in philosophy without knowing it. Here, or anywhere, I can only
offer illustrative extracts from what is at least a fascinating chapter
in the history of ideas.

Richard Wollheim makes the essential distinction, unknown to
Gibbard, between 'simple' and 'complex' projection: within simple
projection, hating my enemy, I ascribe hate to him; within complex
projection, hating him, I find him hateful, or (in a phrase of Wollheim's) 'of a piece with' my hatred.[30] Here the effect is captured by
a new term adapted from the cause ('hateful' from 'hate'). Elsewhere, it may be conveyed by an old term used metaphorically, as
when I find a landscape 'melancholy',[31] or by a wholly new term,

---

[27] *An Enquiry concerning the Principles of Morals* (1777), app. 1.

[28] *Notes on a Case of Paranoia* (1911), *The Standard Edition of the Complete
Psychological Works of Sigmund Freud*, ed. J. Strachey, 24 vols. (London: Hogarth
Press, 1955–74), xii. 63.

[29] More to the point is Freud's description of another kind of projection: 'The
mechanism of hysterical phobia, too, culminates in the fact that the subject is
able to protect himself by attempts at flight against an external danger which has
taken the place of an internal instinctual claim' (*The Metapsychology of Dreams*
(1917), *Standard Edition*, xiv. 224). For the phobic find things frightening, not
frightened.

[30] See *The Thread of Life* (Cambridge: Cambridge University Press, 1984),
214–15; *Painting as an Art* (London: Thames & Hudson, 1987), 82. Simple and
complex projection are confused in a good joke within a piece by Santayana that
rescued Russell from the spell of *Principia Ethica*: 'For the human system whiskey
is truly more intoxicating than coffee, and the contrary opinion would be an error;
but what a strange way of vindicating this real, though relative, distinction, to insist
that whiskey is more intoxicating in itself, without reference to any animal; that it
is pervaded, as it were, by an inherent toxication, and stands dead drunk in its
bottle!' ('Hypostatic Ethics', in George Santayana, *Winds of Doctrine* (London:
J. K. Dent, 1913), 146). 'Drunk' stands to 'intoxicating' somewhat as 'hating' stands
to 'hateful'.

[31] Cf. Henry James, *English Hours* (1905), *Collected Travel Writings: Great Britain
and America* (New York: Library of America, 1993), 251: 'From the garden of the
distinguished cottage, at any rate, it is a large, melancholy view—a view that an occa-
sional perverse person whom it fails to touch finds easy, I admit, to speak of as

which is where 'good', 'beautiful', and the rest make their appearance. Among the differentiae of complex projection are that it can
target inanimate objects without animism, and that there needs to
be a match between mind and world. These features endeared
projection to the Romantics, concerned as they were to rehabili-
tate the human imagination, and to re-enchant the natural world,
after the depredations of Newtonian science. I start with two
Frenchmen. Ernest Renan actually uses our word: 'L'enfant
projette sur toutes choses le merveilleux qu'il porte en lui.'[32]
Baudelaire records less innocent experience, and adds a simile:
'Le hachisch s'étend alors sur toute la vie comme un vernis
magique; il la colore en solennité et en éclaire toute la pro-
fondeur.'[33] Yet the deepest source may lie earlier within our own
poetry. Already in Wordsworth's 1805 *Prelude* we read this of 'the
infant babe':

> From Nature largely he receives, nor so
> Is satisfied, but largely gives again;
> . . . his mind,
> Even as an agent of the one great mind,
> Creates, creator and receiver both,
> Working but in alliance with the works
> Which it beholds.[34]

dreary; so that those who love it and are well advised will ever, at the outset, carry
the war into the enemy's country by announcing it, with glee, as sad.' It is not this,
but the simple projection of melancholy by 'some night-wandering man whose heart
was pierced', that is rejected by Coleridge in 'The Nightingale' (1798).

[32] I have not been able to trace the quotation. Compare Stendhal on the infat-
uations of the young: 'Ces âmes trop ardentes ou ardentes par accès, amoureuses à
crédit, si l'on peut ainsi dire, se jettent aux objets au lieu de les attendre.' They cover
objects as yet unseen with an imaginary charm drawn from their own well (*De
l'amour* (1822), ch. 22).

[33] *Les Paradis artificiels* (1860), *Œuvres complètes*, ed. C. Pichois, 2 vols. (Paris:
Bibliothèque de la Pléiade, 1975–6), i. 430. He thus anticipates, and perhaps disarms,
a joke of David Wiggins. In the original version of 'Truth, Invention, and the
Meaning of Life' Wiggins wrote of values 'put *into* (or *on to* like varnish) the factual
world' (*Proceedings of the British Academy*, 62 (1976), 338). Elsewhere, Baudelaire
writes of 'une lumière magique et surnaturelle' that the artist's eye casts upon 'l'ob-
scurité naturelle des choses' (*Salon de 1859*, *Œuvres complètes*, ii. 645). Gérard de
Nerval had written already of 'les rayons magnétiques émanés de moi-même ou
des autres' that form 'un réseau transparent qui couvre le monde' (*Aurélia* (1855),
quoted by Pichois, *Œuvres complètes*, i. 841).

[34] II. 267–75. A much earlier source is Edward Young, who writes that our senses
'half create the wondrous world they see' (*The Complaint; or, Night Thoughts*
(1742–5), Night VI, 'The Infidel Reclaimed, Part I'). But he would appear to have
in mind no more than Locke's theory of secondary properties.

And Coleridge telescopes the exchange: 'O Sara! we receive but what we give.'[35] Though they were also influenced at the time by animism, they are guiltless of the confusion alleged by Gibbard. To dismiss such language as metaphorical would be to make a number of mistakes, not least about metaphor (which is not, and cannot be, a vehicle of nonsense); yet it remains a theorist's task to make the most of such suggestions. Melanie Klein elaborated a quasi-physiological conception, which Wollheim encapsulates as follows:

The initiating phantasy represents the emotion as being expelled from the body and then spread or smeared across some part of the world, and the primitive nature of the mental functioning to which projection belongs is revealed in the highly physical or corporeal way in which . . . the expulsive phantasy envisages mental phenomena. Emotions are in effect envisaged as bits or products of the body which can be spewed out or excreted and then deposited in the world.[36]

When I first tried to think about this, I quite succumbed to the alliance of Wollheim's mandarin prose and Klein's peasant faith.[37] I now have cold feet, for various reasons. First, hardly anyone believes it. Secondly, it leaves it mysterious how there is scope for projection of a kind where there is none for simple projection. Projected *into* another person, my emotion can become his (in my eyes); projected *onto* an object (or person as object), it can only become its own correlate (as when *hate* becomes the *hateful*, *love* the *lovable* or *lovely*). Precisely when the projection is literal and physical, though a phantasy, this seems a metamorphosis, as if an *ear*, removed by a surgeon, changed into a *sound*. Thirdly, it is unclear how private unconscious phantasy feeds into public linguistic invention. The Kleinian story would be implausible as an error theory revealing a delusive content implicit in our evaluations; it must rather tell part of the aetiology of our linguistic practices. But until the whole tale is elaborated, however speculatively, we cannot tell whether it may cohere around phantasy as an essential core.[38]

---

[35] 'A Letter to ——' (1802), line 296.   [36] *Painting as an Art*, 84.
[37] 'Three Types of Projectivism', in J. Hopkins and A. Savile (eds.), *Psychoanalysis, Mind and Art: Perspectives on Richard Wollheim* (Oxford: Blackwell, 1992).
[38] None of this tells against a different strand in Freud and Klein that traces the origin of the superego to the internalization of external prohibitions; for this process is the converse of simple projection, and a creature of communication. When the

I still have hopes of some notion of projection. Values are *sui generis*, and may continue to seem queer until we can say where conceptions of them might come from. Anxiety may only be stilled by 'genetic-psychological' speculation that supplements 'analytic-philosophical' investigation.[39] We should recognize that philosophical puzzlement is not always resoluble by philosophy alone— unless philosophy is protean. Is there a way forward that does not presuppose anything so concrete and controversial as Kleinian doctrine? It may help to focus upon an aspect of complex projection, that of *correspondence* between mind and world. Not that we should speak of 'correspondence' *instead of* 'projection'. That would risk obscuring two interrelated points: mind and world are not laid out for comparison (from what viewpoint?) like the two halves of a tally; and mind does not confront world with an inner structure given in advance. Rather, a mind is essentially a window upon the world. Yet we need not conceive of the window as *either* transparent *or* opaque. A mind is a point of view from which the world shows up in ways that both reflect a mentality, and capture a reality.[40] With these caveats, we may ask: what is this correspondence?

Wollheim has written that, within a maturing psychology, 'Those parts of the environment upon which feelings are projected are now selected because of their affinity to these feelings.'[41] Again, we

voice of the superego is adopted through identification as a voice of one's own, conscience is born (see Wollheim, *The Thread of Life*, 218–19). Here is a living aspect of the prehistory of morals.

[39] Strawson, 'Perception and its Objects', in G. F. Macdonald (ed.), *Perception and Identity* (London: Macmillan, 1979), 42. He adds a warning: 'It will be important to run no risk of characterising mature sensible experience in terms adequate at best only for the characterisation of some state of infantile experience.' We must not bring the effect down to the level of the cause; but, if we can spell out a history *from* cause *to* effect, we should be less tempted to reduce effect to cause.

[40] See Wiggins, 'Truth, Invention, and the Meaning of Life', Sect. 6; rev. in Wiggins, *Needs, Values, Truth*, 3rd edn. (Oxford: Clarendon Press, 1998). Think upon this analogy: colour-concepts are internally related to forms of experience; yet experience of red is experience of things *as being red*, and pillar boxes *really are* red.

[41] 'Correspondence, Projective Properties, and Expression in the Arts', in Wollheim, *The Mind and its Depths* (Cambridge, Mass.: Harvard University Press, 1993), 152. When he adds, 'We recognize parts of nature as those on which we might have, or could have, projected this or that kind of feeling' (pp. 152–3), he warns us against supposing that correspondence could be identified independently of projection, and prior to it.

can return to the Romantics. Wordsworth finds a reciprocal fit between mind and world:

> How exquisitely the individual mind
> (And the progressive powers perhaps no less
> Of the whole species) to the external world
> Is fitted; and how exquisitely too—
> Theme this but little heard of among men—
> The external world is fitted to the mind.[42]

Baudelaire's sonnet 'Correspondances' (1857) has made correspondence celebrated, but is less psychological than another sentence of his describing the effects of hashish: 'La sinuosité des lignes est un langage définitivement clair où vous lisez l'agitation et le désir des âmes.'[43] Here the state of mind is intoxicated. In other writers, it is already moralized. Charles Rosen quotes from Schiller: 'Every continuity with which lines in space and tones in time join together is a natural symbol of the inner concordance of the spirit with itself and of the inner coherence of action and feeling; and in the beautiful aspect of a pictorial image or musical composition is painted the still more beautiful one of a morally regulated soul.'[44] Equally creature and not creator of morality is the mentality expressed in a poem by Victor Hugo, 'A un riche', which contains these lines:

> Tout object dont le bois se compose répond
> A quelque objet pareil dans la forêt de l'âme.[45]

But of course Schiller and Hugo believe nature to be edifying: they have in mind process, not stasis. Less cultured correspondences could feed into a genetic story that was stepwise: early movements of the soul alert the infant to aspects of the world that stimulate subtler movements that bring into view finer aspects, and so on indefinitely. So long as these movements are not interpreted mentalistically, but acknowledged to consist not least of facial expres-

---

[42] *Home at Grasmere* (1800), lines 1006–11.   [43] *Les Paradis artificiels*, i. 430.
[44] Review of Friedrich Matthesson's poems (1794), as quoted and translated by Rosen, *The Romantic Generation* (London: HarperCollins, 1995), 130.
[45] (1837), in Hugo, *Les Voix intérieures*. For other parallels, see F. W. Leakey, *Baudelaire and Nature* (Manchester: Manchester University Press, 1969), 239 n. 1. Hugo's sense of proportion, contrasting nature's 'bois' with the soul's 'forêt', is characteristic, but slightly absurd: one wonders along which common coordinates the inner world is supposed to outmeasure the outer.

sions and physical actions (including gestures and vocalizations), the story can be social and not solipsistic: a mind is formed as a language is learned and a tradition assimilated. Culture and psychology, soul and society, must collaborate in what Wollheim has called 'the symbolic, the emblematic, the awareness of match observed and the elaboration of match invented'.[46] With a hunch that they may contain the heart of the matter, I now leave projection and correspondence behind, and turn to other aspects of moral and personal development.

3. *Acrasia and Cognition*

Adjourning any attempt to start at the beginning, let us imagine a child entering a society that already deploys a language of morals. How is she to make that language her own? Aristotle had part of the answer: she must be habituated in acting according to the precepts (universal or particular) that put to use the moral concepts of the language. He also added that she must be trained in finding pleasure and pain in the right things. The ideal conception of acting morally requires that, as he puts it, one know what one is doing, one choose it for its own sake, and one's choice derive from a firm and unchangeable character.[47] How is the child to advance from doing the moral thing towards acting morally? A plausible suggestion is that she should *mimic* the state of character that she intends, or is intended, to achieve. So long as she possesses the natural virtues,[48] she should be able to enjoy not only the fact, but the content, of the mimicry (not that one may not colour the other). To the extent that imitation becomes reality, her use of language is infused by her desires, and her desires are informed by language. Eventually she may hope to achieve *phronēsis*, a state that cannot be forgotten since it fuses conceptual abilities and dispositions of desire.[49] Of course this is a long process: 'It must become second nature (*dei gar sumphuēnai*), and this takes time.'[50] And in actuality, we must add (though Aristotle does not), the development is never complete, and often open to reversal. From occasion to occasion, desire is liable either to drain away from judgement, or to well

---

[46] *The Thread of Life*, 215.
[47] *Nicomachean Ethics (NE)* 2. 4, 1105^{a}28–34.   [48] See *NE* 6. 13, 1144^{b}4–14.
[49] See *NE* 6. 5, 1141^{a}28–30.   [50] *NE* 7. 3, 1147^{a}22.

up without or contrary to judgement. Moralization is an imperfect
system of psychic irrigation, always in need of upkeep.[51]
   Mimicry in the service of self-creation is not hypocrisy. T. S. Eliot
understood this when he wrote of Byron, 'Hypocrite, indeed, except
in the original sense of the term, is hardly the term for Byron. He
was an actor who devoted immense trouble to *becoming* a role that
he adopted.'[52] Yet it does complicate the issue of sincerity. One
extreme is mere animality (or, if you like, innocence). The other is
a state of total 'acceptance', in Wollheim's sense, in which one does
not merely assent to the relevant judgements, but lets them register and reverberate throughout one's being, so that they come
to define how one thinks and feels.[53] Between the extremes lies a
world of approximation, the human world. The adult who lapses
and the child who aspires may be telling themselves things that they
wish or hope, though perhaps among alternative wishes and hopes,
fully to accept; however they act, they may be partly or wholly
serious in what they say. Another agent 'lifts the net' (as Dick Hare
has put it), either for himself or, still more seductively, for a friend;
he can manifest in innumerable ways that he remains faithful to
morality in his fashion. Yet another takes a moral holiday by
imagining that her situation has suddenly assumed an extraordinary face, like Robert Musil's Bonadea: 'During such spells she did
not lose her good intentions, and her firm will for respectability, for
a moment; they then stood outside, waiting, and had simply nothing
to say to this world transformed by desire.'[54] As a notice once read

   [51] I am influenced here by an eloquent and original essay by Sabina Lovibond,
'Ethical Upbringing: From Connivance to Cognition', in S. Lovibond and
S. G. Williams (eds.), *Essays for David Wiggins: Identity, Truth and Value* (Oxford:
Blackwell, 1996).
   [52] 'Byron', in Eliot, *On Poetry and Poets* (London: Faber & Faber, 1957), 205,
Compare the moral metamorphosis achieved through wearing and living a mask in
Max Beerbohm's story *The Happy Hypocrite* (1897). Mimicry can serve other purposes related to self-creation. One is self-discovery: 'Sometimes we pretend in order
eventually to become what we pretend to be. Sometimes we pretend in order to find
out whether we already are something or not' (Alexander Nehamas, *The Art of
Living: Socratic Reflections from Plato to Foucault* (Berkeley: University of California Press, 1998), 54). Another purpose is self-variegation: 'Sometimes a critic may
choose an author to criticise, a role to assume, as far as possible the antithesis to
himself, a personality which has actualised all that has been suppressed in himself;
we can sometimes arrive at a very satisfactory intimacy with our anti-masks' (Eliot,
The Use of Poetry and the Use of Criticism (London: Faber & Faber, 1933), 112).
   [53] See *The Thread of Life*, 237.
   [54] *Der Mann ohne Eigenschaften*, 2 vols. (Hamburg: Rowohlt, 1978), pt. 1, ch. 63,
i. 259.

in a Paris hotel, 'Guests please leave their values at the reception.' Often the case will be ambiguous, and here fiction is true to life. In his programme note to a performance of Molière's *Tartuffe* given in 1996 at the Almeida Theatre in London, Noël Peacock contrasted different interpretations of its anti-hero, whether as 'an entirely comic figure' and 'master hypocrite', or as a 'pale, thin ascetic whose piety was real and not pretended'.[55] It would be an illusion to suppose that a real-life Tartuffe would have to know, or even that it would have to be determinate, which he was. Perhaps this is why Jonathan Kent's production presented him, rather strangely, as a steely and salacious John the Baptist; one was reminded of Rasputin. My companion was a cleric whom I know rather well. He commented that a bad priest can be a man of intense piety; as he explained, it may just be that for him every situation is a new one.[56] Even in less paradoxical cases, human sincerity is seldom simple.

Let me be more analytical. With some speculation, we can spell out why Aristotle may have doubted the possibility of what has been called 'hard acrasia', that is, of intentional action consciously contrary to practical judgement.[57] He seems to envisage that practical reason reaches a conception of the human goal, which he calls *eudaimonia*, through a reflective mingling of *all* the motivations that come with our composite make-up and social acculturation. Forming a conception of one's end is not mechanical, and demands the exercise of intelligence;[58] yet non-rational desires are not just

[55] Cf. *Boswell's Life of Johnson*, ed. G. B. Hill, 6 vols. (Oxford: Clarendon Press, 1887), iv. 289: 'A wicked fellow is the most pious when he takes to it. He'll beat you all at piety' (10 June 1784).

[56] Thus, as Bernard Williams nicely puts it, Odysseus induces Neoptolemus to join in deceiving Philoctetes by inviting him 'to bracket the action from the rest of his life' (*Shame and Necessity* (Berkeley: University of California Press, 1993), 87). It had better not be in this way that ethical particularists would have agents bracket every action.

[57] By a 'practical judgement' I have in mind a judgement with a content of a kind to conclude a piece of practical deliberation, and direct the formation of an intention. A fuller and finer treatment would delineate how language variably admits and inhibits the phenomena sketched here. (a) 'I must ϕ' differs from (b) 'I ought to ϕ', and again from (c) 'It is best that I ϕ', even when all three are meant categorically. (c) is receptive of the rider 'though it is quite all right if I don't', which is a concession preclusive of hard acrasia. (a) conceives of no alternative, deliberate or acratic. (b) is the most pertinent to my purposes: it permits slippage, but brands it as a lapse. Hence 'I ought to ϕ, but I shan't' is merely conflicted, whereas 'I must ϕ, but I shan't' is incoherent. Accepting that one must ϕ can only coincide with intentionally failing to ϕ if the failure is compulsive.   [58] *NE* 6. 11, 1143^{a}35–^{b}5.

a datum but an input. Inasmuch as we are creatures of desire, our goal is characterizable as a way of life that is 'such that one who obtains it will have his desire fulfilled'.[59] An all-in practical judgement comes of applying the total goal to the context of action. So long as the judgement is sincerely meant, then, since it is practical, the desires that influence it must exert equal influence upon action (if nothing prevents); since it is all-in, taking all desires into account, what is decisive for judgement must be decisive for action (if any). Provided that the all-in view is kept to bear upon the context of action—which only perfect virtue guarantees—judgement must prevail.

Much that needs to be said about morality leaves open the possibilities of acrasia. Moral education is a training both in judgement and in desire. In advancing from the mere exclamation 'Hurrah for *x*!', or the mere avowal 'I like *x*', to the evaluation '*x* is good', the child presents itself before a social tribunal, and can be asked to show that it is doing more (in a phrase of John McDowell's) than 'sounding off'. It commits itself to shedding the arbitrariness or idiosyncrasy that we expect of one another when something is merely 'a matter of taste'. As it matures, it must be ready to speak on the side of desiring what, or as, it thinks to be good from a point of view that others can respect. Likes and dislikes can be brute; judgements need to be grounded.[60] As the child inherits a morality by becoming party to a pattern of practical justification, many of its desires take on a general fixity as standing aspects of judgements. It comes, say, to prefer being generous to being mean not just when it feels like it, but with a consciousness of attitudes that it shares with others, and with itself on other occasions. As its personal desires become informed by shared reasons and justifications, they become less childish and fickle.

And yet there always remains some slack between judgement and desire, even when a judgement is practical. A dichotomy, often presupposed in discussions of acrasia, between judging sincerely or insincerely has to be replaced by a spectrum of degrees of

---

[59] *Eudemian Ethics* VI. 5, 1215^{b}17–18. This is compatible with admitting, indeed emphasizing, that desire is transformed by a second nature that does not only develop out of first nature through a prudence that tries to reduce the probabilities of dissatisfaction.

[60] Or, alternatively, grounding: there are paradigm-cases of the application of values.

acceptance. At one extreme, a practical judgement so pervades the agent's psychology that this contains no volitional tendency whatever, whether in the form of a divergent inclination or of a feeling of inertia, towards a failure to act accordingly; he is then totally of one heart and mind. A more probable state of an agent (and one more probably demanded by Aristotle of the virtuous agent) is that he does not feel painfully conflicted either by *wanting* to act otherwise, or through a *strong* inhibition (or the like).[61] Yet no intrinsic feature of the judgement, let alone any adventitious insistency on the part of the judger, guarantees that there will be no conflict, nor even how any conflict will be resolved.

A mismatch between practical judgement and effective desire can arise both for the worse, and for the better. We cannot equate the strength of a desire with the strength of the associated reason (whether this be a reason it creates, or a reason it tracks).[62] So we must allow that a recognition of a reason as overriding may be accompanied by an ineffectual desire, just as a recognition of a reason as overridden (or even of the absence of any reason at all) may be accompanied by an effective desire. Practical grounds that have impinged on reflection without percolating internally may have little effect against contrary desires. Then there are desires that continue to press even after the agent has found no value in their satisfaction. A familiar instance is procrastination, that is, putting things off pointlessly. Many of us are inclined to procrastinate even though we appreciate the pointlessness, and are aware that delay may derive no value from inclination (since yielding to it induces depression as much as relief). There are also desires whose intensity varies independently of any variation in the expected value of their satisfaction. A famous example of J. L. Austin's is the sudden access of temptation that may prompt a man into taking more than his share of bombe at high table.[63] Such transients of desire may effect action without distorting or obscuring judgement.[64]

---

[61] For a distinction between *wanting*, and merely having a desire, see my *Mental Conflict* (London: Routledge, 1995), 43; for argument that Aristotle is not impossibly demanding, see ibid. 123–5.

[62] For the contrast, see Stephen Schiffer, 'A Paradox of Desire', *American Philosophical Quarterly*, 13 (1976), 195–203.

[63] 'A Plea for Excuses' (1956), in *Philosophical Papers*, 1st edn. (Oxford: Clarendon Press, 1961), 146 n. 1.

[64] Irrational yet effective desires may also be generated not by bad habits or

Yet, if such cases count as weakness, there are others where, as we say, the heart is wiser than the head. An acratic impulse may be an intimation of defective practical reasoning, for it may be implicitly perceptive of considerations corrective of one's deliberations. It may be no accident that the judgement that an agent fails to put into effect would not accord with a wiser judgement.[65] Here we may be beholden, but are not bound, to his ensuing attitude: if his head falls retrospectively in line with his heart, we are more likely to consider that his action respected his best reasons. Though still classifying the action as hard acrasia on the definition given above ('intentional action consciously contrary to practical judgement'), we would then ascribe it not to weakness but to sensitivity. However, we may also form the opinion that action has distorted subsequent judgement (as can happen to those who are at once impulsive and self-justifying). Real difficulties arise here in separating psychological diagnosis from ethical assessment.[66]

There is also a more fundamental extenuation of acrasia. Philosophers, as well as moralists, tend to view our common tendency to it as inherently a defect. I believe that, while we must all rue the tendency on occasion, we should not regret it in general. The moral was already implicit in my broadly Aristotelian account of moral development, but it can be spelled out. Suppose that hard acrasia was impossible, not just for angels and devils (who are too good or too bad, and in either case actually inconceivable), but for us, real creatures of imperfectly educated desire. This could only mean one of two things. Either practical judgement would be a reflection of effective inclination, aping the dignity of reason while always echoing the voice of desire.[67] Or else it would be silenced

passing whims, but by drives that are unconscious or unintelligible; see John Cottingham, *Philosophy and the Good Life: Reason and the Passions in Greek, Cartesian and Psychoanalytic Ethics* (Cambridge: Cambridge University Press, 1998), 153–62.

[65] See Alison McIntyre, 'Is Akratic Action Always Irrational?', in O. Flanagan and A. O. Rorty (eds.), *Identity, Character, and Morality: Essays in Moral Psychology* (Cambridge Mass.: MIT Press, 1990). The dilemma of Huckleberry Finn, whose practice towards a runaway slave was more perceptive than his principles, has been familiar to philosophers since Jonathan Bennett's 'The Conscience of Huckleberry Finn', *Philosophy*, 49 (1974), 123–34.

[66] See a warning in Williams, *Shame and Necessity*, 44–6.

[67] One may compare Freud: 'Often a rider, if he is not to be parted from his horse, is obliged to guide it where it wants to go; so in the same way the ego is in the habit

when it was ineffectual, gaining and losing its voice at desire's behest. This intermittency would often escape not only prediction but detection; for we continue to speak, and usually think we mean what we say. Aristotle allows the acratic to say what they like, for they are playing a part;[68] if so, it is a part that is played unawares. I would rather plead that it is acrasia that makes practical judgement possible. For if this is indeed to be *judgement*, it must achieve a reflective distance from desires that frees it from dependence upon their contingencies and fluctuating intensities. Practical judgements cannot claim both to be exercises of judgement, and to amount to acts of will.

Thus desire relates to practical judgement internally (since practical judgement is a creature of educated desire), yet loosely (since even effective desire is not a slave of practical judgement). Another kind of judgement to which desire relates internally is evaluation. Values are supervenient in that no two cases can differ evaluatively without differing subjacently in ways that could in principle be stated neutrally. However, we cannot expect the extension of a value to hang together as an intelligible whole at a subjacent level.[69] We can say more: when the extension does form a unity from a neutral point of view, there is no reason to suppose that it sustains a value at all, rather than merely permitting the application of a term meliorative or pejorative. Such terms bear a special colouring (Frege's *Färbung*), or facial expression;[70] they do not, in addition, connote a special kind of property.[71] How best to distinguish a neutral from an evaluative viewpoint is a question that is complicated by my reflections about sincerity, but perhaps I can still say some things fairly familiar. Imagine a child who has begun to grasp the concept of politeness (say through familiarity with a few maxims or precepts), but has as yet no sense of engagement on its

---

of transforming the id's will into action as if it were its own' (*The Ego and the Id* (1923), *Standard Edition*, xii. 63).

[68] *hypokrinesthai*, the origin of our word 'hypocrite' (*NE* 7. 3, 1147ª18–24).

[69] The thought is far from new; see Bernard Williams, *Ethics and the Limits of Philosophy* (London: Fontana, 1985), 217–18 n. 7.

[70] On tone of voice, see Christopher Ricks, *T. S. Eliot and Prejudice* (London: Faber & Faber, 1988), 133.

[71] Thus the Greek term *barbaros* did not name a disvalue: it was just a mildly denigratory term that the Greeks applied to non-Greeks. It depended for its extension simply upon a sense that it shares with our 'non-Greek', and not upon any distinct sense of its own.

behalf. He must minimally understand it to be a value, that is, he must recognize that it is cited as making a unity of certain ways of behaving, and as telling for or against behaving in those ways. Yet this does not take him far, for until he develops a nose for what is polite that is also a taste, he will be unable to do two things: to advance to an ability to apply the concept to new cases falling under no mechanical rule (say of etiquette), and to reflect about hard cases where decision might go either way. Evaluation rests on perceptions of salience and relevance that we share not just as describers of a causal environment, but as inhabitants of a human quality-space that is also a space of desire.[72] Of course cultures can and do vary (though the fact is barely worth noting so generally); yet it is because we share certain tendencies that incline us, once started somewhere, to go on in one way rather than another, in ethics and aesthetics as well as in arithmetic, that there is any substance to the thought that some ways are reasonable and others perverse.

This brings me finally to a large question: can moral judgements achieve truth? I count myself as an anti-non-cognitivist (after David Wiggins) in that I know no compelling ground for giving up hope. I have briefly explored what some find obstacles to truth: the plausibly projective origin of evaluation, and the connection (loose but not contingent) between practical judgement and motivation; whether an evaluative or practical judgement counts as a moral one depends upon content or context. Let me end with a still briefer attempt at reassurance. Pessimism would be compulsory if moral judgements were bound to have ideas above their station, like a parvenu denying his origins. Yet, even if we adopted a Kleinian aetiology, it would not have to follow that, as I once expressed it, 'unconscious phantasy leaves behind a deposit of falsity to disfigure judgment'.[73] Nor do we have to suppose that it is only to neutral and unmotivating points of view that anything can be reliably apparent.[74] There are two general lines of response to the error

---

[72] However, the desires that quicken an individual's conception of a value may be entertained rather than nursed; they may be ways of feeling that engage his imagination, but not his inclination. A previous distinction needs to be extended: wanting to ϕ is not just having a desire to ϕ, which is not merely entering into a desire to ϕ. Such refinements arise from the multiple aspects of desire.

[73] 'Three Types of Projectivism', 117.

[74] Here I can only pose a question crucial to the aptness of evaluations for truth: may the sense of a term at once relate internally to sentiment, and yet objectively

theorist. One is empirical: we have to look and see—a procedure for which we can depend upon him to lack the patience. The other is a priori (with evident debts to Wittgenstein and Davidson). What speakers mean is what they say, and this is defined by the grounds that they have and give. (This only becomes verificationist if we import a restrictive theory about what can serve as data.) A posteriori statements may count as true in the sense of matching how we can tell things to be;[75] they can only be ranked as failing, all the same, to be true to fact at a deeper level by an interpretation that over-interprets. Any answers to external questions, in Carnap's sense, that are implicit in a linguistic practice can enjoy neither more, nor less, depth and solidity than the practice itself; they are such stuff as rules are made on. Error theories rest on a false picture of mind and meaning. The sense of a term is tied to the criteria that competent speakers count as telling for or against its application; even if we could detect some metaphysical mistakes as floating about inside their minds, these would be irrelevant to what was said in using the term unless they connected with verbal behaviour by affecting how it was applied. It is a principle of interpretation that speakers are prone to local error, but incapable of systematic delusion. Ideology as a failure of transparency may infect certain lines of thought, but not whole modes of thinking.[76]

If so, anti-realism may share a grave with realism. This leaves open genuine questions about cognizability. It may be that the grounds that give sense to certain of our judgements fail to provide a means of resolving disagreement. This is so with matters of taste that are undecidable but not ineffable (we *call* things other than jokes funny or unfunny, and assert or deny, in the outmoded usage of a late uncle of mine, that a girl 'has *it*'). It may also be true of moral claims that display what Wollheim has called 'the

---

determine its application to the world? I believe that it can; see my 'On Criticising Values', in A. O'Hear (ed.), *Philosophy, the Good, the True and the Beautiful* (Cambridge: Cambridge University Press, 2000).

[75] This does not reduce ascriptions of supervenient value to assertions of subjacent fact for the reason I gave earlier: an evaluation rests on a pattern of response that is not redefinable in terms of tracking a subjacent property.

[76] My second line of response is indeterminate to the extent that this distinction is unclear. What, for example, should we say of religious belief? Are we to count it as a failed line of factual thinking, or (with Wittgenstein) as a mode of thinking with its own rules? Not that we can say whatever we like: failure should be detectable *from within*.

presumptuousness, the arrogance, for which morality is such a traditional mode of expression'[77] in imposing themselves upon others
across cultural divides beyond the possibility of persuasion. It may
also hold more generally of practical judgements, which try to
address all relevant grounds for action, than of moral evaluations,
which may supply some of the grounds (and not necessarily the
decisive ones). A conviction that is shared by my two mentors in
moral philosophy, Dick Hare and David Wiggins (and when they
agree, which is not generally, they may surely be right), is that the
only way to resolve the matter is not by metaphysical or meta-
ethical speculation, but case by case in actual ethical argument. A
philosopher who supposes that we have here a point of theory that
he is to settle without taking any real interest in practice is making
a mistake.

[77] *The Thread of Life*, 225.

4

Confidence and Irony

Miranda Fricker

> I believe that in relation to ethics there is a genuine and pro-
> found difference [from science] to be found, and also . . . that
> the difference is enough to motivate some version of the
> feeling . . . that science has some chance of being more or less
> what it seems . . . while ethical thought has no chance of being
> everything it seems.[1]

Sceptical reflection about value tends to open up a disconcerting
gulf between how ethical thought is, and how it seems to be. It is a
good question exactly what it would take for ethical thought to be
everything it seems. The answer will depend on how ethical thought
in fact seems to some relevant 'us'. It is often assumed that the
nature of our ethical experience is determinate enough and fixed
enough for there to be a number of general claims we can make
about it once and for all. But the assumption is questionable. An
important reason to question it is that our ethical experience may
vary with the historical and cultural location of the ethical community—the 'us' to whom morality is seeming one way or another.
J. L. Mackie took our moral experience to be metaphysically objectivist, so that for morality to be all that it seems, values would have
to be objective entities which had action-guidingness somehow
built in—'queer' entities, then, about which scepticism was found
to be in order.[2] If this was once the right answer to our question,
its rightness will be as historically changeable as our ethical phenomenology may be. Mackie did not attend to the idea that our

[1] Bernard Williams, *Ethics and the Limits of Philosophy* (London: Fontana, 1985),
134–5.
[2] J. L. Mackie, *Ethics: Inventing Right and Wrong* (Harmondsworth: Penguin,
1977).

ethical phenomenology might vary with culture and history. Understandably, perhaps, as he was relying on a feature of our phenomenology which might reasonably be expected to be constant: the idea that moral requirements present themselves in experience as coming from 'outside' ourselves. This idea is often, rightly, invoked. But it is very unclear that our grasp of a complex idea as abstract and philosophically problematic as the contrast between 'internality' and 'externality' to the 'self' is determinate enough, or fixed enough, to imply anything very much as to how it figures spontaneously in our ethical experience. If there is a determinate manner in which the idea figures, it must be as the idea is shaped by our particular, ongoing ethical *tradition*.[3]

This means that ethical phenomenology could take different forms. Although we must be wary of overloading ethical experience with intellectualist luggage (a danger which perhaps attends Mackie's account), in a culture characterized by an empiricist outlook, it would not be surprising if the externality of ethical requirements were experienced as metaphysical objectivity. Or, in a culture where a relativist mindset has successfully asserted itself, perhaps one should expect relativity somehow to register in ethical phenomenology. I don't know whether our moral experience is less metaphysically objectifying than it was before the undeniable cultural influence of post-modernism (an influence which can be recognized even by those who would not accept the idea that 'postmodernity' names a special historical moment). But it would surely be surprising if the anxious awareness of social difference within and between different cultures—the psychological logo of postmodernism—had not had any effect upon how ethical requirements present themselves in our experience. Be that as it may, we should allow that how morality seems, and hence the answer to the question whether morality has a chance of being as it seems, is susceptible to cultural and historical change. These matters are, in important part, matters of tradition.

The concept of a tradition is of something social or collective in its nature, and this should shape our understanding of the instability that sceptical reflection about value can bring. J. E. J. Altham has remarked: 'It is possible that for some individuals certain of

---

[3] On the concept of a tradition, see Alasdair MacIntyre, *After Virtue: A Study in Moral Theory* (London: Duckworth, 1981), esp. ch. 15.

their ethical dispositions depend *psychologically* upon a belief that they are objectively grounded, but, upon the whole, ethical dispositions, being part of a person's character, are not even psychologically vulnerable to the results of inquiry into their general metaphysical status.[4] That our ethical dispositions are a matter of character brings considerable practical stability, and this stability is in significant part owing to the fact that personal character is the result of an internalization of an ethical outlook held in common. The stability of character does not mean, however, that scepticism leaves ethical psychology just as it is. For it is not in terms of a practical instability that scepticism should in the first instance be understood as posing a threat. The instability should in the first instance be understood in terms of the destruction of authenticity: the onset of a sense of alienation from our own concepts and attitudes as we go about our normal evaluative and practical business. Wherever sceptical reflection has the power to disconcert ethical thought, that power will not be due to a merely individual motivational psychology, but rather to a shared phenomenology of ethical authority which arises from assumptions and attitudes embedded in the particular tradition. Instability will manifest itself as a form of self-alienation on the part of individuals *qua* members of the society whose tradition it is.

If a given tradition casts the authority of ethical judgements in terms of absolute objectivity—as derived perhaps from some set of values held up as metaphysically objective, or from the law of God, or from the workings of Pure Reason—then, so long as its members are at all likely to go in for sceptical reflection about the supposed source of authority, the tradition sets them up for a fall. It sets them up for the special disillusionment that brings inauthenticity so that, as they shape their actions and judgements according to their ethical concepts, the feeling creeps over them that they are merely acting out, merely going through the motions of something which used to be authentic. If they (we?) have no means of escaping this predicament—a tragic predicament in so far as it makes a charade of commitments depended on for life's meaningfulness—then the authority of ethical judgement will depend upon success in repressing sceptical reflection, or else somehow

[4] J. E. J. Altham, 'Reflection and Confidence', in J. E. J. Altham and R. Harrison (eds.), *World, Mind, and Ethics: Essays on the Ethical Philosophy of Bernard Williams* (Cambridge: Cambridge University Press, 1995), 162.

sealing it off from normative ethical thought, so as to keep the disillusion at bay.

1. *Personifying Alienation: The Ironist*

An important strategy for confining sceptical reflection so that it cannot undermine ethical authority is Richard Rorty's 'ironism'.[5] He divides reflection into 'public' and 'private' stances towards the ethical, so that the subject is divided between two personae: the public liberal (assuming s/he is a liberal), and the private ironist. It is not merely a division of stances, however—as if it were simply a question of two equally irresistible yet irreconcilable conceptions of the ethical subject. It is rather a division between two different and conflicting sets of concerns or interests which the reflective subject will have: 'The core of my book [*Contingency, Irony, and Solidarity*] is a distinction between private concerns, in the sense of idiosyncratic projects of self-overcoming, and public concerns, those having to do with the suffering of other human beings'.[6] Rorty's ironism is essentially an error-theoretical strategy for living with the threat of sceptical destabilization. He says, for instance, that ironists are never 'quite able to take themselves seriously because always aware that the terms in which they describe themselves are subject to change, always aware of the contingency and fragility of their final vocabularies, and thus of their selves'.[7] Contingency for Rorty, then, is understood as posing a threat to 'seriousness'. But contingency brings such fragility only on a very familiar traditional assumption: that acknowledging the historical and social contingency of our ethical outlook will undermine the authority of our ethical judgements. Given this assumption, dividing one's reflection between public and private stances can seem like a good coping strategy. The ironist puts her sceptical thoughts at a safe distance from ordinary ethical deliberation—rather as the weight-watcher may put the chocolate truffles safely out of his reach. The comparison is not intended to trivialize. Given that

---

[5] Richard Rorty, *Contingency, Irony, and Solidarity* (Cambridge: Cambridge University Press, 1989).

[6] Richard, Rorty, *Truth and Progress: Philosophical Papers*, iii (Cambridge: Cambridge University Press, 1998), 307–8 n. 2.

[7] Rorty, *Contingency, Irony, and Solidarity*, 73–4.

the distinction between public and private stances is basically one between different sets of 'concerns', the analogy with the weight-watcher's self-disciplinary tactic is not altogether distorting. The difficulty with Rorty's two stances is that (unlike the Humean division between philosophy in the study and life at the billiard table) there is nothing about human psychology which renders us simply incapable of experiencing our naïve ethical commitments as undermined by sceptical reflection. Is it precisely because we are in fact capable of bringing scepticism to bear on our everyday commitments, producing alienation and inauthenticity, that the private–public distinction can seem well motivated. In the absence of plain psychological incapacity, then, Rorty needs to provide a *justification* for the confinement of sceptical reflection to those particular concerns and projects which define the private stance. And I see little option here besides the roughly prudential justification that if you want to fulfil both public and private projects, you had better keep them apart. If this is right, and the ironist strategy effectively makes prudence an organizing principle of ethical reflection, then ironism shows up as deeply at odds with actual ethical psychology, so that it is hard to imagine how we might make the transition to the 'post-metaphysical' attitude. Further, we can see that such a transition is not even desirable, since an appeal to self-discipline is (as our weight-watcher will know) not a particularly reliable recipe for stability.

There is a different sort of difficulty concerning the relation between public and private stances, which relates to the ideal of transparency in ethics: the ideal that the authority which ethical thought has over us should not depend upon any misunderstanding on our part. At first glance, the figure of the ironist might appear to be a very embodiment of the ideal of transparency: someone who makes no metaphysical pretence of that which is really contingent. We might think, then, that the post-metaphysical society is a place where no one labours under any misapprehension about the authority of ethical judgement. But a more perspicuous description would be that it is a society in which people are, in one (private) area of life, open and explicit about the way in which another (public) area of life involves an ongoing pretence: the pretence that ethical thought is authoritative, when in fact the conditions of authority, conceived still in metaphysical terms, are not met. Thus Rorty describes the ironist as someone who 'would like

to avoid cooking the books she reads by using *any* [metaphysical]
. . . grid (although, with ironic resignation, she realizes that she can
hardly help doing so)'.[8] Looked at in this way, the figure of the
ironist is an embodiment not of transparency but rather of self-
conscious alienation. Ironism, then, does not serve any genuine
transparency. That the authority of ethical thought should depend
upon our psychological movement in and out of denial as to its contingency is not much better than a straightforward dependence on
misunderstanding. For the ironist, ethical thought cannot be what
it seems. Our best hope is in the maintenance of a hermetically
sealed sceptical self-consciousness.

But why, it may reasonably be asked, should we want transparency? Why should it matter whether we go about our ethical
lives aware of the true nature of the authority of our judgements?
So long as we sustain our ethical practice, so long as we carry on
the conversation, isn't that enough? These are sensible questions,
and it is not the case that transparency must be striven for no
matter what. Further, there are different strengths of transparency
one may or may not hope for. Bernard Williams distinguishes a
modest from an excessive sort when he says, 'It is one aspiration,
that social and ethical relations should not essentially rest on ignorance and misunderstanding of what they are, and quite another
that all the beliefs and principles involved in them should be explicitly stated.'[9] The more modest, and essentially anti-ideological,
aspiration that our ethical life should not depend on ignorance or
misunderstanding is the model we shall have in our sights here.
That is all we need to satisfy the hope that ethical thought might
be what it seems.

One obvious reason to value transparency of this kind is that any
general misunderstanding about the authority of ethical judgement
inevitably comes under suspicion of serving an ideological function.
(In a situation where there is no strongly objective authority available for ethical thought, we must not fail to ask why it is that some
people want to insist there is one. Is it, for instance, that they
hope—consciously or unconsciously, cynically or ingenuously—to
bring us to regard their particular ethical views as absolutely
authoritative?) The possibility of ideologically contaminated moti-

    [8] Rorty, *Contingency, Irony, and Solidarity*, 76.
    [9] Williams, *Ethics and the Limits of Philosophy*, 102.

vation will typically provide sufficient ethical reason to eradicate the misunderstanding, and so achieve transparency. At the very least, then, transparency is valuable in virtue of its place in anti-ideological thinking. It must be acknowledged of course that some sceptical theorists are suspicious of the very idea of ideology. Their scepticism is not metaphysical but sociopolitical: it revolves around the suspicion that lurking behind all appearances of ethical authority is a will to power. For them the notion of ideology is at best no longer relevant, and at worst itself an instrument of power, because the very idea of ideology depends on the possibility of a contrast between truth and ideology, authority and power, from which they wish to demur. Thus Foucault:

The notion of ideology appears to me to be difficult to make use of . . . like it or not, it always stands in virtual opposition to something else which is supposed to count as truth. Now I believe that the problem does not consist in drawing the line between that in a discourse which falls under the category of scientificity or truth, and that which comes under some other category, but in seeing historically how effects of truth are produced within discourses which in themselves are neither true nor false.[10]

But there is no reason to concede in advance that ethical authority can only be a channel for the will to power, any more than we must concede that it can never be more than a vain metaphysical hope.

Even granted the anti-ideological value of transparency, however, it would not be wholly fair as an objection to ironism that it fails, as it does, to produce it. For what transparency is made to give way to, given the ironist understanding of our predicament, is the greater good of keeping our ethical practice going at all—and that is obviously a reasonable order of priority. The point, then, is not to use transparency as a stick to beat the ironist with, but rather to see why transparency remains a reflective ethical ideal, and so remains a motivation for seeking an alternative, non-ironist understanding of our predicament. We should look for an alternative

---

[10] Michel Foucault, *Power/Knowledge: Selected Interviews and Other Writings 1972–1977*, ed. C. Gordon, trans. C. Gordon, L. Marshall, J. Mepham, and K. Soper (Hemel Hempstead: Harvester Wheatsheaf, 1980), 118. For a diagnostic discussion of the reductivist post-modern view (which Foucault is careful here not to express), see my 'Pluralism without Postmodernism', in M. Fricker and J. Hornsby (eds.), *The Cambridge Companion to Feminism in Philosophy* (Cambridge: Cambridge University Press, 2000).

conception of what it takes for ethical thought to be authoritative, and hope thereby to move beyond the fragility that motivates ironism. If the philosophical situation were really as is presumed in Rorty's account, one would be glad to have rehearsed the schizophrenic possibilities of the public–private split. But I shall try to show that we need not conceive our predicament in this way. Philosophy, for all its limitations, offers resources to conceive the requirements of moral authority more modestly (genuinely non-'metaphysically'), and so to modify our excessively objectivist tradition which sets us up for the alienation Rorty assumes we must learn to live with. The task is to see if we can locate a conception of ethical authority which is modest enough to be realistic, critically well equipped enough to be politically acceptable, and yet forceful enough to match, indeed to help shape, our experience of ethical necessity.

2. *Reflective Conditions of Confidence*

If we hope to surpass ironism as a response to the threat posed to ethical authority by sceptical reflection, what alternative non-objectivist model of authority is there available which might protect us against alienation? Williams has proposed something called 'confidence' as a model of ethical conviction. Conviction and authority are of course different ideas: ethical conviction is a psychological state, whereas ethical authority is a property of ethical judgement. But they are importantly connected in that a judgement's having authority is a requirement for entitlement to conviction about it. The basic idea will be that the authority of ethical thought derives from the ethical community's approximating the best sort of reflective state; and I agree with Williams that, concerning the ethical, the best sort of reflective state to be in is confidence. Further, given hospitable social conditions, this more modest, less objectivized conception of ethical authority might have some impact on our ethical tradition, and so (indirectly) upon the nature of our spontaneous ethical experience. The envisaged strategy, then, is one of active critical engagement with tradition: to help prepare the way for a non-objectivist turn in the ethical tradition which has set us up for alienation and inauthenticity. There need be no forgetfulness of philosophy's limitations. Clearly, philosophy alone cannot bring about any such change; rather, its role is to help set the intellectual stage.[11] Williams offers us confidence as a model of conviction, and my thought is that in so far as this model might come to find its place in our tradition, so might our experience of ethical conviction (and thus of ethical authority) come to move in a non-objectivist direction that makes for transparency and hence stability.

The strategy exploits the fact that tradition is both the necessary starting-point for ethical thought and also, as MacIntyre makes clear, something with which we should have a critical relation. A tradition is, or should be, a site of argument. In exercising a critical capacity with respect to our own tradition we can, to some extent, direct and re-create it. Naturally we are passive recipients of a backlog of history; yet we make history too (whatever we do), and to this degree we have a certain responsibility—albeit very indirect—for how ethical requirements present themselves in experience. This has an immediate bearing on the question whether, and how, we might aim for transparency—a match between how ethical thought is, and how it seems. On Mackie's view, the question is immaterial, since a number of deeply entrenched habits of thought mean we cannot help our objectivizing ethical psychology.[12] Our helplessness has the advantage that scepticism's threat to ethical authority is only academic. But it has the disadvantage that our ethical experience cannot be corrected as to its objectivizing 'error'; not only does it rest on a misunderstanding, it must. If, by contrast, our ethical experience is to some extent changeable via the changeable context of tradition, and if by philosophizing we participate in the ongoing process of re-creating our tradition, then the question of our aiming to bring ethical experience into line with the truth about ethical authority can arise within philosophy as a more than merely academic question.

Again, we must avoid intellectualist presumption as to philosophy's impact on tradition. It is to be avoided not simply by refraining from excited overstatement, but also by ensuring that our notion of a tradition is suitably complex. An ethical tradition cannot be simply intellectual and institutional. 'Tradition' here is to

---

[11] Exactly how much or how little philosophy can do will itself be a social-historical question. Philosophy's impact, or lack of it, on a given ethical tradition will depend (mundanely) on how much attention is paid to philosophical ideas in the culture in question.   [12] Mackie, *Ethics*, 42–6.

be understood as a whole cultural entity, to include not only our intellectual inheritances, and the social practices and institutions that sustain an ethical way of life, but also our cultural symbolism, our *imaginary*.[13] The idea of the imaginary is an invaluable critical and explanatory tool, not least because it has application across diverse arenas of the imagination: notably, ethical and political, psychoanalytic and philosophical. The imaginary is an important domain in which ideology can be at work, so that careful scrutiny of the imaginary (as manifested in common understandings of the social world, or in literature, or in philosophical texts) can reveal residual social meanings that serve unjust power relations.[14] Imaginary meanings which are politically and ethically suspect need not be strictly ideological, since they need not work in a broad and systematic manner to the advantage of one social group at the expense of another. None the less, the imaginary is *inter alia* a depot of oppressive residual meanings that no longer fit well with the self-image we project to ourselves in explicit avowals and in our public rhetoric. An example profoundly relevant to our ethical imaginary might be drawn from the politics of disability, where the drive towards equality and a properly informed social understanding is at odds with our still powerful imaginary association between physical abnormality and wickedness or evil.[15] The imaginary, then,

[13] The inclusion of the imaginary in the conception of an ethical tradition marks an obvious departure from MacIntyre. There are various different and interrelated notions of the imaginary. In particular, I do not invoke Jacques Lacan's notion, clearly, which takes its meaning precisely from a contrast with the symbolic order. Sources for the notion I intend are Michèle Le Doeuff's seminal (*sic*) *The Philosophical Imaginary*, trans. C. Gordon (London: Athlone Press, 1989); and Moira Gatens's *Imaginary Bodies: Ethics, Power and Corporeality* (London: Routledge, 1996). For a discussion of Luce Irigaray's notion of the imaginary (and of how it too is distinct from Lacan's), see Margaret Whitford's *Luce Irigaray: Philosophy in the Feminine* (London: Routledge, 1991), ch. 3.

[14] See Susan James, 'The Power of Spinoza: Feminist Conjunctions', interview with Moira Gatens and Genevieve Lloyd, *Women's Philosophy Review*, 19 (1998), 6–28. In her *Imaginary Bodies* Gatens ends a discussion of how, in a society which ostensibly endorses gender equality, it can still be brought as a consideration in favour of the defendant in a rape that when a woman says 'no' she often means 'yes': 'The ethical problem concerning the legal treatment meted out to women . . . is a political problem. . . . There is a multiplicity of embodied habits, customs and laws which continue to bear the scars of [women's political] exclusion. . . . As far as the present is concerned, there are some . . . who unreflectively endorse and perpetuate a sexual imaginary in which women embody the paradox of being considered as *both* free and rational members of a democratic political body *and* beings under the "natural" authority of men' (p. 141).

[15] Examples are ubiquitous in children's stories of ugly wicked witches and so on,

may be understood as an unofficial store of collective meanings, which functions as a kind of historical buffer zone: the locus of a critical lag between past and future, from where a residue of not quite expelled meanings exercises a surreptitious influence on social understanding. If you want to know a tradition's private motivations, its secret rationalizations, its possibly shameful origins—then explore the cultural imaginary. Perhaps we should think of an imaginary as the synchronic counterpart to a genealogy.[16]

Anti-Conservative Reflection

What, then, is confidence? Williams introduces it as 'basically a social phenomenon',[17] though it is also a normative notion, and not a merely social-psychological description.[18] If confidence is a good state to be in with respect to the ethical, it must inhabit a midway position between bad kinds of conservatism on the one hand, and neurotic or otherwise exaggerated kinds of self-questioning on the other. A bad kind of conservatism might be a conservatism of mere thoughtless complacency; or it might be one of brute dogmatism; or again it might be a conservatism motivated by ideology. That confidence is distinguished from these bad conservatisms shows that it is a normative state, and it shows, in particular, that confidence requires the sort of critical thinking which safeguards against

but also in literary culture quite generally. One unforgettable example is found, for instance, in Laclos's *Les Liaisons dangereuses*. Upon the exposure of the cruel intrigue spun by the Marquise de Merteuil and Vicomte de Valmont, we learn that Merteuil contracts a disfiguring disease which costs her one eye and renders her, everyone agrees, 'vraiment hideuse'. Her fate prompts an unnamed marquis to remark that the disease had turned her inside out, so that she now wore her soul on her face: 'que la maladie l'avait retournée, et qu'à présent son âme était sur sa figure' (Pierre Choderlos de Laclos, *Les Liaisons dangereuses* (Paris: Flammarion, 1981), 378).

[16] Friedrich Nietzsche, *On The Genealogy of Morals*, trans. Walter Kaufmann and R. J. Hollingdale (New York: Random House, 1967).

[17] Williams, *Ethics and the Limits of Philosophy*, 170.

[18] Williams makes the normativity separate from confidence itself, though consequently more explicit as a requirement, in 'Who Needs Ethical Knowledge?' (in A. Phillips Griffiths (ed.), *Ethics*, Royal Institute of Philosophy suppl. 35 (1993), 213–22), where he introduces what in *Ethics and the Limits of Philosophy* is simply called 'confidence' as 'reasonable confidence': 'A desirable state for one to be in with regard to one's ethical views is confidence. . . . But we do not want the confidence of bigotry—if there is to be confidence, it should be reasonable confidence' (p. 213). As I shall use the term, confidence is something we possess only if we are entitled to it.

our ethical concepts' colluding with the forces of ideology. It will be a cultural-historical question whether this safeguard can be achieved through merely reactive critical reflection (so that we mobilize our critical powers only after some complaint has been expressed) or whether a more proactive reflective attitude is called for. If at some moment in a given tradition there is reason for pessimism about the credentials of the relevant thick concepts,[19] or about the good order of the discursive climate, then clearly a more proactive attitude will be required than if there is reason for optimism about such things. Whether the order of the day is optimistic or pessimistic, however, the crucial aspect of our reflective attitude is that it should be politically astute. One must have a nose for the ideological if one is to achieve confidence. If we fail to detect that a given concept has an unjust ideological function, so that it should be modified or phased out, then we will have failed to safeguard against a bad kind of conservatism. For example, contrary to an (incredibly) still popular marriage vow, we are not entitled to confidence in the concept of wifely obedience, because this concept presupposes a relation of subordination to a husband which is oppressive to women. The airing of such a critical consideration exemplifies the workings of immanent critique in our ethical lives: we judge our concepts by our best ethical standards. Anti-ideological refection will be of special importance so long as it is in the nature of human society for there to be a marked risk of ethical concepts' evolving under the sway of unjust power relations. So long as this is the case, safeguarding against ideological function will require more than merely reactive critical reflection.

Our reflective activity (whether proactive or reactive) is not supposed to underpin any strongly positive conclusion as to our concepts' desirability or justification. The suggestion is more modest, and in tune with Williams's view that no objective justification is available, or necessary. The requisite critical reflection is such that a thick concept's survival of it is sufficient to show that one is not being badly conservative in living by it. Thus the reflection which licenses confidence is basically negative. It is immanent in our own

---

[19] I take the defining rough contrast between thick and thin ethical concepts to be that the former are substantially world-guided, in that they have significant descriptive content, whereas the latter are not. Examples of thin concepts are 'right', 'wrong', 'obligation' (probably), and 'duty' (possibly); examples of thick are 'courageous', 'charitable', 'kind', 'cowardly', 'spiteful'.

ethical outlook—though always involving the exercise of social imagination as we entertain possible alternative ways of going on.[20] It essentially involves asking the question: is this is an acceptable way to organize and interpret our social world? For example, should we—as in that marriage vow—conceive of a wife's behaviour towards her husband as falling under the concepts 'obedient' and 'disobedient'?; should we reserve the concept of a 'family' to contexts of heterosexual parenting?; should we think of a parent's punishing a child with a slap as 'discipline' or 'assault'? We will draw our (defeasible) conclusions to such specific questions *en route* to confidence. Confidence itself, however, will not be the conclusion to any line of critical reasoning; it is rather a by-product of critical reflection. If critical reflection must be self-conscious, confidence need not be. Confidence is a *stance* we achieve towards our ethical concepts, and should be construed, as it were, adverbially.

If this account of its relation to reflection is correct, then confidence is in one respect a stronger notion than knowledge: members of the fictional hypertraditional society, where there is next to no reflection, are perfectly capable of ethical knowledge (knowledge gained through the correct employment of thick concepts); but their somnambulant unreflectiveness will render them incapable of satisfying the conditions of confidence. In another respect, however—and according to certain comments made by Williams (not in *Ethics and the Limits of Philosophy* but elsewhere)—confidence is characterized in a way which would make it a weaker notion than knowledge.[21] The core idea is that we can have confidence in our thick ethical concepts provided that their way of carving up our social world is all right. But Williams says that we can also have confidence in judgements made using *thin* ethical concepts, even though we cannot have knowledge at this level. It is important for Williams that there should be a model available for

---

[20] For a Wittgensteinian account of the nature of our responsibility for our own conceptual practices, see Sabina Lovibond, *Realism and Imagination in Ethics* (Oxford: Blackwell, 1983).

[21] See Williams's reply to Altham, in which he says the idea he had in mind in *Ethics and the Limits of Philosophy* was that 'granted the nature of modern societies, we would face a good number of ethical tasks with the help of unsupported thin concepts, and, since there was not going to be knowledge in that connection, it would be as well if we had confidence' (Altham and Harrison (eds.), *World, Mind, and Ethics*, 207).

ethical conviction concerning judgements couched in terms of thin concepts, because he holds that, not to put too fine a point on it, thick concepts are on the decrease. Modern society is, for Williams, characterized not merely by a climate of intense self-inquisition but also by an increasingly exclusive dependence on thin concepts. He suggests this independently from philosophical considerations, as a historical claim for which he then offers a philosophical explanation. The explanation is that reflection tends not only to drive individual thick concepts from use, but to do so without replacing them with new ones, so that the overall ratio between thin and thick concepts becomes ever greater as reflection and history roll on.

The idea that reflection depletes our stock of thick concepts motivates the claim that we can have confidence in judgements couched only in the thin. There would not be much comfort, after all, in claiming confidence in only our thick concepts if we were in any case doomed to rely largely on thin ones. And since it is reflection which is thought to diminish our stock of thick concepts, there is not a lot the reflective society can or should do about the depletion. If that were how things stood, it would indeed come as a relief to find we could have confidence in the unsupported thin. But I do not see how we can have confidence in thin concepts independently from a confidence in a set of thick concepts that orchestrates their use. In the case of thick concepts, the suggestion has been that we gain confidence in them only if they survive appropriate levels of appropriate sorts of critical reflection. But it is hard to see how the reflective condition is to be met in the case of unsupported thin concepts. What would it be for a thin concept—'wrong', 'right', 'good', 'bad'—to survive reflection where survival demonstrates non-conservatism? Presumably the required reflection would address not feckless questions such as 'should we carry on with the concept of wrong?', but rather questions such as 'should we carry on using the concept of wrong in relation [for example] to wives not doing-what-their-husbands-tell-them-because-their-husbands-tell-them-to?' The unconvincingly longhand character of the questions which would have to be asked in order to win confidence in unsupported thin concepts may lead one to suspect that one is not really succeeding in testing a thin concept here at all, but only an ungainly conjunctive artefact whose function, if any, would be rather that of a thick concept. This suspicion gives rise to the further doubt that there could ever really be a situation of unsupported thin concepts. Certainly, thin concepts are singularly unsuited to carving up anything but the most hermeneutically bland of social worlds. It is hard to see how, in a situation where our only obviously evaluative concepts were thin, there would not have to be some other, less obviously evaluative concepts carving up our social world for us, thereby functioning much as the bygone thick ethical concepts did. In this situation, apparently non-evaluative concepts—'family', say—might be used in a way which is implicitly evaluative. This is not hard to imagine, since implicitly evaluative practices are already perfectly common: as when someone might withhold the concept of a family from two parenting adults and the child they are jointly bringing up, on the ground that the adults are of the same sex. But it remains very hard to imagine a situation in which the employment of thin concepts was wholly unsupported by other concepts functioning basically as thick ethical concepts do.[22]

Be that as it may. We need not be concerned with the question whether an ethical community could live, confidently or not, by thin concepts alone, for we need not quite accept Williams's motivating idea that the modern world is characterized by an increasingly exclusive reliance on thin concepts. We may accept instead the closely related claim that the modern era is characterized by a marked preoccupation with certain thin concepts (in the context of liberal democracy, the concept of a right particularly comes to mind). On this view, there is no presumption that thick concepts are decreasing overall, but only that modernity has led us to attach comparatively little importance to them. We continue to acknowledge that reflection tends to put particular thick concepts out of use, but we leave open the possibility that it tends equally to introduce new ones. Perhaps reflection is usually best described not as discarding or introducing any concepts, but as modifying them by changing their application. (This would, for instance, be so in the case of 'obedience' as applied to wives, since reflection obviously does not point to making the whole concept of obedience redundant, but specifically the obedience of wives to husbands. Or, again, consider the case of 'family', or 'cruel', where the issue is one of

---

[22] Thus I agree with Susan Hurley's 'non-centralism' about reasons for action (see her 'Objectivity and Disagreement', in T. Honderich (ed.), *Morality and Objectivity: A Tribute to J. L. Mackie* (London: Routledge & Kegan Paul, 1985)).

how broadly the term should be applied.) If this is right, then we need not accept that reflection tends to deplete our stock of thick concepts, leaving us to rely increasingly on the thin. And so we need not be concerned if, as I have suggested, the reflective conditions of confidence are not such as to be met in relation to thin concepts unsupported by a system of thick ones organizing their use.

Rejection of the historical claim which Williams is inclined to accept is neutral with respect to the related and important idea that reflection, by putting certain thick concepts out of use, can destroy knowledge—an idea which, although controversial,[23] is surely right. No doubt it has been controversial for many reasons, but one explanatory factor must be that it exemplifies a general fact about knowledge which mainstream epistemology is singularly ill equipped to acknowledge: that access to knowledge can be affected, and independently from its effect on the inquirer's rational standing, by a very non-epistemic-looking factor: *who one is*. A matter of 'mere' social identity—one's place in history and culture—can present an obstacle to possessing knowledge, even when it presents no obstacle to satisfying the rational conditions of knowledge (the possession of a justified true belief, perhaps). As history rolls on and culture changes, critical reflection can lead us to disown, or (less strongly) to cease identifying with, certain of our concepts, so that some knowledge which was once ours is no longer ours. Knowledge we once possessed is put out of our reach by a social-psychological gap opened up by reflection, and so may with some literal accuracy be described as 'destroyed'.

It may be that talk of 'destruction' is, however, unhelpfully provocative, for it can encourage the misunderstanding that reflection is being said to cause a rationally retrograde step of some kind. Take the example of 'female chastity', which is no longer (in the main) one of our concepts. A proposition such as 'the princess is chaste', where the princess in question is some historical figure who was indeed 'chaste' and where we have good reason to believe it, cannot constitute a piece of our ethical knowledge, even though we stand in the proper rational relations to it. None the less, there remains a sense in which it is not simply the case that knowledge

<hr />

[23] See, for instance, A. W. Moore's 'Can Reflection Destroy Knowledge?', *Ratio*, new ser., 4 (1991), 97–107; and Simon Blackburn, 'Making Ends Meet', a Discussion of B. Williams, *Ethics and the Limits of Philosophy*, *Philosophical Books*, 27 (1986), 193–203.

has been destroyed since the concept lost its ethical currency, for we can of course still grasp such propositions in thought—certainly we haven't lost *that* ability . What we have lost is the ability to *own* (as opposed to disown) such a proposition, with the result that we can no longer possess it as a piece of ethical knowledge. The metaphor of 'ethical currency' is an apt one. Our relation to rejected thick concepts is analogous to our relation to shillings and farthings. Since we put them out of use, they are not our money any more. We can still grasp them in our hands all right, but not as currency—they are not current, but historical. Instead of talking only in terms of destruction, then, we might add that what was once a piece of ethical knowledge has been replaced by a piece of historical knowledge—knowledge about our forebears' ethical life. Reflection through time has *displaced* the ethical knowledge that the princess was chaste along two planes: horizontally (it's now about someone else's way of life), and vertically (it's now knowledge at the reflective level). The result is, we no longer know that the princess was 'chaste' as a piece of knowledge *in* our ethical way of life, but rather as knowledge *about* an ethical way of life, and not our own (hence the appropriateness of inverted commas). We might wish to emphasize, then, that wherever reflection destroys ethical knowledge, it gives way to a replacement item of historical knowledge. This means that reflection will not have brought any overall rationally retrograde step. Thus understood, the idea that a piece of *ethical* knowledge can be destroyed when concepts required for it are expelled from our outlook should not be epistemologically jarring.

This picture of the destruction of ethical knowledge shows up the relation between the question what sorts of reflection earn confidence, and Williams's idea of stability under reflection. I have been presenting confidence as a route to stability under sceptical reflection, in virtue of the fact that the anti-ideological vigilance required for confidence inevitably aims at transparency. But it is clearly not the case that confidence brings stability under all other kinds of reflection. The reflection required to sustain confidence will bring a general stability, but locally—in connection with particular concepts—some *in*stability is demanded. For we have seen that confidence requires the sort of anti-conservative reflection which will sometimes alter thick concepts' application, or even make them redundant. Without the local instability this causes, we should be suspicious that we were not in fact in a state of confidence at all, but of a bad conservatism instead. Here, the fact that our relation to history should not be merely receptive but critical and creative shows up in reflective practice. We are seen to make history by forcing certain conceptual practices into the past. In fulfilling the conditions of confidence, we play an active role in the development of our ethical tradition.

Reflection as Collective Critical Activity

So far I have been exploring how confidence—'basically a social phenomenon'—is also intended as a normative phenomenon. And I have tried to say something useful about its normativity through an account of the sorts of critical reflection it might require. Another way to approach confidence's sociality is under the aspect of a contrast not with 'normative' but with 'individual'. Thinking of confidence as an ideal epistemic state to be in regarding the ethical encourages a characterization of ethical judgements as deriving their authority from the agent's social setting—from something outside the individual, then. This inspires hope that the notion of confidence will help to make sense of our externalizing ethical phenomenology—our experience of the practical necessity of ethical judgement as originating outside ourselves. If the authority of ethical thought is derived from our confidence in our ethical concepts, then the necessity in question comes from something not simply in the individual, but in the collective. And this is precisely what we need to give an explanation of our externalizing ethical experience which (unlike Mackie's error theory[24]) is also a vindication.

But a vindication of our externalizing ethical experience will only be forthcoming on a strongly social understanding of confi-

---

[24] Mackie does acknowledge that the sociality of the ethical means 'the attitudes that are objectified into moral values have indeed an external source, though not the one assigned to them by the belief in their absolute authority' (Mackie, *Ethics*, 42–3), and he also says that when someone expresses moral demands, 'he is expressing demands which he makes as a member of a community, which he has developed in and by participation in a joint way of life' (p. 44). But because he does not consider the possibility that our moral experience could be externalizing but *not* metaphysically (or otherwise strongly) objectifying, Mackie fails to allow that our externalizing experience might be vindicated (found free of error) by an account which conceives the authority of ethical judgement as deriving from a state of the collective—for instance, the collective state of confidence.

dence—stronger, I think, than Williams intends. The strongly social understanding depicts confidence as a collective analogue to an individual's psychological state of confidence. The word *analogue* makes the crucial point. It means that confidence would not be properly understood as the aggregate of independent individual confidences. The notion would not be properly explained by saying that it is what a society has when enough of its individual members have it, for the order of explanation would be the other way around. Individuals can have confidence, for sure, but they do so in virtue of being socially constituted: it is *qua* members of a society where there is confidence that individuals can have confidence. This seems in tune with Williams's claim that

the conclusion of practical necessity . . . [seems] to come 'from outside' in the way that conclusions of practical necessity always seem to come from outside—from deeply inside. Since ethical considerations are in question, the agent's conclusions will not usually be solitary or unsupported, because they are part of an ethical life that is to an important degree shared with others.[25]

However, my strongly social interpretation seems incompatible with something else Williams says about confidence:

It is basically a social phenomenon. This is not to deny that when it exists in a society, it does so because individuals possess it in some form, nor that it can exist in some individuals when it is lacking in society. When this happens, however, it is in a different form, since the absence of social confirmation and support for the individual's attitudes must affect the way in which he holds those attitudes.[26]

As I understand it, this quotation shows that Williams's own understanding of confidence is methodologically individualist (the order of explanation is bottom-up so that individuals' possession of confidence is prior), and that it is not necessary that a society possess confidence for one of its members to possess it, if in a different form. If so, then Williams's idea of confidence is weakly social— assimilable, for instance, to the model of a speculative market, where if enough individual dealers have confidence in the pound, say, then this will be contagious so that others come to share the confidence, resulting in a general confidence where the climate of

---

[25] Williams, *Ethics and the Limits of Philosophy*, 191.
[26] Ibid. 170. I am grateful to Adrian Moore for pointing this remark out to me, and more generally for helpful discussion.

reciprocation could be said to transform that of the individuals. The sociality at stake here is (as we might call it) severalist, as opposed to collectivist.

But there are at least two reasons in favour of the collectivist, or strongly social, conception. Firstly, it can better accommodate the division of reflective labour. Clearly, it cannot be a requirement of confidence that every individual who possesses it fulfil the overall reflective conditions. As with most other spheres of epistemic practice (e.g. the empirical-scientific), in the ethical sphere individuals can piggyback on the deliberations of others regarding the credentials of shared concepts. There is a delicate balance to be found between the need to rely on others in this way and the exigencies of personal responsibility for one's own evaluative thought, but that there be some significant degree of non-individual responsibility through the division of reflective labour is a matter of quotidian necessity. Without such a division, the achievement of confidence would make full-time ethical theorists of us all—a price certainly not worth paying.[27] The strongly social conception of confidence allows us to make proper sense of the fact that reflective advances are held in common, as a shared ethical resource available to individuals even while they are looking the other way, variously getting on with the thing that gives all this reflection its point: life. The work of critical reflection, and especially that most politicized branch of ethical reflection we might call conceptual activism, will tend to be unevenly undertaken. This unevenness reveals an important epistemic consequence of social differentiation within the collective, inasmuch as it will be the social experience of women which particularly affords a critical perspective on certain marriage vows, or particularly that of lesbians and gay men which affords a critical perspective on the narrow application of 'family'. None the less, the confident stance towards the relevant concepts is won generally, at the collective level (and conceptual activists do a considerable ethical-epistemic service to their less critical contemporaries). On the severalist conception, the key relations between bearers of confidence are inter-individual relations of 'confirmation and support'. This makes it hard to explain the fact that it is possible for unreflective individuals—who have scant critical thoughts

---

[27] 'Confidence is merely one good among others: it has a price, and the price should not be set too high' (ibid.).

available to be confirmed or supported—none the less to use common ethical concepts with confidence.

The second reason to favour the strongly social conception of confidence is that it is better placed to give the hoped for vindication of our externalizing ethical phenomenology. It surely won't be enough to understand confidence as social simply in the sense that it usually involves social confirmation and support. That understanding does not give us the idea we need, namely, that the authority of ethical judgements derives from something which transcends the individual. The way in which ethical authority features in our spontaneous experience as coming from outside us cannot be justified by the idea that it is supported by *more* individuals, simply. Mere intersubjectivity—mere confirmation and support—is not enough. What is needed to vindicate our externalizing experience is something different from the mere aggregate of individuals: the collective. There is nothing metaphysically mysterious about this idea. A collective is composed, naturally enough, of individuals. The crucial difference is simply over the question whether an individual can have confidence independently from her belonging to a collective where there is confidence. And the driving thought remains the familiar one that individuals can satisfy the conditions of confidence only through critical participation in a shared way of life, a tradition. Indeed, conceived in abstraction from some such specific cultural-historical setting, the question whether an individual has confidence does not arise, so the right conception of the individual, for those asking that question, must be as of someone who is already a participant in a collective practice where there is or is not confidence. No weaker conception of confidence's sociality, it seems to me, is capable of honouring Williams's idea that the seeming externality of ethical necessity derives from the fact that it comes from an 'outside' which is 'deeply inside'. The only thing 'deeply inside' that could authorize ethical necessity is the collective practice which constitutes individuals by shaping their character and socializing them into a particular ethical outlook.

On the collectivist conception, collective confidence is necessary, though not sufficient, for individuals to share in it. On this point, an analogy with money may, again, be helpful. Individuals can possess money only if they belong to a collective which operates the requisite institutions and practices, though membership of such a collective naturally provides no guarantee that any particular individual will have any money. So it is, I am suggesting, with confidence: an individual can only have it if the collective has it, though he might not have it even then. He might, for example, be prey to neurotic self-inquisition, perhaps because he believes, falsely, that that is the only way to avoid ethical imperialism. (An individual among us can have too low, as well as too high, an opinion of our ethical thought.)

Reflection as Socially Differentiated

Anti-individualist arguments from *conception*, however, only get us so far. At this stage of the argument, one may still legitimately demand to know why a lone reflective individual in an otherwise unreflective society is not able critically to assess her culture's ethical concepts so that, on finding them to be all right, she might achieve confidence. This is surely a conceptual possibility, even on the collectivist conception: a collective ethical practice could, in principle, contain one remarkable participant who alone makes confidence-earning use of generally neglected collective critical resources. However, in relation to many of our thick concepts there is a powerful reason for denying that this is an *epistemological* possibility (whatever the starting conception). Our thick concepts are part of the hermeneutic constitution of our shared social world, and we have seen that confidence requires us to safeguard against bad kinds of conservatism. But individuals are differentially placed in that social world. There is a plurality of social identity positions that make a difference to social experience, so that a lone reflective individual in a society where collective levels of reflection fall short of confidence will not be in a position to achieve the safeguarding. One is not in a position to regard one's ethical practices as free from bad kinds of conservatism if there are social groups who are (perhaps subtly) prevented from going in for the kind of reflection about their own social experience which would equip them to rebel against a conceptual practice that did them an injustice—for example, by characterizing them as 'naturally' subordinate and so fit for obedience to another group, or by characterizing their sexual orientation as 'unnatural' and so shameful. Thus, for many of our thick concepts, being justified in believing that they are all right requires participation in reflective activity going on more generally in society by people who are differently socially positioned.

Naturally the lone reflective individual's lack of justification applies directly only to those ethical concepts which are at least *candidates* for doing an injustice to someone's social experience. However, the candidature inevitably spreads fairly widely among our concepts, since we cannot assume we are able to tell exactly *which* of our concepts are the ones we should regard as suspect. (What straight person was in a position to see that one might question the justice of an exclusively heterosexual application of the concept 'family' before gay people forced the issue into public view?) Social imagination is of course essential in ethics, and it can get us a very long way; but it cannot get us to place from which the lone reflective individual is able to survey her concepts and the social world they help construct, and be justified in a unilateral rubber-stamping.

Where reflection is distributed across social difference sufficiently for confidence,[28] an individual's reflective activity will show up as dependent upon that of the collective, not simply in the sense sustainable by the insight from the philosophy of mind and language that using concepts at all is a fundamentally public activity, but rather in the sense sustained by the epistemological insight that different individuals' critical reflection will make different contributions to fulfilling the anti-conservative conditions of confidence. Thus we see that a socially differentiated division of ethical reflective labour is not merely convenient, but crucial to the achievement of confidence. The fact of social difference, then, combined with the requirement of anti-ideological reflection, presents an insurmountable epistemological obstacle to the lone individual's earning confidence. But it poses no obstacle to a properly distributed collective reflective practice in which, to a sufficient degree, everyone has their say. The conclusion to be drawn here is that it is only through participation in a collective critical practice which is democratic enough to earn confidence that an individual may earn confidence.

The main idea argued for here is that the basic source of

[28] Clearly, adequate distribution across social difference will be a less than perfectly socially differentiated distribution—lest we set our standards for confidence too high.

authority in the ethical is a particular kind of collective ethical practice: one in which there is confidence. This idea is importantly different from the idea that ethical practices in which we confidently participate constitute *an ethical authority*—as if tradition were something which, when in doubt, we could consult for a ruling. To see things that way would be to forget that a tradition is a site of argument, and so to construe the kind of authority it can embody too positively and too concretely. A tradition is the precondition of any consideration's weighing with us as an ethical reason for or against doing something. Once a consideration presents itself as a *reason*, there is nothing further to be said about its authority outside the immanent critical thinking of the confidence-earning kinds I have been at pains to identify. Thus, location in a tradition is the precondition equally of ethical conservation and ethical change (even revolutionary change—all criticism is immanent, and some is radical). The suggestion has been that confidence, conceived now as basically a collective phenomenon, is essential for a tradition's being in good shape; and if a tradition is in good shape, then its ethical thought is authoritative and an externalizing ethical phenomenology can be vindicated.

An Irony of Critical Engagement

Earlier I suggested that anti-ideological reflection aims *inter alia* at transparency about the nature of ethical authority. The achievement of transparency would render us insusceptible to the special disillusion which otherwise threatens to follow sceptical reflection. If we are free from misunderstanding about ethical authority, then sceptical reflection cannot show us anything we don't already accept. The special disillusionment we thus avoid is such as to cast all ethical judgements in the same mould: as claiming a false authority. So the achievement of transparency in ethical thought safeguards our ability to employ a fundamental distinction required for critical reflection: that between genuine authority and false authority. This is a distinction we mark out whenever we modify or discard a thick concept because we have discovered its function is ideological, or in some other way unacceptable. The observation that the anti-ideological reflection required for confidence presupposes a contrast between genuine and bogus authority brings into view the proper place of irony in ethics. Post-modernist cynicism about authority has co-opted the ironical attitude so that it can seem as if its only form is sceptical. But this is not so. In the literary Modernist tradition, the idea of the unreliable narrator is essential, where this takes the form of an ironic stance on the part of the author to the testimony of the narrator, an irony which is then taken up by the reader. Such an ironical stance presupposes the contrast between reliability and unreliability in a narrator, and is therefore a conceit wholly foreign to any general scepticism about the very idea of the authority of the authorial (*sic*) voice. Yet it is also a stance which encourages, indeed requires, the reader to be alert to the possibility of unreliability—of false authority. This sort of irony, then, is part and parcel of the reflection required for confidence: to attend, with some political perceptiveness, to the ways in which a given concept may serve an unjust social function, and so to question with appropriate suspicion the purported authority of any judgement employing it. The irony of someone who is critically engaged in the ethical is an irony of vigilance as to the potential for false authority. It is an irony of self-conscious engagement, not sceptical disengagement.

I have tried to elaborate Bernard Williams's idea of confidence in order to present it as part of a proposal for moving beyond what we can now see as the *contingently* destabilizing power of scepticism about objective value. Confidence—construed as a strongly social notion but still not a strongly objectivizing one—has been presented as the basic (because preconditional) source of authority in ethical judgement. Williams talks in terms not of authority but of conviction. I favour approaching the issue from the point of view of authority because it wears on its sleeve the normative dimension of the sort of conviction which has always been hoped for in ethics: conviction which is not only practically efficient, but also well grounded; conviction which is located in individual psychology, and yet which flows from a source that transcends merely individual patterns of motivation. More broadly, the proposal here has been that the explication of authority in terms of confidence might be the centrepiece of a strategy for reshaping our ethical tradition—a tradition which, as it stands, renders ethical authority unnecessarily vulnerable in the face of certain traditional sceptical goadings. The proposed strategy is directed towards an ideal of transparency, because the kind of reflection that confidence requires is inevitably so directed. In such a situation there would be no risk of disillusionment, for ethical authority would at last seem just as it is.[29]

[29] My thanks to Pamela Anderson, Tom D'Andrea, John Dickie, Edward Harcourt, Stephen Law, Hallvard Lillehammer, Sabina Lovibond, Adrian Moore, Keith Wilson, and an anonymous reader for Oxford University Press for their helpful and encouraging critical responses to earlier drafts; and also to participants in seminar discussions at the Universities of Manchester and Southampton. For invaluable discussion of the issues addressed here, and for much else besides, I am deeply indebted to Bernard Williams.

5

Morality, Ideology, and Reflection; or, The Duck Sits Yet

Peter Railton

I

Should we see morality as an ideology? And, if so, what are we to conclude? Morality *does* make an almost irresistible target, a sitting duck, for *Ideologiekritik*. For it presents itself as a set of evaluations and commands of lofty impartiality or universal validity; yet a glance at history shows instead a succession of norms—all at one point or other widely viewed as moral—that have sanctioned slavery, the subjugation of women, and a host of other purported rights and duties that seem to us in retrospect to correspond more closely to the prevailing distribution of power, privilege, and interests than to conditions of absolute value or universal reason.

None the less, we seem to have a soft spot for morality and moral theorizing. Professional philosophers and historians not excepted, we by and large continue to think of our own morality as something possessing considerable authority (with allowance for the usual slippage between what we practise and what we preach). This social and cultural deference has inspired some of our most incisive intellects—Marx and Nietzsche, to take an interesting pair—to critique morality mercilessly.

'The ideas of the ruling class are in every epoch the ruling ideas,' Marx wrote, and are 'nothing more than the "ideal expression" of the dominant material relationships.'[1] Every ruling

---

[1] K. Marx and F. Engels, *The German Ideology*, trans. W. Lough, ed. and abridged C. J. Arthur (New York: International Publishers, 1970), 64. Hereinafter *GI* in parenthetic page references in the text.

class will 'represent its interest as the common interest' and 'give its ideas the form of universality, and represent them as the only rational, universally valid ones' (*GI* 65–6). As soon as Marx makes a distinction between 'theoretical' and 'philosophical' communists, we know which ones to take seriously on the subject of morality:

Theoretical communists, the only ones who have time to devote to the study of history, are distinguished precisely because they alone have *discovered* that throughout history the 'general interest' is created by individuals who are defined as 'private persons'. They know that this contradiction is only a *seeming* one because one side of it, the so-called 'general', is constantly being produced by the other side, private interest . . . (*GI* 105)

Philosophical communists, by contrast,

innocently take on trust the illusion . . . that they are concerned with the 'most reasonable' social order instead of the needs of a particular class and time . . . With perfect consistency they transform the relations of these particular individuals into relations of 'Man'; they interpret the thoughts of these particular individuals concerning their own relations as thoughts about 'Man'. In so doing, they have abandoned the realm of real history and returned to the realm of ideology. (*GI* 104, 109)

Theoretical communists 'do not preach *morality* at all' (*GI* 104).

Nietzsche, for his part, did not doubt that interests far from universal underlie existing morality, though he hardly thought of them as élite interests. In morality 'high and independent spirituality, the will to stand alone, even a powerful reason are experienced as dangers; everything that elevates an individual above the herd and intimidates the neighbor is henceforth called *evil*; and the fair, modest, conforming mentality, the *mediocrity* of desires attains moral designations and honors'.[2]

Many elements of the full critiques Marx and Nietzsche have lodged against morality are uncomfortably convincing. Even the seeming contradictions to be found between their accounts do not evidently disqualify the key insights of either, or both. Morality is no one phenomenon, homogeneous across time and place. What we experience every day as morality has diverse roots and a continu-

---

[2] Friedreich Nietzsche, *Beyond Good and Evil*, trans. and ed. Walter Kaufmann (New York: Random House, 1966), 201.

ing dynamic; Marx and Nietzsche might well be credited with picking out contradictory elements within morality itself.[3] Even shot full of holes, however, the duck sits yet. What are we to make of this situation? I will venture the suggestion that this situation is, in a sense, as it should be. But I do so with some awareness of the paradox this appears to involve. As Rousseau once said concerning humankind 'living in chains', in his own characteristically paradoxical way: 'How did this situation come about? That I will not say. What could make it legitimate? That I will.'[4]

But why try to defend or legitimize morality's continued standing (or sitting)? Why not think it an unfortunate but predictable fact of life, like the continued standing of many popular conceptions—religious, pseudo-scientific, and so on—that flourish despite devastating critiques? Morality, it seems to me, is remarkable for the number of people who are not the sorts attracted to Old Time Religion or New Age Spirituality, but who tacitly or explicitly affirm it. Perhaps they know something?

2

Morality certainly does seem to possess many of the symptoms of an ideology. Indeed, these often become more acute the further we go up the scale of philosophizing about morality—even (perhaps especially?) when the philosophy in question calls itself 'critical philosophy'.

The man (or woman) in the street would almost certainly say 'yes' if asked whether morality should be an important factor in life. Perhaps he'd simply be embarrassed to say anything else, but more likely he'd sincerely be of the opinion that he wants to see

[3] And there might in fact be less tension between Marx's and Nietzsche's critiques than these few passages might suggest, since the two appear to use the term with a different scope—the 'morality' Nietzsche most famously stigmatized is more specific historically.

[4] Translated freely from Jean-Jacques Rousseau, *Du contrat social*, ed. François Bouchardy (Paris: Egloff, 1946), 42. It seems to me plausible to depart from the more standard translation of *ignorer* as 'do not know', since in his Second Discourse Rousseau offers a theory of just how our situation came about. It seems more apt to see Rousseau as announcing that he does not see the doctrine of social contract itself as a form of *historical explanation* of man's social bondedness (and so he wishes to set aside at the outset such questions of explanation), but rather sees it as a way in which social bondedness *might*, under certain conditions, be legitimized.

more rather than less of it in the world at large. But how many pedestrians would readily assent to the philosophical opinion that moral thought and action are *rationally mandatory*, and those who act against the requirements of morality are *ipso facto* irrational? Popular reification of morality may be rampant, but the question whether there might in a given situation be reasons that outweigh moral considerations seems hardly to be strictly *unintelligible* to the average person.

I, for one, was brought up in a very moralistic household, but without the intrusion of professional philosophy. In that household, it could be a source of pride that one would get one's head cracked for acting on a principle of justice. But you could have knocked me over with a feather when I first heard—in graduate school, as it turned out—that the very principles which seemed to require so costly a transformation of one's life to take fully to heart were actually requirements I would simply be irrational to evade or ignore. Either the world contains a surprising amount of irrationality even in its most sensible and successful corners, I thought, or morality must be a lot happier with the present state of the world than any morality worth its salt could be.

Perhaps, though, the very moralism of my household distorted my perspective by giving me too elevated a notion of what morality asks of us. How then can I pretend to speak from first-hand experience of morality in general? In asking about morality and ideology, it would perhaps be better for us not to start off with anyone's full-fledged moral concepts or experiences, but to attempt instead to identify some relatively central and uncontroversial elements in moral discourse and practice. In doing this, we will focus largely on moral *discourse* and especially the moral discourse of philosophers. This is somewhat regrettable. However, it is the philosophers who have been most explicit about what they take morality to be. Moreover, they are (if anyone is) the intellectual cadres of secular ethics. If their moral conceptions can be seen as ideological, then we will have made a good start on the way to a general ideological critique.

3

In recent years the term *ideology* has once again acquired currency. Though it has always borne a range of senses, the range appears to be shifting in some ways that I certainly wish I better understood. For present purposes, a conception of ideology along fairly classical lines as laid out within the Marxist—or *marxisant*—tradition seems best able to express the concerns about morality I hope to explore. In any event, this conception continues to inform much contemporary discussion.

An ideology is in the first instance a set of beliefs or values held by individuals or groups,[5] not a set of propositions considered in itself. The same descriptive or evaluative proposition could be held for quite diverse reasons,[6] and this points us to a key element: whether a belief or value (as held by someone) is ideological will depend upon the nature of the explanation of why he or she has it.

A given set of descriptive or evaluative propositions as held by a certain individual or group might be more or less questionable, but it will count as ideological only if there is an explanation of these beliefs and other attitudes according to which their prevalence is attributed (to a significant degree) to the fact that holding them serves certain non-epistemic interests—especially, perhaps, interests in *legitimation*. The interests in question need not be the interests of all of those holding the beliefs. They may, for example, be the interests of the socially or culturally dominant class. An *ideological diagnosis* (as we might call it) of why certain attitudes are held typically involves showing that they serve a legitimizing function because they represent particular institutions, practices, or norms as good—or as obligatory, natural, universal, or necessary. Equally, they may represent alternative institutions, practices, or norms as bad—or as unnatural, impermissible, foreign, or, especially, impossible.

Although this diagnostic notion of ideology is at root explanatory in ambition, it has a potential normative relevance that has been

---

[5] That a group can properly be said to have a belief that is not simply the collected beliefs of its members has been nicely shown by Margaret Gilbert, *On Social Facts* (London: Routledge, 1989).

[6] I mean to use 'proposition' fairly neutrally here. No commitment to cognitivism about value is presupposed, only the admissibility of the following sort of dialogue: '*Bill.* Shortening the work-day is a good thing. It will make people more well-rounded. *Joe.* I agree with your first proposition, but not your second. I doubt people will become any more well-rounded in their spare time than they already are, but I do think it will help reduce unemployment.' Whatever is expressed by 'Shortening the work-day is a good thing', and which Joe is claiming to be of one mind with Bill about, is what I will call an 'evaluative proposition'.

salient throughout its career. For example, to attribute the currency of a belief chiefly to *non*-epistemic interests is hardly a form of epistemic endorsement. As Pascal's wager illustrated, it is evident that beliefs can satisfy various sorts of interests without being true or well warranted—indeed, in certain contexts true or well-warranted belief might be antithetical to an individual's or group's strongest interests.

Now it cannot be the whole of ideological critique to claim that there is a contrariety between a belief's functioning ideologically and the belief's truth or warrant. For there are many cases in which epistemic and non-epistemic interests point in the same direction: often our non-epistemic interests will be advanced more effectively by true belief or reliable belief-forming practices than by error or arbitrariness. A belief's truth or a belief-forming mechanism's reliability can be part of an explanation of why I get so much out of it, and it sometimes seems quite possible for me to 'see through' a largely non-epistemic explanation of my belief to an epistemically vindicatory picture of why that non-epistemic story works.[7]

However, we also find cases in which the attempt to 'see through' to the non-epistemic explanation is naturally destabilizing of belief. Suppose that, like most automobile drivers, I consider myself well above average (on a 0 to 10 scale, I have heard it said, drivers on average rate themselves about 7.5). This belief not only feeds my vanity and legitimizes my conduct—it also gives me the nerve to venture out on the roads, to trust my children to my hands, and so on. Let us suppose that I could be shown rather quickly that this belief of mine really stems almost entirely from these non-epistemic interests—e.g. that I have been grossly selective in my attention to evidence and highly biased towards my own case in interpreting what evidence I do notice. Can I 'see through' this non-epistemic explanation of my belief to an 'epistemic explanation' that would provide reasonable warrant? No. Neither can I attribute the effectiveness of the belief in advancing my interests to its truth. (The main contribution of the belief is to enhance my mobility and confidence. Even as a below-average driver I may well benefit on the whole from this.) This sort of non-epistemic explanation invokes a mechanism that depends to some extent on its lack of

---

[7] A situation of this kind seems to exist in Bayesian 'Dutch Book' justifications for conforming to the probability calculus in one's subjective credence assignments. This argument has been seen as a way to *defend* Bayesian epistemology as such.

transparency. The belief is therefore more likely to be destabilized than reinforced on reflection.[8]

This destabilization itself calls for a bit of explanation, lest it seem to be simply a psychological quirk without normative relevance. For example, certain beliefs might not survive two weeks of fasting and chanting, but that need not be relevant to their epistemic status. We need to have some picture of how destabilizing effected by an *accurate reflective awareness of the causal explanation of one's beliefs* could even be a candidate for special normative epistemic relevance.

Belief that *p*, as a propositional attitude distinct from pretending or supposing or merely accepting that *p*, is distinguished in part because it not only represents *p* as true, but it represents *itself* as an attitude responsive or accountable to *p*'s truth.[9] This representational claim need not be understood as a claim about a conscious mental act. It can be understood counterfactually: a believer that *p* who is confronted with contrary evidence will feel 'cognitive pressure' either to weaken (qualify, hedge) that belief or to undermine or dismiss the evidence.[10] Reflective awareness that a belief of mine is to be explained ideologically tends by the nature of its content to exert this sort of pressure, even if the belief in question remains attractive to me.

We might note, for example, the special place in our mental

---

[8] This raises, however, a delicate question for ideological critique to which we will return: What if, as a psychological matter, the belief for which no vindicating explanation is found none the less seems to remain stable on reflection (as typically seems to be the case when it comes to self-ascriptions of driving skill)? Is the issue in ideological critique whether a belief *is* destabilized, or *should be*?

A more realistic psychological portrait of the situation would allow for higher-order beliefs. A belief in the above-average quality of one's own driving may indeed be very robust under all manner of reflective exposure to evidence, but one can more readily shed certain second-order beliefs in the light of this evidence. For example, does one take one's firm first-order opinion that one is an above-average driver with a grain of salt when deciding how much insurance to buy, or whether one's family would be safer in marginal driving conditions with oneself at the wheel, or someone more experienced?

[9] This sort of thought has been emphasized by Bernard Williams, 'Deciding to Believe', in Williams, *Problems of the Self* (Cambridge: Cambridge University Press, 1973). David Velleman gives a seminal account of the ways in which this self-representation distinguishes belief as a propositional attitude in 'The Guise of the Good', *Noûs*, 26 (1992), 3–26.

[10] This is something that can properly be said to be understood—for example, by a young child—before a 'self-representation of one's beliefs' becomes self-consciously available.

economy for what we call 'belief *in*'—'Though I can see only too well that the reasons why I believe in God are not evidential, I will none the less continue to believe in God [or in my driving, or in my child's innocence, or in the possibility of universal brotherhood]'. 'Belief in' often marks locations of a kind of *structural tension* or *incompatibility* within the domain of our beliefs. Not outright mutual exclusion—it is not *impossible* for us simultaneously to believe that *p* and believe that the explanation of this is ideological. Indeed, we seem quite capable of believing both that *p* and that not-*p*, so long as they aren't presented to us in the same way at the same time. But we are imagining a context of full, reflective awareness, and there the claim of incompatibility is more credible: to sustain genuine belief that *p* (rather than a hopeful 'belief in *p*') requires somehow undermining, supplementing, or detoxifying the non-vindicating explanation.

4

Thus far we have been speaking primarily of belief in general. What, then, of *morality*?[11]

To begin, we need to re-emphasize that the interests a given ideology serves need not be interests of all those who hold the ideology. The 'ruling ideas' of which Marx spoke, for example, are held by ruler and ruled alike. And Nietzsche held that potentially great individuals were being kept back in their development in part by their own assimilation of ideas that express the standpoint of the 'herd'.

Nor need the interests served by an ideology be the interests of particular individuals. Ideological analysis is not to be confused with the sort of cynicism that attributes everything to self-interest. On the contrary, ideological analyses have often focused on structural interests, interests belonging to individuals only *qua* members of groups, classes, or institutions. Individuals may acquire or lose these interests as their roles change, since the interests in the first instance attach to the roles themselves—to the conditions favourable to the preservation or strengthening of a given role, say,

---

[11] As before, we are assuming that we can speak of 'moral belief' or 'belief in moral statements or propositions' innocently, without thereby presupposing a cognitivist moral meta-theory.

rather than to the conditions favourable to the preservation or strengthening of the particular set of individuals who happen to occupy that role at a given time. Thus the bourgeois entrepreneur ardently champions the market, even though increased competition may mean *his* elimination from the role of bourgeois. A patriotic German father of three joins the army in the Great War, even though he and his progeny would probably benefit more if he could contrive to stay at home and leave the fighting to others. Yet he willingly shoulders his Mauser and marches off to the front to defend the Fatherland, his head full of grand and dangerous ideas.

How can we identify *moral* convictions within the welter of convictions that help constitute a society—assuming, as we will, that this is a reasonable thing to attempt to do? Just as the term 'ideology' has a descriptive and a normative sense, so does the term 'morality'. We speak of morality descriptively when we try to give an empirically accurate account of certain norms and notions current within a given society, the extent to which they are observed, the ways they are taught and sanctioned, etc. We speak of morality normatively when we ask whether actions, practices, and so on are indeed right or wrong, better or worse, appropriate or inappropriate.

Should we use 'morality' in the normative sense to delineate which of the convictions abroad within society are the moral ones? That would seem to be the wrong approach for present purposes, since it would deem a widespread conviction a moral one only if it really would pass muster with us evaluatively. But if only legitimate norms and convictions will be counted for our purposes here as moral ones, then we have a quick, entirely definitional answer to the question whether ideological criticism can delegitimize morality. Better for our purposes to adopt a less normative approach to distinguishing morality, based upon some relatively uncontroversial ways in which our culture itself identifies the distinctively moral, and leaving open at the outset whether these prevalent norms and convictions will be judged by us to be appropriate at the end of the day.

It would be too ambitious empirically and too problematic philosophically to attempt to answer the question, What are the criteria of 'the moral' as found in our traditions of discourse and practice? Let us try for something more modest, which will still be ambitious enough. Avoiding the problematic term 'criteria', and restricting our focus to the mainstream philosophical traditions, can we identify certain core elements that serve to distinguish moral evaluation from other species? We can then ask whether these elements might be vulnerable to critique as ideological.

Here, then, are some central truisms of various philosophically self-aware traditions within modern thought. Moral evaluation is:

(a) *impartial* (or, as I would prefer to say, non-partial)—it takes into account all those potentially affected;

(b) *universal* (or, as I would prefer to say, non-indexical)—it claims a legitimacy and scope of application that goes beyond any particular set of social boundaries or conventions;[12]

(c) *beneficent*—it assigns prima facie positive deliberative weight to the well-being of those potentially affected, negative deliberative weight to their suffering.

I said 'traditions' within modern moral philosophy, but have I just written a recipe for utilitarianism? The utilitarian does think that (a)–(c)—fully fleshed out—suffice for the essential framework of morality. But numerous others think of (a)–(c) as expressing necessary conditions of moral thought.[13] Thus, on a fairly orthodox Kantian conception, morality is unquestionably impartial and universal, and, moreover, a precondition of the rational acceptability of moral demands is that following them will in the end be compatible with the well-being of the individuals and communities who do so. And Rawls's less orthodox Kantianism, which has its own forms of non-partiality and non-indexicality, also involves an underlying beneficence, as a concern for one's index of social goods

---

[12] Universality in this sense must be distinguished from *non-relationalness*. The particular principles, motivations, virtues, etc. that are morally appropriate in a given social or historical context might be quite diverse, and might make a place for a number of essentially *individual* variables—e.g. one's spouse, one's children, one's friends, etc. But this does not morally privilege particular individuals as such (i.e. is non-indexical). I may have special moral obligations to my children, but *your* special moral obligations are to yours.

[13] Recently, there has been an emerging critique of (a) and (b) in particular as essential to moral thought. Partial and particularist conceptions have been defended as (none the less) morally principled. One might, in the present context, see this critique as attempting to remove some of the *pretence* of morality that leaves it so vulnerable to ideological criticism.

is combined with ignorance of one's particular place or prospects in society.

There is, however, another truistic aspect of morality, which (*a*)–(*c*) do not capture, and which has figured most prominently in non-utilitarian thought. Elements (*a*)–(*c*) are in effect constraints on third-personal moral *evaluations* of states of affairs—how things look from a moral point of view. But this standpoint is not the whole core of moral thought or the point of view of the moral agent in choosing. Just as an alchemist might identify both a *passive* and an *active* essence in any given substance, so must we notice an active element in moral thought. This active element is reflected in a truism:

(*d*) Morality is *practical*—it purports to provide answers to the agent's questions 'What ought I to do?' or 'How best to live?'

How this fourth truism is to be understood in any detail is highly contested, and no one interpretation could answer to our need to identify relatively consensual elements of philosophically-minded moral thought. Arguably, it is as much by their answers to the question 'What is the practical nature of morality?' as anything else that moral philosophers differentiate themselves from one another. For here we find disputes over internalism versus externalism, the priority of the right over the good, the priority of action versus character, the relationship of morality to practical rationality, the overridingness of moral judgments, the conditions of moral agency, and so on.

What does seem to be elemental in (*d*) is the notion that moral discourse affords some first-personal directive content for agents deliberating about what to do. Such *directive*[14] judgements might be expressed as recommendations, commands, or permissions, but they are in any event thought of as *non-hypothetical* in form and *non-optional* in scope. To say they are non-hypothetical is not to claim that they are commands of pure reason, but only that they are not conditional upon the particular desires or preferences an individual happens to have at the moment. Thus they have the form 'You should . . .' rather than 'If you happen to go in for this

---

[14] I owe this term to David Wiggins; see his 'Truth, Invention, and the Meaning of Life', rev. in Wiggins, *Needs, Values, Truth*, 3rd edn. (Oxford: Clarendon Press, 1998).

sort of thing, you should . . .'. Many sorts of directives are non-hypothetical, from the laws of the state of Michigan to the rules of cricket. But unlike these directives, moral directives are also thought to be 'non-optional' for normal adult human agents. That is, I can (as various unsavoury but wealthy individuals do) remove myself from the scope of the laws of Michigan by moving to a country that has no extradition treaty with it and is not a signatory to certain international accords, and I can keep myself out of the reach of the rules of cricket by the simple expedient of never venturing to play it (thus in using a notebook computer at the moment, I am not either in violation of, or compliance with, the rules of cricket prohibiting electromechanical assistance). Moral directives leave us no such way out. Were I to decide to have done with life, and to end my normal human adulthood in suicide, this decision itself would be within the scope of moral norms, and would remain forever so even if I succeeded in wholly annihilating myself a moment afterwards. These features of non-hypotheticality and non-optionality characterize moral directives, but do not suffice in themselves to define morality. For epistemic directives, prudential directives, aesthetic directives, rational directives, etc. also seem to have these characteristics. They differ from morality more in substance—as given in the moral case by (a)–(c)—than in form.

I have spoken of 'normal human adult agents' rather than, say, 'rational agents as such'. Even as we had to be careful not to ally elements (a)–(c) too closely to utilitarianism, we must be careful not to ally (d) too much with Kantianism. A utilitarian or perfectionist who asserts that 'the right follows the good' is making a directive judgement, despite the priority being assigned to an evaluative standard. She is claiming that acts are to be guided by the ends they might embody or bring about, and she is doing so in a way that is both non-hypothetical and non-optional. For there is nothing in the utilitarian's or perfectionist's claim to restrict its application only to those who happen to want to follow it, or to permit normal adult humans to opt out through the exercise of choice. Even virtue ethics, which in some cases dispenses with the notion of *moral obligation*, is hard to imagine without directive judgements—e.g. the wise instruction to follow the path of developing, sustaining, or heeding virtues in our lives, rather than be distracted into other directions of personal development and decision. Virtue theories may do this—indeed, may have elaborate accounts of proper moral instruction and education—without grounding the enterprise in the motivational scheme of conscientiousness and guilt that seems characteristic of (and perhaps problematic about) moral obligation. More likely, they will ground it in ideals of a good life, 'fit' for normal adult humans. We may require instruction and education to appreciate these ideals—their normative bearing in guiding our lives need not be hypothetical upon whether we now are attracted to them. If we claim somehow to have decided to opt out of their scope, we will have accomplished no more than to deceive ourselves about our real nature—just as we can continue to deceive ourselves about the nature of the world in general, without thereby changing anything about how things are or should be. So directing choice non-hypothetically and non-optionally is common ground across major moral theories.

But how does a non-hypothetical, non-optional directive judgement in accord with (*a*)–(*c*) actually engage us, and 'guide action'? An early printing of Mackie's *Ethics* had on its cover an image of an immense hand descending from heaven, pointing the way to a traveller at a crossroads. This sort of device may caricature certain aspects of popular thinking about morality, but surely it cannot be what Mackie had in mind when he claimed that morality, if genuine, would have to possess 'objective prescriptivity'.[15] For even if the other heavenly hand (the one not seen on the book cover) holds a mighty thunderbolt, poised to be hurled at the traveller the moment he disobeys, and even if the puzzled traveller at the crossroads knows this, the tableau remains one of external rather than moral guidance or directive force. Things would be no different if the unseen hand held a golden reward for travellers who comply. In either case the reason the traveller has been given to comply is powerful, but not in itself a moral one.[16]

If genuine moral direction cannot simply be a matter of coercion or reward, what is to be the force that directs agents or guides moral

[15] See J. L. Mackie, *Ethics: Inventing Right and Wrong* (Harmondsworth: Penguin, 1977).

[16] Mackie's own view on this matter is not entirely clear. At one point he suggests that, if God were to exist, then so could 'objective prescriptivity'. But though God might provide an *external incentive* to act in accord with moral requirements, or might afford an awe-inspiring spectacle of command, there is no suggestion in Mackie's text as to how God or God's commands might actually ground *moral* authority.

action? The time-honoured Aristotelian and Kantian answer is to say 'the force of reason', but there is also the time-honoured Humean answer that reason itself could possess no such force, and it must instead come from certain reasons in conjunction with certain distinctive sentiments, e.g. sympathy. Clearly we cannot say that there is an uncontroversial common ground on the question of 'moral motivation', beyond the consensus that it cannot come down to mere coercion or reward—even if well disguised. Yet this is none the less enough for us to carry on our discussion of morality and ideology, since an ideological critique of morality often takes the form of attributing what a populace calls 'moral motivation' precisely to structures of power and interest, of coercion and reward—albeit well hidden from direct view by 'false consciousness', which talks of Reason, proper function, human nature, duty, impartiality, universality, sympathy, supersensible selves, and the like. If the critics are right that purportedly moral motivation can be given a fundamental 'unmasking explanation' of this kind, revealing the discourse of moral motivation to be superficial and naïve, that would be sufficient to place Aristotelian, Kantian, and Humean moral traditions alike in a most uncomfortable spot.

5

We will come back to morality shortly, but first let us pick up the thread of our discussion of ideology and belief. We had briefly discussed how a philosophical explanation of the destabilization of belief under reflection might go: in the relevant cases, reflection on the ideological origins of belief will be destabilizing not merely by some quirk, but because belief by its nature 'aims at' truth. The fact of destabilization thus seems to possess a kind of normative relevance *internal* to epistemology, even if it is not in itself normatively determinative (it is, after all, just a fact). Might there be an analogue on the moral side, such that if ideological criticism in fact tends to undermine moral commitment, this is more than a mere curiosity but rather possesses internal normative relevance to morality?

To be sure, ordinary, 'descriptive' belief has a central place in moral thought and practice. It is easy to say a priori that moral evaluation 'floats free' of descriptive belief, so that people could have all the same descriptive beliefs yet differ arbitrarily much in their moral evaluations, but in fact this is seldom or never the case. Historically, beliefs about the nature of action, the psychology of motivation, the likely causes and outcomes of acts and practices, the teleological structure (or lack of it) of the world, the distribution of human differences and similarities, and so on, tend to be found clustered with particular moral points of view, rather than distributed arbitrarily across the moral landscape. Arguably, some of the most profound historical changes in moral opinion have been precipitated precisely by changes—seemingly very 'normatively relevant', if not 'logically compelling'—in underlying descriptive beliefs about the existence of natural hierarchies, human variability, cosmological origins, and so on. And much of ideological critique is focused directly on these areas of belief, from Feuerbach's criticism of religion to contemporary feminist criticism of the naturalizing of gender distinctions.

To grasp the nettle, however, we need to ask explicitly whether the effect of the 'reflection test' in changing moral opinion can be underwritten in a way *normatively internal* to morality. After all, some quite humane values might as a matter of fact fail to survive a ruthless preoccupation with personal failings or with the loss of national prestige suffered as a colonial empire crumbles. How would this tend to disqualify these values morally?

We need, then, to locate a path of disqualification that is relevant according to distinctively moral standards of relevance. We began in the case of belief with the *attitude* of belief, and the norms said to be 'internal' to it. Let us proceed similarly with the attitude of valuing, and moral valuing in particular.

The attitude of valuing typically involves some sort of desiring, it seems, but is distinct from *mere* desiring, much as believing that p typically involves some sort of 'finding oneself drawn to believe that p', but also involves something more. Belief that p characteristically involves various commitments and claims of authority, usually tacit: one accords p a degree of confidence in one's actions and interactions; one gives p a certain weight in assessing one's own beliefs, new evidence, or the beliefs of others; one seeks to render p, and one's commitment to it, consistent with one's other beliefs; one is inclined to feel defensive about one's attitude towards p and to be disquieted by learning that the explanation of why one believes that p is not truth-related—that one's belief that p cannot be seen as *attuned to* evidence for p. At this point one may freely recognize that one still is drawn as strongly as ever to believe that p, but one's attitudes of epistemic commitment to p and claimed authority regarding p will not comfortably remain undiminished. Putting things the other way around, one might find that one is not much 'drawn to believe' this uncomfortable explanation of one's belief that p, but that, given the evidence, one is none the less inclined to accord it epistemic authority.

Similarly, I can desire A without the sorts of commitments or claims of authority that valuing A characteristically—and, again, usually tacitly—involves. When I value A, other things equal: I am inclined to accord A some weight in regulating my deliberation and choice, and also my judgements of others and recommendations to them; I seek to reconcile my plans, goals, and ends with A; I am inclined to invoke A to justify or defend myself, and to treat it as in turn justified and defensible; thus I typically feel uneasy when I perceive A to be threatened, and defensive when I take A to be challenged. One way in which A might be challenged is by an explanation of my valuing A that removes any element that I would count as an appropriate ground of value, such that my valuing could not be seen as an *attunement* to relevant value-making features. In the absence of any other backing for A, I could still acknowledge that my desire for A is undiminished, even as I will no longer be easy in according A the same regulative role in running my life or judging myself and others. Put the other way around, I may come to see the taking of not-A as an end as appropriate—as attuned to value-making features—even though I do not now much desire not-A at all.

An example of this 'internal' purport of the attitude of valuing might help, and for our purposes the relevant domain of evaluation is the moral. Given the amount of content in conditions (a)–(c), above, and the regulative practical role (d), we can see how moral evaluation cannot 'float free' of other attitudes and beliefs. Consider someone brought up in a racial or caste system, who initially deemed it morally appropriate to keep 'higher' and 'lower' groups from mixing. Were he ever to be attracted to a member of a 'lower' group, this individual would likely find that attraction 'unclean', 'intrinsically degrading'—an appropriate source of guilt, and not to be permitted to regulate his choice of social relations. Were he to learn that his sister had formed a romantic relationship with a 'lower' group member, he would think her 'disgraced' and 'for ever stained', and be very ashamed for himself and his family. Suppose now that this individual learns that the supposed historical and bio-logical basis of the caste or racial distinctions is bogus: the groups are virtually indistinguishable genetically and the actual origin of the subordination–superordination relationship is a brutal con-quest unrelated to any moral concerns. This individual might well continue irresistibly to *feel* that there is something in itself 'off' or 'shameful' when members of the different castes or races intermix, but would be unlikely to think that moral 'righteousness' lies in reinforcing this feeling to prevent any intercaste or interracial attraction from having a regulative role in action. He might still find himself acutely uncomfortable when his sister presents her new spouse, but he would feel quite differently about whether or why she now should be driven from the family.

Moral evaluation, then, finds its place in a complex constellation of non-moral beliefs and attitudes, and indeed *supervenes* upon them, yielding the final element of the moral point of view to be mentioned here:

(*e*) one is committed to defend one's moral evaluations by citing non-moral but morally relevant value-making features.

This sort of supervenience has been seen by moral philosophers of all stripes as a conceptual, a priori, or otherwise fundamental truth about valuation—one would simply not grasp the idea of value if one thought that values could simply be 'added' to a state of affairs or 'pasted' to them (such that two states of affairs could be identi-cal in all non-moral characteristics, yet, properly, receive different moral evaluations). When allied with elements (*a*)–(*d*), the result is that moral evaluation hardly 'floats free' of our best account of how the world works, why we believe what we do, and so on. Thus, while these various constraints are logically consistent with the persis-tence of moral disagreement in the face of many factual agree-ments, factual agreements that concern matters within the scope of (*a*)–(*e*)—such as learning that there is no difference between the races and castes of a given society that could affect characteristics relevant to well-being, capacity for rational action, etc.—impinge forcibly on moral opinion, not as a psychological curiosity, but by the nature of the moral attitude itself.

Of course, even in the presence of an explanation indicating that the only reason I value *A* is one that counts as morally irrelevant under (*a*)–(*e*), I could insist that there must be *some* morally relevant ground for *A*, and I could be right. None the less, lacking any defence of *A*, and with a favourable attitude towards it already explained in a non-justificatory way, I may have difficulty impressing anyone with my authority in continuing to urge *A* in moral decisions. I am likely to appear more dogmatic than upright, closer kin to an unquestioning 'believer in *p*' than to a responsible 'believer that *p*' whose attitude is to be accorded some normative authority.

And that alternative attitude is often resorted to in just such circumstances. Absent any further ground for valuing *A* than, say, learning that I picked it up from my family's traditions, I could continue to make it a fundamental matter of faith that I 'believe in *A*', and will conduct myself accordingly. What is likely to drop away in humane individuals is the conviction that those from different family environments, with different evaluative traditions, are in a *morally indefensible* position when they disagree with me about *A*. One can, that is, retreat from the domain of mutual moral condemnation and affirm one's conviction only on behalf of a personal, familial, or cultural ideal or preference.

Reducing reflective disequilibrium can take yet other forms: I might on further reflection reject the non-justificatory explanation as lacking sufficient credibility; I might arrive at an independent justification for *A* (one that does not depend upon how I acquired the value); or I might simply live in a certain *mauvaise foi*—not clearly rejecting the explanation, not clearly repudiating the value, trying not to dwell on the tension between the two, bluffing my way through until I myself am no longer much troubled, buffering my self-esteem with the usual rationalizations. Being in bad faith makes one vulnerable in certain ways, but it is a very familiar sort of vulnerability.

6

We now are in a position to begin to apply our characterization of what (at least in part) makes a set of views an ideology to our account of what (at least in part) makes a set of views a morality.

It is already easy to see why it is so tempting to apply an ideological critique to morality. But spelling this out a bit will help us to say something about a quite general question, 'What is the nature of ideological critique itself?' It will also enable us to pose a more particular question, 'Does the weight of ideological critique, such as it is, fall uniformly upon moral notions, or are there some elements that are much more vulnerable than others?'

Marx spoke of ideologies as standing things on their heads: representing the particular as general, the local as universal, the contingent as necessary, the profane as sacred, the effect as cause. Although he diagnoses ideologies as in fact expressing a particular standpoint in a contingent and historically evolving world, he insists that they do not—indeed, cannot—represent themselves as such. A given class (for example) will 'represent its interest as the common interest' and 'give its ideas the form of universality, and represent them as the only rational, universally valid ones'.[17] It is essential to a functional ideology that those holding it and passing it along to others by and large take it to heart. That is, if (say) partial, conventional, contingent norms are to be reified as disinterested, natural, and necessary, then this reification must have a deep grip on the ideologues themselves. That is what entitles us to take the rather grandiose but typically sincere philosophical conception of ethics as manifest in (*a*)–(*e*) as paradigmatic.

We have identified both passive and active elements in our philosophical understanding of morality. Each is at risk, in its own way, from ideological criticism. But to the same degree?

Shared risks first. The passive, evaluative component (comprising (*a*)–(*c*) and (*e*)) claims to perceive things comprehensively and coherently, from a point of view that is not merely descriptive, and yet is not the point of view of anyone or any time in particular— no individual, group, or society. This seems not only grandiose, but potentially nonsensical. Points of view do not need to be perfectly coherent, but surely they cannot be as incoherent as the jumble that would result from simply aggregating individuals and their

---

[17] In a sense, Rousseau pioneered this sort of understanding, when he argued that every group with a distinctive set of interests tends to develop a *moi commun*—a collective 'me'—that purports to speak on behalf of the good of the whole. His remedy is to fight ideology with ideology, recommending the inculcation in the populace of a 'civil religion' of deference to civil authority, and recommending to lawgivers that they purport to have received the laws from a divine source (Rousseau, *Du contrat social*).

ends across time and space. A point of view is by its nature selective, offering a perspective on the landscape rather than the landscape as such. The moral point of view *is* supposed to be selective, glimpsing only that which is relevant to moral evaluation—typically, philosophers have spoken of the general interest and the intrinsically good. Yet Marx and Nietzsche each argued in his own way that actual societies are scenes of conflicting interests, and that actual goods have their value not inherently, but in virtue of their relation to subjects. Without subjects, nothing would be of value. Not because there would be no one to see or appreciate it, but because, without subjects, there would be nothing that could *constitute* value. Absolute or non-relational value, value that stands apart from subjects and calls forth their pursuit, is a *fetish*.

One can, of course, readily see the legitimizing function of a claim made on behalf of a particular standpoint that it is universal, impartial, attuned to objective, intrinsic value-making features. Such a claim privileges a particular standpoint, and privileging is the secular equivalent of canonization. Yet it is altogether too easy in retrospect to see past claims of universal validity as unwarranted projections of the local and particular into the eternal and sacred, and thus supposedly beyond question or challenge. Philosophical conceptions of the good, too, seem in retrospect expressive of their context. Not much imagination is required to see in the Aristotelian notion of proper function a reflection of the Greek caste system. Or to see in medieval notions of noble and base, or honour, the reflection of an aristocratic warrior society. Or to see in the utilitarian ideas of happiness as individual desire-satisfaction and of a universal metric of value the reflection of modern bourgeois commodification and market society.

The issue here is not, or at any rate not yet, whether this constitutes a telling reason for rejecting these notions. And it would take an altogether different level of engagement with history to say anything about the credibility of these claims. But at the moment our concern is merely hypothetical: since previous conceptions of the good bear some of the superficial marks of ideologies, we should ask whether and to what extent this diagnosis, if borne out, would disqualify them. Before investigating further, we need to have a similarly preliminary look at the active element in morality's alchemy.

The active side of morality has characteristically found expression during the modern period[18] in the notion of *obligation*, which in turn has been voiced in two terminologies. First, a terminology familiar from emergent civil society: rights, laws, duties, requirements, contracts. Of course, however much they resemble civil notions, moral rights and laws are, according to this conception, natural or rational rather than conventional. We understand the 'force' of these notions in civil society to lie in their civil embodiment: mechanisms for verifying and enforcing contracts, advantages of mutual trust, the institutionalization of property, etc. As natural or rational notions, we must see these as owing their force to something else, such as the abstract notion of respect for others, reasonableness, or fairness.

Secondly, we find a terminology of religious and, ultimately, I suppose, familial origin: a language of commands and imperatives issued from some authoritative source. This language we understand tolerably well if attached to an actual (presumptively authoritative) issuing subject using the imperative voice. And we can grasp its 'action-guiding' force if we imagine that the issuer is someone we wish, or are constrained by some interest or incentive, to please. But moral commands or categorical imperatives are supposed not to be issued by a lesser force than Reason itself, or rather, that part of each of us which embodies Reason.

It is, again, not difficult to see the potential contribution to legitimation of such 'denatured' notions of obligation or imperative. Yet as philosophers since Hobbes and Hume have urged, it is problematic whether these notions can really have application apart from a background of actual institutions, sanctions, etc. Kant's critical philosophy sought to move from a metaphysical conception of the ground of obligation to a 'practical' one, but even for him a background teleology of reward and sanction remained in place as a necessary postulate of practical reason. Historical perspective may well convince us that what is in fact going on is less an expression of divine teleology than of local social circumstances. The distinctive notion of natural property rights as individual entitlements that demand respect, which gains ascendancy in early modern

---

[18] It would enrich our discussion to be able to consider more teleological conceptions of the active side, such as those found among the Greeks. But, apart from noticing in passing the interesting legitimizing relationships among organic conceptions of proper function and hierarchy in society, the body, and the soul alike, we will leave these questions aside.

moral philosophy, seems to have a great deal to do with the emergent forms and conflicts of modern civil society, but it hardly affords the *only* or *natural* condition under which humans have lived together with some semblance of peace and flourishing, or mutual respect.

So has the mainstream moral philosophy of Hobbes and Hume already done the work of ideological critique for it? Not the whole job, surely. For the philosophical critique of 'naturalizing' obligation and property has made use of its own 'naturalizing', which Marx and others have deemed to be equally dubious: a theory not of Reason but of Human Nature (and allied theories of 'natural appetites' or 'sentiments'). Hobbes of course offered his conception, and asked contemporaries who might doubt it simply to look into their own hearts. There they might indeed find that which Hobbes describes, Marx could assert, but this introspective device cuts off inquiry or insight into the social and historical origins of that 'human nature'. If the anthropologist Karl Polanyi is right, however, never has a conception less faithful to the history of mankind been more prophetic of its future.[19] Hume, for his part, spoke confidently of origins, and of natural versus artificial sentiments, but for the most part innocently of any anthropological or evolutionary evidence. Indeed, his quasi-anthropological remarks are the clearest cases of his uncritically projecting the attitudes of a metropolitan culture, and thus among the most acute sources of embarrassment for his contemporary admirers.

The philosophical critique of natural law, brilliant as it was, did not in Marx's eyes bring an end to ideology in ethics, but rather ushered in a new ideology, of 'human nature' or 'natural sentiments' as an exogenous constraint on human history and practice, rather than a (partial) product thereof. Claims of human nature or natural sentiment afforded a fixed point of criticism that was itself beyond criticism, and afforded the basic vocabulary which determined all that could—or could not—be achieved socially or collectively in the name of morality. But who knows how much human practice (e.g. the history of sexual selection) has shaped our evolution, or will continue to shape it (now that genetic engineering is a possibility)? Marx chided Feuerbach for taking the cherry tree outside his study window as a recurring image of 'nature' in his

---

[19] K. Polanyi, *The Great Transformation* (New York: Rinehart, 1944).

writings, without seeing the extent to which that very tree was the product of generations of human hybridizing practice.

Although often placed in a realm apart from reason and argument, sentiment has been seen by its champions as not without force in justifying morality. Indeed, it holds out the prospect for a compact account of the 'action-guiding' character of morality—'ought' implying 'can', as it does—since sentiment *drives* action. One can view a theory of sentiments as telling us where, if anywhere, the motivational infrastructure requisite for justification is to be found. A theory of sentiments is well suited to play this 'limit' role in setting the horizons for the modern imagination, for is not contemporary society the expression *par excellence* of the priority of private sentiment, of the elevation of personal preference to the point where it seems more authoritative for the individual than some Platonic Form or something called the Laws of Reason?[20] At any rate, this is how a Marxist diagnosis might go.

We are obviously moving absurdly briskly here, but the goal is only illustration. On the surface at least, modern moral philosophy—even modern critical moral philosophy—is grist to the mill of ideological analysis. The particular character or content of the reifications involved varies between passive and active elements in morality, and with the evolution of the various schools of moral thought. But in general it is possible to begin to tell a story in which the particular is being taken as universal, the conditioned or relational as absolute, the contingent as necessary, and the socially and historically local as natural. And in all cases we can see how these stories could have a legitimizing function, at the least by turning back certain challenges to legitimacy.

7

But what are we to do with these bald claims? Let us simply suppose for the moment that something like them is true.

Ideological (self-)criticism is normally understood to involve posing to ourselves the question: Can our commitment to particular views and practices be (sincerely, and with awareness) sustained

[20] Cf. the paradigmatic 'modern' response to attempts at the objective justification of morality, 'So what?'

in light of a full social-historical understanding of where those
views, practices, and commitments come from, how they operate
within us (e.g. their psychological or psychodynamic mechanism),
and what their actual or likely consequences are (e.g. which interests they effectively promote or hinder)?

At the outset I mentioned the remarkable degree to which even
philosophers critical of past moral theorizing or practice have
defended continuing commitment to morality.[21] One usually has to
look outside mainstream philosophy—to Marx or Nietzsche, say—
to find attitudes more openly dismissive of the core of conventional
morality.[22] Suppose, as I just did, that the ideological diagnosis is
largely true. Which response—the sceptical or the defensive—
seems more appropriate?

Asking this question seems, however, to be stepping outside the
framework of ideological critique. For it suggests that we have
a *second* sort of test in mind. In the first test we ask whether
or to what extent our convictions do in fact survive critical self-
awareness. In the second test we ask what to make of that—
whether this response on our part is or is not appropriate. When
put this way, it seems as if the second test is the locus of all the
epistemic action—the first test is just one more piece of empirical
psychology, which might figure in the second as a kind of evidence
but which lacks normative standing in its own right.

Or is the 'second test' really separate? Deeming one's responses
appropriate appears to be just one more normative conviction. Are
we now asking whether this conviction itself will in fact be retained
when we are fully aware? Yet ordinarily we distinguish questions
of the appropriateness of a response from questions of whether in
fact we have it under such-and-such conditions. Perhaps we can
clarify this as follows. Consider the following 'second-order' ideological argument.

You say we should reflect on our commitments by asking
whether they would survive in the harsh light of historical and
social self-understanding. Fine. But where did the commitment

---

[21] Even Mackie, who finds morality to be based upon a fundamental error, offers
a reconstruction of moral practice.

[22] Hobbes and Hume remain distrustful of social innovation, and come to the
rescue of established property and hierarchical relations—urging citizens strongly
(if not, in Hume's case, exceptionlessly) to respect for private property, contractual
obligations, and political authorities.

that expresses come from? It has all the trappings of an Enlightenment ideal of a transparent self and of psychologically frictionless belief-acquisition. It shows a touching faith in the curative or therapeutic power of knowledge and self-awareness, and in the *psychological* unity of knowledge—genuine knowledge can always sit comfortably beside other knowledge. Though adding knowledge may have some dramatic and unwanted noncognitive effects on us (reducing self-esteem, say), it is supposed not to be destructive of existing knowledge. Moreover, this seeming Enlightenment ideal also shows a deference to the notion of *historical fact* and the context of *third-party explanation* rather than (say) *social construction* and *self-narration*. The ideal invests authority in a 'bird's (God's?)-eye view' of ourselves, our history, and our psychology. And is it to be imagined to be a genuine possibility that we actually take this perspective? We are being asked to accord normative standing to our responses in this notional condition. But why should we not distrust this conceit, too, and the deference it involves? Perhaps this transition cannot be negotiated, and we can only replace one self-narrative by another, still grander in ambition and still further from the situatedness that gives at least some genuine content to our thought and activities. One might hope that the transition could be attempted in good faith, and yield some genuine gains in knowledge. But mightn't it have more or less severe epistemic costs at the same time? Mightn't it also be destructive of some epistemic value?

How might we make sense of this last possibility?

Bernard Williams, in his influential book *Ethics and the Limits of Philosophy*, raises what I take to be a similar concern about the easy supposition that a distanced perspective destroys prejudice but nothing of real epistemic value.[23] This looks like a normative issue, for it requires us to ask not 'What is *altered* by reflection?' but 'What *of epistemic value* is at peril?' or 'What do we have *epistemic reason* to make of this alteration?' It begins to look, therefore, as if we can normatively problematize ideological critique itself by a reflective process that asks where our confidence in the authority of changes wrought by such critique might come from.

---

[23] B. Williams, *Ethics and the Limits of Philosophy* (London: Fontana, 1985). He gives special attention to 'confidence' in an ethical outlook.

Are we trading here upon mysterious claims? Consider then the following very mundane story. Somewhere in the depths of the medieval English countryside is a village huddled around a large clocktower. The clock's mechanism was the work of an itinerant clockmaker, Cruikshank, who built many clocks that stand in towers across the broad countryside in those parts. Unfortunately, Cruikshank was more a master of building impressive-looking clocks that could enhance the self-esteem of a village than of the delicate business of gears and escapements. So his clocks keep very poor time and are so often in some state of disrepair that one can seldom form a reliable judgement about the time by glancing up at the clocktower. However, in our little village, which we'll call Wrell, an accidental feature of the way the clock's weights were suspended has had the surprising effect of making a Cruikshank timepiece run like clockwork. Residents of this village can form reliable judgements of the time by consulting this clock, and often do. They have come to rely on this clock, and have done so successfully over the years. Although they have not formulated elaborate reflective beliefs about 'the reliability of this sort of mechanism', they do count on their Cruikshank clock in a way that villages elsewhere do not, and that they themselves would not were the clock typically inaccurate. It seems to me pretty clear that the residents of Wrell can know it's noon from observing the single, ornate hand at twelve.

A traveller who has visited the other towns where Cruikshank had travelled and left clocks in his wake is well acquainted with both their singular appearance and their unreliability. When he arrives in Wrell, he, too, sees the clock's hand at twelve. But he does not thereby acquire the knowledge that it is noon, for he recognizes the clock to be a Cruikshank. The villagers can learn that it is noon from looking at the clock, but he can't. He knows too much.

Might there be a model here for moral lore and practices, with a similar possibility of being 'wised up' in a way that cuts one off from certain genuine ways of knowing? We might think of ourselves in the contemporary world as akin to travellers who've become aware of the wide historical and geographic diversity in certain norms, of the particular contingencies so many seem to reflect, and of the ways in which they typically garner the support of their communities as natural and evident—however arbitrary in content they may seem to us. We're struck by the disparity between the cosmic purport of these normative systems and the particularity of the forces that shape and sustain them.

It is unsurprising that the first great wave of anthropological fieldwork in the late nineteenth and early twentieth centuries precipitated many relativist thoughts and sentiments. The possibility thus arises that in our home society we have a working moral 'clock' that none the less is to a significant degree the result of historical accident. That is, our morality does indeed permit mutually beneficial social co-ordination, promote individual flourishing, and reasonably allocate benefits and burdens. Yet perhaps we have come by exposure to a wider world to 'know too much' about the real origins of moralities to be able to know (as perhaps we did before) that an act is good or fair by knowing it to be in accord with our established practices.

Suppose, moreover, that part of the very way the practices in our home society have made so many good lives together possible is that the worm of reflection has not (at least, until recently) begun to gnaw at our hearts. Perhaps one setting (maybe one of the few) in which a moral life is compatible with moral knowledge has been lost to us. If moral lives and moral knowledge are endangered species, we have not done much to promote their survival by removing one of their few habitats! This does not look like much of an advertisement for the normative authority of reflective self-awareness or ideological critique. After all, part of the explanation of why, in the pre-anthropological home society, people held the moral beliefs they did *is* that they did not problematize their moral assumptions, by insisting on prying into questions of origin, and becoming as a result disequilibrated by an awareness of the role of morally irrelevant or unsavoury factors in the history of their moral opinions.

8

We can, however, give this argument—and these two examples— one more twist. Return first to Wrell. Not all explanations are debunking. Despite our initial, justified scepticism, we as travellers *could* acquire confidence in the clocktower that would permit us to learn from it after all. When we enter the town we know too much to learn the time from the Wrell Cruikshank—but also not enough.

If we knew more, we would know that it is in fact reliable. Perhaps we could observe its co-ordination with another timepiece we know to be accurate, or with the movement of the sun. This co-ordination would, however, remain a mystery for us in a way that it is not for the Wrellians—for we know the faultiness of Cruikshankian handiwork. To whatever extent they may have reflected on the question of the reliability of clocks of this type—which need not be much, I would think—they have had no reason to think that it is otherwise than part of the order of nature that clocks like this would be reliable. Does this lack of reflection upon reliability or insight into mechanism impugn their claim to be able to know the time by looking at the clock? That would be a severe judgement. We daily gather knowledge from countless indicators in our environment that are indeed reliable, even if we have not formed reflective beliefs on their reliability or on how it might be brought about.

Our own situation with regard to Cruikshank clocks is, however, different. The reliability of such clocks has been explicitly *problematized* for us—and not in a gratuitous or generically sceptical way. Forming judgements based upon the reading of the Wrell clock strikes us as a perilous business, needing justification. At the outset we can only regard it as a happy coincidence if the clock's hand is at twelve when the sun is directly overhead. Why should we expect the clock's agreement with local solar time to be robust or enduring—this is after all a Cruickshank clock—before we at least have some more extensive experience with it and are aware of the possibility of an explanation in which accidental features of a clock's installation or idiosyncrasies of its location can (for example) offset built-in characteristics of its mechanism? This is a contingent, relational kind of reliability, of course, but it is none the less a kind of reliability. We see what a poor proxy for 'arbitrary' the notion of 'contingent' really is. And we see how poor a word 'relativistic' (which suggests observer dependence) is for 'relational' (which suggests contextual dependence). Whatever the source of the Wrell clock's reliability, my initially sceptical frame of mind only made *me* unable to rely upon it rather than making *it* unreliable in any way.

Now let us return to the other imaginary example, in which we suppose that existing moral practices in our home country are highly appropriate from a moral point of view, but we have become uneasy about relying upon them owing to reflective awareness of their arbitrary origins and of the extent to which social practices in general are variable or arbitrary. Can our pre-anthropological moral knowledge be rewon? Moral inquiry can no longer for us take the form of asking with great care, 'Is tradition being followed?', even if this question did occupy the centre of pre-anthropological debates over a practice's wisdom or fairness. We must be able to see established moral practices as yielding certain regular outcomes—contingently, relationally—in our evolving context. And we perhaps must also have some idea of how it could be that practices of arbitrary origin whose surface appearance or formal features do not as such distinguish them from other, morally unreliable practices might none the less, in a given social and historical setting, be robustly dependable morally. Of course, our participation in any such reflective, vindicatory process may now have tainted us or our society: we have lost the innocence that was a key ingredient or a saving grace, and an ideally full self-understanding that would overcome this could be for ever out of reach in practice. But even this unfortunate result need not preclude our knowing that the pre-anthropological practices were good. So normative moral knowledge perhaps need not be an altogether closed book to the cosmopolitan mind.

We are working here with the idea of a *vindicatory explanation* of a practice, as opposed to a debunking explanation. Vindication may take many forms. The explanation can be 'direct': we might show that, though the origins are arbitrary in various ways, the practice (or artefact, phenomenon, etc.) has certain features which, in its context, make it robustly reliable in particular respects. Or, the explanation can be 'indirect': the practice (artefact, etc.) exists as it does and where it does (or plays the role in people's lives that it does) because of a *selection mechanism* that favours reliability of the relevant sort. The explanation can also combine the two, as our story of Wrell does: a direct explanation of the clock's reliability along with an indirect explanation of why people in Wrell pay attention to what its hand says (unlike residents of other villages with other Cruikshanks). Direct explanations are often of the 'existentially quantified' form: we have reason to think there is *something* about this practice (or artefact, etc.) in this setting that yields reliability. Indirect explanations are often highly speculative: we have reason to think this practice (or artefact, etc.) wouldn't continue to be used if it didn't play such-and-such a role at least as well as salient, available competitors. Not much is clear about *how much* vindicatory explanation one must possess once a practice (artefact, etc.) has become as deeply problematized as talk of objective moral knowledge has been for us moderns. No doubt the answer is pragmatic in the sense that how much vindication we need depends upon the centrality of a practice (artefact, etc.) to our lives and the seriousness and specificity of the problematization.[24] What perhaps does seem clearer is that Wrellians themselves need not (at least, not before they hear about the other clocks) possess a vindicatory explanation of their Cruikshank's reliability in order to know the time from looking at it, but that *our* need for such an explanation is greater. It is one of the burdens of knowledge.

We might think that telling time is of little direct relevance to the moral case because of the existence of objective indicators to check correlations independently. And we might also think that, in the story of the pre-anthropological home society, the real issue for moral epistemology has just been assumed away—the practices are described as if they unproblematically bore identifiably moral properties. This, too, would yield the possibility of objective indicators and independent ways of checking, but only because we have fixed the moral criteria. What if our concern—what has been problematized by the ideological critique of a Marx or a Nietzsche—is with the criteria themselves, or their very possibility? Where then is the objective indicator or independent check?

9

To move further along in answering such questions we need to be more self-aware in thinking about the critical reflection test itself. How well does *it* survive critical reflection? First, we must ask, what

---

[24] Some have thought that philosophical scepticism of the 'the world might have been created five minutes ago to look just like this' sort doesn't need much of an answer, because it so unspecific in its problematization and because its practical implications are slight. I am grateful to David Lewis and Jim Joyce for reminding me of this.

does it (at least, in its classic form) seem to presuppose? Here is a partial listing:

(1) there exists a relatively determinate causal history of our beliefs and values;

(2) there exist real needs and interests, capable of shaping behaviour on the individual and social level in the manner ideological explanations require, and also such that we can make sense of the claim that a purported general interest is in fact not so;

(3) we are capable of acquiring reasonably warranted beliefs about (1) and (2), despite our own particular interests and historical and social situatedness;

(4) the failure of certain beliefs and values to survive reflective exposure to these warranted beliefs constitutes some degree of warrant for rejecting or revising them, whereas survival constitutes some degree of warrant for continued acceptance.[25]

Don't (1)–(4) themselves run afoul of the critique of objectivity and of the reification or fetishization of value?

What sorts of ambition must a theory of belief or value have in order to underwrite talk of warrant or objectivity? These are very large and contentious questions, and we will have to content ourselves with looking only at one aspect: how *rationalistic* must the ambition be? Hume famously argued at the end of part 1 of the *Treatise of Human Nature* that a strict rationalistic project failed even in its own terms: 'understanding, when it acts alone, and according to its most general principles, entirely subverts itself, and leaves not the lowest degree of evidence in any proposition, either in philosophy or in common life'.[26] Kant, coming along behind Hume, attempted to rescue rationalism by rendering it *critical*

---

[25] On at least some accounts, a further, important presupposition is also present:

(5) Beliefs and values that survive reflection are not only warranted, but also are such that holding them and acting upon them tends to promote genuine, usually general or 'emancipatory', interests.

For further discussion, see Raymond Geuss, *The Idea of a Critical Theory* (Cambridge: Cambridge University Press, 1981).

[26] David Hume, *A Treatise of Human Nature*, ed. L. A. Selby-Bigge (Oxford: Clarendon Press, 1888), 267–8; hereafter *Treatise* in parenthetic page references in the text.

rather than dogmatic, grounding claims of objectivity and warrant in a priori necessities inherent in thought and action rather than metaphysical necessities inherent in the world. Many in the tradition of *Ideologiekritik* can be thought of as pressing this critical rationalist project beyond Kant, situating it socially and historically. But it would appear to sustain after all a commitment to the attainability of objectivity and warrant through an operation of reflective understanding—as exemplified in (4). In a word, a faith in *reason*.[27]

But the critical reflection test does not belong to any particular philosophical tradition, and is just as important to Hume as it is to Kant. For by the end of part III of the *Treatise* Hume summarizes his 'accurate proof of this system of ethics' in just these terms:

> It requires but very little knowledge of human affairs to perceive, that a sense of morals is a principle inherent in the soul, and one of the most powerful that enters into the [human] composition. But this sense must certainly acquire new force, when reflecting on itself, it approves of those principles, from whence it is deriv'd, and finds nothing but what is great and good in its rise and origin. Those who resolve the sense of morals into original instincts of the human mind, may defend the cause of virtue with sufficient authority; but want the advantage, which those possess, who account for that sense by an extensive sympathy with mankind. According to the latter system [i.e. Hume's sort of system], not only virtue must be approv'd, but also the sense of virtue: And not only that sense, but also the principles, from whence it is deriv'd. So that nothing is presented on any side, but what is laudable and good. (*Treatise*, 619)

Descending from Hume we have a compatibilist conception of freedom, a relational conception of value, and a contingent conception of the operation of human motivation and understanding. A de-escalated version of the Kantian synthetic a priori regulative principles of thought and action results. Hume argues, against outright scepticism, that we cannot even begin to think—even to think sceptical thoughts—without attributing some prima-facie warrant to reasoning and experience, and that we cannot even begin to act—even to act on sceptical thoughts—without attributing some prima facie commending force to what we aim at. But, much as a

---

[27] And, of course, in the case of (5) (see n. 25), in the power of reason to set us free.

Bayesian claims that epistemic rationality consists not in starting from demonstrable truth or certainty, but in starting from one's existing beliefs (one's *priors* for both propositions and new evidence), and proceeding to condition them in a potentially self-correcting way upon new experience, which may lead us arbitrarily far from our original starting-point, Hume does not assume that prima-facie warrant and commending force is tantamount to a priori *necessary* or *unrevisable* warrant or commending force. Indeed, for Hume, even the 'principle of human nature . . . that men are mightily addicted to *general rules*, and that we often carry our maxims beyond those reasons, which first induc'd us to establish them' (*Treatise*, 551) knows some limits, as sentiments of sympathy and credibility (and 'a serious good-humour'd disposition') continually act as countervailing forces, capable of undermining a rigid compliance with rules and bringing us back to our senses.

Reification seems inessential in any of this, though it is always a danger. Hume may strike us as overly complacent, but it is important to record that he thought scepticism should never be wholly set aside (*Treatise*, 270).

In any event, the crucial step lies in repudiating such thoughts as those equating subjectivity or contingency with arbitrariness. Subjects are parts of the world, possessing at a given time more or less definite properties, as well as the capacity to remake themselves in various ways. Sentiments as well as reasoning are products of a long-term interaction between organism and the natural and social world, and both sentiment and reasoning may be more or less impartial and object-oriented. When critical reflection brings them together, it may accomplish something neither could accomplish on its own. If we call that which relates to subjects *subjectual*—as we now call that which relates to objects *objectual*—we can see at once how misleading the equation of subjectual with arbitrary can be. Ideological criticism draws upon this very thought: while the subjectual cannot simply be reified as merely objectual—subjects have ways of seeing themselves that then contribute to the explanation of how they behave—subjects none the less are implicated in the world and interactive with it in ways that may make them more or less capable of seeing themselves or the world as things are. We might call this *objective subjectuality*, a condition that requires effort and good fortune, to shake the complacency of our ordinary self-conceptions, but is in no way incoherent. Ideological analyses contribute to the shaking of our complacency by indicating how deeply things might not be as they seem.

There is a remarkable similarity between the critical machinery of ideological analysis, Hume's 'accurate proof' of his ethics, and Rawls's notion of (wide) reflective equilibrium as a form of justification.[28] All three operate with the thought that we concede normative authority to conclusions which show a certain kind of stability in the light of fuller information, greater sensitivity and awareness, and movement away from various kinds of parochialism. Such a picture presents the appearance of illicit movement, from an 'is' (that which in fact is stable) to an 'ought' (that which we should believe or value)—from brute fact to normative authority. But the fact isn't very brute (it is reflective, critical) and the authority isn't absolute (it is provisional, and dependent upon rationally optional natures and purposes).

We do of course start off with what we believe and value, and where we end up may depend more or less heavily upon that. But rationality in belief—as philosophers of science have long emphasized—must be a matter of *where one goes from here*. For surely neither alternative is rational: to go nowhere (because one cannot start anywhere) or to start from where we aren't (with what we *don't* believe).

If morality, the sitting duck for ideological critique, is still afloat, that is because we have been able both to criticize and to rebuild it—as we have rebuilt scientific belief—from normatively available materials to meet the empirical onslaught of experience. Moral thought itself furnished the essential ingredients to give rise to challenges of partiality, false factual assumptions, or parochialism about the good life. These have been recognized grounds of criticism within moral practice, stemming from its objective purport. But moral thought has also evolved under these criticisms, becoming less partial, less factually benighted, less parochial. As criticisms have become normatively intelligible (e.g. charges of parochialism of various kinds), so has a morality rebuilt in response to them.

We ask a lot of morality for it to be in good standing because we

---

[28] See John Rawls, *A Theory of Justice* (Cambridge, Mass.: Harvard University Press, 1971).

grant moral assessment a good deal of authority. Perhaps this will be vindicated over time to a significant degree. Further knowledge and reflection do seem unlikely to unsettle altogether such ideas as these: that lives can go better or worse for those who will live them; that institutions and attitudes can be less or more partial; and that practices can be more or less widely, reciprocally, or equally beneficial to those affected by them. Perhaps the reluctance of philosophers in the modern epoch to consign morality to the depths where notions of honour, divine order, and natural teleology now repose reflects their sense that morality has proven remarkably adaptive, remarkably effective at co-opting its critics. A sitting duck, morality is also Neurath's duck.[29]

[29] With special thanks to David Hills and James Joyce for helpful comments and conversations. Thanks, too, to Edward Harcourt for organizing the conference at which this paper was presented, and for his thoughtful and patient editing of this volume. A fellowship from the National Endowment for the Humanities helped support the writing of this paper (Grant FA-35357-99).

6

Naturalism and Genealogy

Bernard Williams

I. Naturalism

In ethics, 'naturalism' has two different kinds of associations. One set of associations flows from Moore's unfortunate appropriation of the term in the expression 'naturalistic fallacy'. The others go with the use of the term in other areas of inquiry, and they circle round the slogan that human beings are part of nature. That the two are not the same comes out if one considers the view that moral requirements are the commands of God: such a view may well be naturalist in Moore's use—that is to say, it may commit the naturalistic fallacy—but it is clearly non-naturalist in the other use.

Moore's use of the term is not my concern here, but it is perhaps worth making one further point about it. Nowadays the naturalistic fallacy is often explained in terms of the relations between fact and value: the fallacy is said to be the mistake of trying to reduce value to fact. But for Moore himself the opposition between fact and value would involve a cross-classification: facts about value are one kind of fact. A distinction between fact and value as such (or, rather, the further explanations you would have to give in order to deliver such a distinction) offers, rather, one account of why the naturalistic fallacy is a fallacy, if it is.

I am concerned with the other, more traditional understanding of 'naturalism'. There is a well-known quite systematic difficulty—which has nothing in particular to do with the case of ethics—in stabilizing the idea of 'nature' so that naturalism in a given area is not either trivially true or implausible to such an extent and in such ways as to be uninteresting. It is trivially true if 'nature' contains whatever there is. Reacting against this, we may say that what naturalism recognizes are just those things recognized by the natural sciences. But then is biology a natural science? If biology is, is ethology? At this point it may be that the screw is turned again, and naturalism is required to represent all the things it recognizes in terms of the universally applicable natural science, physics. So the project of naturalism gets tied to physicalistic reductionism. Not only is this an implausible undertaking in itself; it also cannot be that the interests of a naturalistic approach in ethics, for instance, should be essentially tied to it.

We should get away from the preoccupation with reductionism. It cannot be that the concerns of those who have wanted to understand human beings, in their ethical as in other aspects, as part of nature, are essentially bound up with the prospects for the Encyclopedia of Unified Science. In trying to do better than this, we may consider the case of life. Living things are, one might think, part of nature if anything is: the study of them is, or used to be, called 'natural history'. So how could there possibly have been a question about naturalism in biology? To put it another way: if there is a question about the roles of physics and chemistry in biology, that cannot be a question about naturalism. However, this is to neglect a significant piece of history. Until the twentieth century, and into it, vitalism was an option. It was agreed that there were living things, but there was great unclarity about what kind of property life was, in particular how it related to properties described by the other sciences. Hence there was a question whether life was part of nature, where that meant the *rest* of nature. That question has now been answered positively, and the characteristics of living things can now be clearly understood in a way that is continuous with biochemistry. Thus we can see in scientific terms how living things could have come to exist.

Granted this, it seems to me that there is no need either to assert or to deny that life has been 'reduced' to biochemical phenomena: the question has simply gone away, ceased to be of any interest. (Perhaps it is a general rule that talk about reduction has a grip only when we do not yet understand how things, processes, facts at one level relate to items at another level and can be explained in terms of them. Perhaps the idea of reductionism always represents a problem and not a solution, like the ideas of supervenience and of synthetic necessary truth.)

Questions about naturalism, like questions about individualism in the social sciences,[1] are questions not about reduction but about explanation. Of course I recognize that this leaves almost everything open. But that is as it should be, because the questions that are substantial and interesting *are* open. The point is that the questions concern what we are prepared to regard, at each level, as an explanation. Moreover, we have no reason to think that what is to count as an explanation at each level, from bits of nature describable only in terms of physics to human beings and their cultures, is at each level the same kind of thing. This is one reason (but only one) that underlies a truth which distinguishes naturalism from reductionism: that 'is reducible to' is a transitive relation, while 'can be explained in terms of' is not. The question for naturalism is always: can we explain, by some appropriate and relevant criteria of explanation, the phenomenon in question in terms of the *rest* of nature? (We might call this the creeping barrage conception of naturalism.)

2. *Human Beings*

When we get to the peculiarities of human beings, the terms of the discussion change somewhat. The overwhelming innovation represented by *Homo sapiens* is the significance of non-genetic learning, which is in the first instance an ethological difference. Every species has an ethological description, and *Homo sapiens* is no different; the exception is that in this case, uniquely, you cannot tell the ethological story without introducing culture (consider, for example, what is immediately involved in answering the question 'In what sorts of things do they live?') Consequently, the story is likely to differ significantly between groups of human beings, and in ways that typically involve history; in many cases, the human beings who are being described will also be conscious, to varying degrees, of that history. All of this follows from the peculiar ethological character of this species.

Individual members of the species must of course typically, standardly, or in the right proportion, have the characteristics that enable humans to have this ethology, to live under culture. The

---

[1] See Susan James, *The Content of Social Explanation* (Cambridge: Cambridge University Press, 1984).

questions then become: what are those characteristics? What is the best, most revealing and explanatory, description of them? Granted such a description, how might those characteristics have come into existence? In the case of some of them, the answer may well be in terms of transmitted social influences operating on general learning capacities, but in the case of some (such as the general learning capacities themselves) they must have genetically evolved, and the question then must be, how? This obviously applies to the language acquisition capacity.

A special case that interests us is the capacity shown, in some form or other, by humans in all cultures to live under rules and values and to shape their behaviour in some degree to social expectations in ways that are not under direct surveillance and not directly controlled by threats and rewards. Call this, begging many questions, (the minimal version of) living in an ethical system.

Living in an ethical system demands a certain psychology. But, importantly, it does not follow that all ethical systems demand the same psychology—moral psychology may be opportunistic (an example would be the supposed difference between shame and guilt societies). Nor need it be the case that one and the same ethical system demands (exactly) the same psychology of each participant. At this level, variation might be not simply individual, but, more interestingly, systematic: this would be the case with our prevailing ethical system, if Gilligan's hypothesis were true, that it involves different psychological formations from men and from women.[2]

Granted that there must be a psychology or psychologies underlying any ethical system, we can ask: what do these psychologies have to be like? What is involved in them? Our immediate question is: what is it for an answer to those questions to meet the demands of naturalism?

3. *Convention*

In trying to give this last question a frame, it is worth mentioning the notion of convention. There is an ancient opposition between

[2] See C. Gilligan, *In a Different Voice: Psychological Theory and Women's Development* (Cambridge, Mass.: Harvard University Press, 1982).

nature and convention, and it might therefore be thought that someone who supposed that 'convention' significantly explained the nature and existence of ethical systems was opposed to naturalism about ethical systems. But this is obviously not so: those who regard ethical systems as 'conventional' typically do so as part of giving a naturalist account. This is because they make two assumptions, one obviously true, the other more dubious. The obviously true one is that, as was first pointed out by Plato (or, just possibly, Democritus), it is the nature of human beings to live by convention: this is just the point about human ethology being cultural. The second assumption is that to live under convention requires no psychology other than would be ascribed to humans *anyway*. That is more dubious. Indeed, what might be meant by 'anyway'?

We can get to this question by recalling the shape of the naturalist's question at the previous stages. A naturalist will claim that what is involved in human beings living in ethical systems can be coherently related to the rest of nature. But what exactly is, now, the rest of nature? In the case of vitalism, it meant nature up to living things; in the case of consciousness (which I have not so far mentioned), it will mean all of those things, together with living things, up to conscious living things. So what does 'the rest of nature' mean in the present case? Does it mean: everything, including conscious living things, up to human beings? If this is what is meant, the focus of the naturalistic question will be: is the human capacity to live in ethical systems closely related to characteristics of other, non-human, species? Can it, and its emergence, be explained in terms familiar from our understanding of other species?

The naturalistic question about ethics has often been put in this way. Some of those who have discussed it in these terms have answered it in the negative. In particular, there have been those who have been very keen on characterizing human ethical capacities by contrast to other animals ('the brutes', as they were sometimes called in such traditions).

Others have understood the naturalistic question in this same way, but have given a positive answer to it. These are typically people who are impressed by sociobiology, and (for instance) see the capacity needed for living under ethical systems as 'altruism' in some sense in which a character called by that name can be selected for in other species. But 'altruism' cannot be brought across from other species to human beings without taking into account the differences between the two, which form a major part of the problem.

The crudity of both these approaches, the negative and the positive, suggests that their shared form of the naturalistic question—the way in which they interpret 'the rest of nature'—is misguided. Before getting to the psychologies that are distinctively presupposed by ethical systems, we need first to allow for the fact that culture affects almost all of human psychology. We cannot consider the most basic instinctual drives of human beings, the drives they manifestly share in some sense with other species, without allowing for the influence of the cultural on them and on their expression. This in itself is simply an application, admittedly a far-reaching one, of an ethological platitude: that the way in which a given instinct or drive displays itself in a given species depends on that species' way of life. It is hardly surprising that the reproductive behaviour of the red deer differs spectacularly from that of the hedgehog or the stickleback, since their ways of life are notably different. If we are going to think in naturalistic terms, or the contrary, about the psychology of human beings as it is most immediately related to their living in ethical systems, we should think in the first place about the relations of that psychology to other aspects of *human* psychology.

There is of course a kind of false abstraction involved in this. I have already said that human beings live under culture—something that follows from the central significance of their capacity for non-genetic learning. I have also said that living under culture involves, roughly speaking, living in an ethical system. If so, we cannot ultimately separate the business of living under culture, together with all the effects that this has on other aspects of human psychology, from whatever it is that enables humans to live in an ethical system. Ultimately, it is true, we cannot. Perhaps, however, we can fruitfully postpone considering all these things together.

There are reasons why it is worth trying to do this. There is a characteristic that is absolutely fundamental to these human peculiarities, namely language use, and we can allow for the involvement of that in other aspects of human psychology first. Moreover, the acquisition of language use looks like something for which the naturalist demand might be met: in particular, we may be able to give an account of how it could have evolved.

When we put those two ideas together, this can encourage a thought which is plausible, or at any rate familiar: that the relation of at least some basic instinctual drives in human beings, even as they are necessarily modified by language and by culture, to functionally similar drives in other species is more transparent than the psychologies that support ethical systems are. This has helped to encourage, no doubt, those who have traditionally thought in terms of an 'animal part' of human beings, as opposed to their rational powers or ethical motivations.

Given these ideas, the naturalist question about ethics will emerge as something like the question of how closely the motivations and practices of the ethical are related to other aspects of human psychology—to the ways, as one can very loosely and inaccurately put it, human beings are 'anyway'. With regard to this particular aspect of the very peculiar ethology of this species, this is the special form taken by the recurrent naturalist question which we have identified as arising elsewhere, e.g. in the case of life: how does the phenomenon in question intelligibly relate to the *rest* of nature, and how, in particular, might it have come about? As one might put it, we are asking about human ethical life in relation to the rest of human nature.

If we can make sense of this undertaking, of explaining the ethical in terms of an account of human beings which is to the greatest possible extent prior to ideas of the ethical, then there is a project of ethical naturalism which is intelligible, non-vacuous, and not committed to a general physicalistic reductionism which is at least dubious, and anyway ought to be a separate issue.

4. *History*

The next suggestion I want to make corresponds to the second half of my title. This suggestion is that the undertaking of the naturalist project with regard to ethics, as it has now been outlined, may well be best carried forward with the help of certain kinds of historical or quasi-historical inquiry. What I have already proposed is to a considerable extent independent of these further suggestions:

it may be that a naturalistic account of ethics would have to satisfy the kinds of conditions I have proposed, without its taking the particular forms that I am now going to suggest. But I think that there are reasons for thinking that it is, in part, likely to take such forms: those reasons I am, to some extent, going to have to leave to emerge on this occasion rather than argue them in detail.

In fact, the suggestion is rather more complicated than I have so far indicated. At least in relation to our own ethical life, the ethical life of modernity, part of the account will consist of real history, which will be to some extent, as Foucault put it,[3] 'gray, meticulous, and patiently documentary'. The reason for this is that our ethical ideas, as contrasted, for instance, with the ethical life of an isolated traditional society, is a complex deposit of many different traditions and social forces, and that it has itself been shaped by self-conscious representations of those facts. (This is not to say that traditional societies are not shaped by history: but the history is less complex, less variously influenced, less mediated by self-conscious representation, and largely unknown, and all this makes a great difference to the account that can be given of it, and to what will count as explanations.)

Moreover, it is likely to be true, sticking in particular to our own case, that the impact of these historical processes will be to some extent concealed by the ways in which their product conceives itself. There is more than one reason for this, but the most general, perhaps, is that a truthful historical account is going to reveal a radical contingency in our current ethical conceptions, both in the sense that they are what they are rather than some others, and also in the sense that the historical changes which brought them about are not obviously related in a grounding or epistemically favourable way to the ethical ideas they encouraged. (There is a contrast with teleological history here, both Hegelian and Marxist.) But a sense of such contingency can seem to be in some tension with something that the ethical system itself demands, a recognition of that system's authority.[4] The tension here is actually made

---

[3] Michel Foucault, 'Nietzsche, Genealogy, History', in Foucault, *Language, Counter-Memory, Practice*, ed. D. Bouchard, trans. D. Bouchard and S. Simon (Ithaca, NY: Cornell University Press, 1977), 139.

[4] I argue elsewhere that there need be no inherent conflict between our being identified with an outlook and our understanding its contingent history: see 'Philosophy as a Humanistic Discipline', Third Annual Royal Institute of

worse by a feature of modern ethical systems, that they try to combine authority with transparency, and their valuation of transparency, which is one of their own products, is likely to encourage the naturalistic impulse itself. All this is connected with the idea that there is likely to be something disobliging or disrespectful or critical about such accounts.

However, it is not simply a matter of what I have called real history. There may also be a role for imaginary history, a fictional developmental story, which helps to explain a concept or value or institution by showing ways in which it could have come about in a simplified environment which contains certain kinds of human interests or capacities, which, relative to this story, are taken as given. The paradigm example is of course state of nature stories about the origins of the state; another is Hume's account of the artificial virtue of justice. A very interesting recent example is E. J. Craig's illuminating account of the concept of knowledge.[5]

It is a very interesting question how it is that entirely fictional stories in this manner can explain or illuminate anything. It is not a question I can take very far here, but I shall sketch an outline. The stories that concern us here apply to concepts or values or institutions, and what the story peculiarly does is to explain how these items can emerge and provide new reasons for action. It does this in terms of existing reasons for action which are taken as given, and the story performs a special function because the new reasons for action stand in a rational or intelligible relation to the original reasons or motivations, a relation which is not simply instrumental—or at least, it is not instrumental in giving individuals reasons for action which they could in principle acquire individually. A special, and important, case is the construction of something which, once constructed, needs to be regarded as an intrinsic value.[6]

Philosophy Lecture, *Philosophy* 75 (2000). Such problems arise, rather, as I claim below, from the particular content of our outlook.

[5] See Edward Craig, *Knowledge and the State of Nature* (Oxford: Clarendon Press, 1990).

[6] There is more than one kind of reason why an individual could not reach the end-point instrumentally. One, as in Hume's account of justice, is that it involves solving a co-ordination problem; and another, where the story constructs an intrinsic value. It is different again when the process could not be consciously acknowledged at all, as in the example of morality and *ressentiment*, discussed in Sect. 6 below.

There is more than one thing than can be learned from the fictional story. The fact that it does without certain resources may suggest that there could be some actual and much less tidy account which also did without them, and called on no more input.[7] Moreover, the story may help to sketch a functional account of the product, which will help us to interpret the explanandum in the real world in terms of some features that are more basic and others that are the result of secondary elaboration—and actual history and social science are likely to help in identifying these different features.

5. *Nietzsche*

An account which offers one or another or, typically, both of these historical and quasi-historical stories is a genealogy, a term which of course signals that the ideas involved owe a lot to Nietzsche, whose *On the Genealogy of Morality*[8] (*GM*) is the best-known and most spectacular contribution to the genre. *GM* has the property of being at once extremely compelling, in particular because it seems to hit on something with great exactitude, and at the same time of being infuriatingly vague. It offers a vivid phenomenology of *ressentiment*, which traces certain moral ideas to a psychic compensation for the lack of power. It also has something to do with history, though it is far from clear what history: there are some vaguely situated masters and slaves; then a historical change, which has something to do with Jews or Christians; there is a process which culminates perhaps in the Reformation, perhaps in Kant. It has been going for 2000 years. (*GM* I. 7.)

There is a blend here of psychology and history which surely owes something to Hegel's *Phenomenology*: there is a set of relations between ideas or outlooks or attitudes which express themselves both psychologically and historically, such that there is an

---

[7] This can be so even though the story is not only fictional but impossible, as it is in the genealogical cases. In other areas, a fictional story may provide a possible mechanism by which a given result could have come about, and thus show that a certain kind of theoretical explanation is possible. This is the point of 'Just So' stories in evolutionary biology.

[8] As it is called in the Cambridge edition, trans. K. Ansell-Pearson (Cambridge: Cambridge University Press, 1994). The title is more familiar as *On the Genealogy of Morals*.

essential connection between the two expressions. We are bound to be dissatisfied with this, in particular because it is associated with features of Hegel's idealism which, like Nietzsche himself, we are bound to find unacceptable. But it can still do a lot for us, if, so to speak, we spread it out more.

One—certainly only one—way of doing this, in relation to one part of Nietzsche's story, would be this:

(*a*) There is a feature of our own outlook, our morality, which is psychologically and conceptually suspect: will or perhaps free will, construed in a certain radical self-creating style, which has links with practices of blame, ascribing responsibility, moral as opposed to secular value, and so forth. This has appeared repeatedly as a theoretical and practical trouble spot, a place of fissures and ruptures. There is a history, a sober real history, of these troubles.

(*b*) There is a sober real history of an actual contrast to these ideas, earlier worlds which lacked them. No doubt there are other contrasting worlds as well, but what particularly matter to us are the worlds that are ancestors of ours.

(*c*) There are all sorts of moral reactions which are tied to (*a*) and its associated practices, and they typically involve a high level of affect.

(*d*) There is, or we hope that there may be, further sober real history which helps us to track the transitions from those earlier worlds to our present situation, and helps us to explain (*c*).

Now Nietzsche himself gives us, centrally to his story, a phenomenological representation, which seems to present a psychological process leading from the earlier ethical condition to something like the outlook in the later ethical condition (the explanandum). If this were a psychological process, it should be recognizable in an individual. But an actual process that led to the actual explanandum could not happen in an individual, since the outcome consists of socially legitimated beliefs, and they could not be merely the sum of individual fantasies. Rather, this is a social process which in actual fact no doubt has many stages, discontinuities, and contingencies, but which—the idea is—can be illuminatingly represented on the model of a certain kind of psychological strategy. Not all genealogies, I suggest, need to contain such a phenomenological representation. This further element in Nietzsche's particular genealogy is, rather, a special case of what was recognized before:

(*e*) a fictional story which represents a new reason for action as being developed in a simplified situation as a function of motives, reactions, psychological processes which we have reason to acknowledge already.

6. Bad Origins

We encountered earlier the idea of a genealogy's being damaging or disobliging: that it reveals what Nietzsche himself called a *pudenda origo*.[9] Foucault remarked on the point that a genealogy in terms of actual history is almost bound to be critical to some extent. As he says, and I agree, this is not because 'the past actively exists in the present, that it continues to animate the present'.[10] The basic idea was that the concepts or values under explanation are likely to claim an authority which rejects the appearance of contingency, and so resist being explained in real terms at all. But this is true to a greater extent of some values and institutions than others. As Nietzsche remorselessly pointed out, it is true to a much greater extent of the morality system than of some other ethical formations, because of its desperate need to be in more than one way self-sufficient. Not every ethical outlook is so resistant to being made transparent. Others may more happily coexist with a consciousness of how they came about. They are more, as one might say, stable under genealogical explanation.

This is so to an even greater extent with fictional developmental stories. Here the relevant question is whether one could understand the explanandum in terms of the fictional history and still (more or less) accept in their original terms the reasons for action which the explanandum provides. In the example of *GM*, the phenomenological fiction of *ressentiment* does not permit this: once again, this is a result of the special demands of the morality system, that it should present itself as separate from and higher than such motives. This expresses its deep involvement in what Nietzsche called 'the

---

[9] See F. Nietzsche, *Daybreak*, trans. R. J. Hollingdale (Cambridge: Cambridge University Press, 1982), sect. 102, p. 59.

[10] Foucault, 'Nietzsche, Genealogy, History', 146.

metaphysicians' basic belief, *the belief in the opposition of values*.[11] (It is an important feature of such a case that the process that the story deploys would have to be, even in the story, unacknowledged. This is one version, a special one, of the feature possessed, as I said, by all such stories, that they given an account of a reason for action which could not be instrumentally derived by an individual.) But some other fictional stories might represent their explanandum in terms which left it stable under reflection, as in this case it is not. This might well be so, for instance, with regard to a story about the origins of the state.

There is a good question, whether and why it matters whether a value or institution is stable under a given genealogical explanation. In fact there are two questions here. One applies only to fictional genealogies, and is an application of the general question of how explanation in terms of a fictional story can be explanation at all, or do anything for our understanding of the actual. Here I must leave that question, saying only that to the extent that such stories do succeed in relating a value which gives us some reasons for action to other reasons for action which, as I very roughly put it, we have 'anyway', to that extent there will be a question—one might say, a relevant thought experiment—of whether we could, if we knew such a story to be true, go on giving the derived value the kind of respect we give it.

The second question is more general. Suppose a given value is not stable under genealogical explanation. It does not necessarily follow that we give up on it, or lose confidence in it. We may merely stop reflecting on it, not address ourselves to the explanation, give up on transparency. A basic reason for this is that we have to go on somehow, try to live by something, and if there is no alternative we will try to keep what we actually have, even if it does fail under reflection. Nietzsche diagnosed the condition of modernity as one in which we, at once, have a morality which is seriously unstable under genealogical explanation; are committed (by that very morality, among other things) to transparency; and find very little to hand in the way of an alternative.

I do not know how far we agree with that diagnosis. But when we consider such questions, there is one further Nietzschean thought which certainly we should keep in mind. Whether there

---

[11] Friedrich Nietzsche, *Beyond Good and Evil*, I. 2, Nietzsche's emphasis.

is an alternative is not something that will be obvious to us, and whether we shall move over in its direction is not a question for deliberation or practical reason. The question is, whether some other ways of living, something which includes other ways of thinking about living, will help us, or human beings who follow us, to live, and one of Nietzsche's most important lessons is that this consideration does not function as a criterion. It is not a matter of choosing some concept or image on the ground that it will help us to live. It is a matter of whether it will indeed help us to live, and whether it will have done so is something that can only be recognized first in the sense that we are managing to live, and then later at a more reflective level, perhaps with the help of renewed genealogical explanation.

Liberal Double-Mindedness

John Kekes

I. Introduction

Double-mindedness is best understood in contrast with single-mindedness. To be single-minded is to have a strong enough motive to override any other motive that may conflict with it. To be double-minded is to have two strong motives that exist in a state of tension because acting on one excludes acting on the other. The agents feel the strength of both motives, but neither obviously overrides the other. Consequently they waver, they are ambivalent, they are of two minds about what they should do.

Double-mindedness may be a temporary state or a lasting disposition. As a temporary state, it is a common experience that most agents have when they try to decide, as they must, between immediate and more distant satisfactions, between the demands of morality and self-interest, between institutional and personal loyalties, between duty and pleasure, and so forth. Such a state is intrinsically undesirable because it involves frustration, but if it is temporary and occurs infrequently, it does no great harm, for reasonable agents can tolerate much frustration and still live a good life. If, however, double-mindedness is a lasting disposition, if it is an essential feature of the psychological profile of agents, then it is a threat to their prospects of living a good life, because it habitually and predictably dooms them to frustration. It is reasonable, therefore, to want to avoid it.

The aim of this paper is to offer an internal criticism of liberalism: liberals are unavoidably and lastingly doomed to double-mindedness because they must acknowledge the strength of two mutually exclusive motives. Liberals are thus forced to be either inconsistent, or conflicted, frustrated, and thus dissatisfied with a crucial aspect of their lives. The psychological cost of being a liberal who is faithful to incompatible motives is therefore great enough to present a serious obstacle to living a good life. If reasonable liberals become aware of the cost of their double-mindedness, they will want to avoid bearing it, if they can. And they can, but only by giving up liberalism.

2. *The Personal Versus the Political*

Rawls has formulated 'the problem of liberalism' as follows: 'How is it possible that there exists over time a stable and just society of free and equal citizens profoundly divided by reasonable religious, philosophical, and moral doctrines?'[1] The solution proposed by numerous contemporary liberal thinkers rests on a basic idea which may be expressed in a number of ways.[2] One is neutrality: the liberal state ought to be uncommitted to any of the conceptions of the good that motivate its citizens. It ought to create conditions in which all reasonable conceptions can be pursued, but no conception ought to be privileged over others, and only those conceptions ought to be excluded that violate the conditions that all reasonable conceptions require. Another way of expressing the idea is that in the liberal state the right ought to have priority over the good. The

---

[1] John Rawls, *Political Liberalism* (New York: Columbia University Press, 1993), p. xxv.

[2] See, for instance, Bruce Ackerman, *Social Justice and the Liberal State* (New Haven: Yale University Press, 1980); Ronald Dworkin, *Taking Rights Seriously* (Cambridge, Mass.: Harvard University Press, 1977) and *A Matter of Principle* (Cambridge, Mass.: Harvard University Press, 1985); Charles E. Larmore, *Patterns of Moral Complexity* (Cambridge: Cambridge University Press, 1987); Thomas Nagel, *The View from Nowhere* (New York: Oxford University Press, 1986) and *Equality and Partiality* (New York: Oxford University Press, 1991); John Rawls, *A Theory of Justice* (Cambridge, Mass.: Harvard University Press, 1971) and *Political Liberalism*; Thomas Scanlon, 'Contractualism and Utilitarianism', in A. Sen and B. Williams (eds.), *Utilitarianism and Beyond* (Cambridge: Cambridge University Press; Paris: 'Editions de la Maison des Sciences de l'Homme, 1982) and 'The Significance of Choice', in Sterling M. McMurrin (ed.), *The Tanner Lectures on Human Values*, viii (Salt Lake City: University of Utah Press, 1988). For a powerful political criticism of these versions of liberalism, see George Sher, *Beyond Neutrality* (New York: Cambridge University Press, 1997). Another criticism is John Kekes, *Against Liberalism* (Ithaca, NY: Cornell University Press, 1997). The argument of this paper differs from these criticisms in being based on considerations derived from moral psychology, rather than politics.

right is embodied in the institutional arrangements that provide the protection and the resources that all citizens need for pursuing what they regard as good, quite independently of what their conceptions of the good happen to be. A third expression of the same idea is that the liberal state ought to be able to justify its institutional arrangements to all of its citizens regardless of their conceptions of the good.

The liberal state thus protects the freedom of its citizens to live according to their conceptions of the good, maintains just institutions that distribute the needed resources, favours conditions in which the widest possible plurality of lives can be lived, guarantees everyone's right to live in this manner, and thus treats all citizens with equal respect. The liberal view underlying equal respect is expressed by Dworkin as 'From the standpoint of politics, the interests of the members of the community matter, and matter equally';[3] by Nagel as 'to give equal weight, in essential respects, to each person's point of view';[4] and by Vlastos as 'the human worth of all persons is equal, however unequal may be their merits'.[5]

It is clear from the writings of Dworkin, Nagel, Rawls, Vlastos, and other liberals that equal concern is taken by them to imply not just the protection of the freedom of individuals to pursue their individual conceptions of the good, but also the distribution of economic resources that makes their pursuit possible. Equal respect, therefore, affects both freedom and welfare rights.

If the citizens of a liberal state understand that the justification of liberal institutional arrangements is to maintain the conditions that they and their fellow citizens need for living according to their different conceptions of the good, then they will support these institutional arrangements. When agents are motivated in this way, they have *political* reasons to treat all citizens and all reasonable conceptions of the good with equal respect, where 'equal respect' embodies conformity to the conditions just adumbrated. Agents, of course, are not motivated solely by political reasons. They are motivated also by their specific conceptions of the good. They want to

---

[3] Ronald Dworkin, 'In Defense of Equality', *Social Philosophy and Policy*, 1(1983), 24.

[4] Thomas Nagel, 'Equality', in Nagel, *Mortal Questions* (Cambridge: Cambridge University Press, 1979), 112.

[5] Gregory Vlastos, 'Justice and Equality', in Richard B. Brandt (ed.), *Social Justice* (Englewood Cliffs, NJ: Prentice-Hall, 1962), 43.

live according to them, and political reasons motivate them, at least in part, because they make it more likely that they can live as they wish. Political reasons motivate them, therefore, partly because they are also motivated by *personal* reasons, which they derive from their conceptions of the good.

In a liberal state the main political reasons are the same for everyone, whereas personal reasons vary with individual conceptions of the good. If two agents have the same political reasons, it is because they support the same institutional arrangements. If two agents have the same personal reasons, it is because they have the same conception of the good. We shall see later that this view leads liberals to treat political reasons as moral and personal reasons as non-moral because the former are and the latter are not impartial. Nevertheless, the justification of both political and personal reasons derives from the conceptions of the good that motivate agents, but political reasons hold equally for all reasonable conceptions, whereas personal reasons hold only for the specific conceptions that are the agents' own.

Perhaps it is not pedantic to stress that the distinction between the personal and the political should not be confused with the distinctions between the private and the public, or the subjective and the objective, or the self-regarding and the other-regarding. The personal has to do with individual agents living according to their individual conceptions of the good. Such conceptions, however, can be, and often are, as public, objective, and other-regarding as any institutional arrangement that political reasons may lead agents to value. The difference between the personal and the political is that the personal is concerned with specific agents living in specific ways, whereas the political is concerned with the conditions that enable any agent to live in any way, so long as it is reasonable.

By way of illustration, consider religious or sexual attitudes. The liberal state is committed to arrangements that recognize a plurality of reasonable religious and sexual attitudes, protect the right to live according to them by providing the needed resources, and treat all reasonable attitudes with equal respect. The political reason agents have to support such arrangements is that they foster whatever religious or sexual preferences citizens happen to have. The personal reason is that the arrangements will help the agents themselves to live as Catholics, atheists, or Buddhists, or as heterosexuals, homosexuals, or celibates.

If agents had no personal reason to live in a particular manner, then the political reason for protecting the conditions required for living in that manner would be less likely to motivate them. If they recognized only personal but no political reasons, then they would undermine the conditions that their personal reasons ought to lead them to want to protect. For reasonable agents, therefore, personal and political reasons ought to coexist harmoniously, even if different considerations give them the force of reasons. The trouble with liberalism is that for liberals personal and political reasons do not coexist harmoniously. The two kinds of reasons routinely motivate them to act in incompatible ways. This is what makes liberals either inconsistent, or conflicted, wavering, ambivalent, and thus double-minded.

3. *The Problem of Double-Mindedness*

To show that this is so, consider the psychological condition of agents who are committed to living according to some reasonable conception of the good. This conception will shape their beliefs and feelings about significant features of life as it is lived in their particular context. They will have beliefs and feelings, which may or may not be conscious or articulated, about race, religion, sex, violence, beauty, authority, family, work, death, and so forth. Call particular clusters of these beliefs and feelings 'formative attitudes'. They are formative because a normal human life cannot be lived without having beliefs and feelings about such matters and because the particular beliefs and feelings agents have are crucial elements of their conceptions of the good.

Formative attitudes are internally complex. They are not simply what agents happen to believe and how they happen to feel about some feature of their lives, such as having children or dying. They include also the importance they attribute to the particular feature. And that is not just a matter of their regarding some feature as important or unimportant in their lives, but also of their judging their importance in comparison with other significant features of life towards which normal agents in normal circumstances will also have some attitude or another. To understand others—or oneself—depends on understanding the hierarchical structure of their formative attitudes, to know what they believe and what feelings they have about the significant features of life. Because the features are significant, the agents' beliefs and feelings will be powerful. The formative attitudes embodying these powerful beliefs and feelings constitute perhaps the strongest personal reasons agents have for doing whatever they do.

Such personal reasons motivate agents to evaluate ways of living and acting as on balance good, bad, or indifferent. What conforms to their formative attitudes they tend to regard as good, what violates them as bad, and what neither conforms to nor violates them as indifferent. What is important in the present context is that in a liberal state even the most liberal of agents will often encounter ways of living and acting that their formative attitudes prompt them to regard as bad. There will be people who, according to these liberals, are racists, sexists, specieists; people who maltreat children, women, and homosexuals; people who scorn the achievements of non-whites; people who side with corporations rather than the workers, who are moved by greed rather than by solidarity, who believe in making use of American power rather than accepting guilt for the terrible things America is supposed to have done. These are common and well-known liberal attitudes, and they provide strong personal reasons for those who hold them to regard their targets as bad. And they are regarded as bad even if they stay within the bounds of the law. They are condemned on moral grounds.

Contrast now the motivating force of strong personal reasons with that of political reasons. Nagel puts the point thus:

the basic insight that appears from the impersonal [i.e. what is here called political] standpoint is that everyone's life matters, and no one is more important than anyone else. . . . at the baseline of value in the lives of individuals . . . everyone counts the same. For a given quantity of whatever it is that's good or bad—suffering or happiness or fulfillment or frustration—its intrinsic value doesn't depend on whose it is.[6]

Those who share Nagel's basic insight unavoidably find their political and personal reasons in conflict. Their political reasons prompt them to regard their own conceptions of the good, their own formative attitudes, their own judgements about what is on balance good, bad, and indifferent as having exactly the same importance as the conceptions of the good, formative attitudes, and

[6] Nagel, *Equality and Partiality*, 11.

judgements about what is on balance good, bad, and indifferent of others, even if the conceptions, attitudes, and judgements of others are incompatible with their own. Political reasons thus often oblige agents who agree with Nagel to act contrary to their personal reasons.

For liberals, this conflict between personal and political reasons is not a rare occurrence, a consequence of pushing the logical implications of a political theory too hard, but a regular and predictable feature of daily experience. Liberals live in a society and must respond to the countless people they encounter. If their responses are motivated by political reasons, they will treat others with equal respect, regardless of whether they live and act in ways that liberals have personal reasons to find good, bad, or indifferent. If, on the other hand, their responses are motivated by personal reasons, then they will not treat with equal respect those whose lives and conduct they find good, bad, or indifferent. If liberals remain consistent, they will be normally motivated by their personal and political reasons in mutually exclusive ways. This will make them double-minded. However they respond to others, they will act contrary to one or another set of their own reasons.

4. Forced Choices

Liberals are aware of this problem. Nagel, who in numerous publications has struggled with it perhaps more than anyone, says:

It is clear that in most people, the coexistence of the personal standpoint with the values deriving from the . . . impersonal [i.e. political] standpoint produces a division of the self. From his own point of view within the world each person, with his particular concerns and attachments, is extremely important to himself. . . . But from the impersonal standpoint which he can also occupy, so is everyone else: *Everyone's* life matters as much as his does, and his matters no more than anyone else's. These two attitudes are not easy to combine.[7]

---

[7] Ibid. 14. But see also Larmore, *Patterns of Moral Complexity*, chs. 3–4; Stephen Macedo, *Liberal Virtues* (Oxford: Oxford University Press, 1990), chs. 2 and 7; Samuel Scheffler, *Human Morality* (New York: Oxford University Press, 1992), ch. 8; and Michael Walzer, *Thick and Thin* (Notre Dame, Ind.: University of Notre Dame Press, 1994), ch. 5.

Liberals labour mightily to overcome this problem and to combine the personal and political reasons that their position obliges them to have. But their efforts fail because they underestimate both the seriousness of the psychological burden that double-mindedness imposes on them and the acuteness of the conflict between their personal and political reasons.

To show just how serious is the psychological burden of double-mindedness, consider an illustration of the kind of conflict that contemporary liberals may encounter. Take a liberal woman who learns that her son's schoolteacher believes that there are inherited racial characteristics, that intelligence is one of them, that blacks are on the average significantly less intelligent than whites, that this makes whites as a group superior to blacks as a group, and that this superiority ought to be reflected in policies affecting education, employment, private association, and other areas of life. The teacher is vocal in his views, and, although he breaks no laws, he is, in the woman's opinion, a racist. She finds his racial attitudes deplorable, she does not want him to be teaching either her son or other students, and she regards the racial views he expresses as deeply offensive. For all of this, she has perfectly good personal reasons, which derive from her conception of the good and from her formative attitudes.

If she is a consistent liberal, she will also have political reasons to regard the racist teacher with the same respect as her son's other teachers, or indeed as she is obliged by her political reasons to regard any other citizen in her society. Her political reasons will tell her to think with Dworkin that the views of the teacher 'matter, and matter equally';[8] with Nagel 'to give equal weight . . . to each person's point of view',[9] including the teacher's; and with Vlastos to treat the teacher with equal respect, since 'the human worth of all persons is equal'.[10]

This conflict cannot be minimized by fastening on the unlikelihood of encountering a racist teacher. That case is meant merely to illustrate one way in which the conflict may arise. It arises also in countless other ways and with great frequency for liberals, as they encounter what they regard as bad formative attitudes

---

[8] Nagel, 'Equality', 112.
[9] Dworkin, 'In Defense of Equality', 24.   [10] Nagel, 'Equality', 112.

in others about abortion, capital punishment, suicide, euthanasia, bussing, reverse discrimination, corporal punishment of children, foreign aid, taking drugs, prayer in schools, pornography, and so forth. Liberals live with others and they cannot help learning about the details of their lives. They must respond to the details, and their personal and political reasons prompt incompatible responses. On the basis of their personal reasons, liberals must often find attitudes contrary to their own morally suspect. On the basis of their political reasons, however, they must respect these attitudes equally to their own, they must be guided by the thought that the 'attempt to give equal weight, in essential respects, to each person's point of view . . . might even be described as the mark of an enlightened ethic'.[11]

Liberals therefore are bound to be frequently double-minded about whether they ought to treat others in accordance with their personal or political reasons. They must routinely choose between responding to others in a way that reflects their own moral attitudes about what is good, bad, and indifferent and responding to them with equal respect, regardless of the moral qualities their lives and actions are thought to have. The point is not that liberals cannot choose. They can and they often do. The point is rather that liberals must choose and whatever they end up choosing, they will act contrary either to their personal or to their political reasons. This makes them double-minded.

5. *Unavoidable Serious Conflicts*

There is a way in which liberals may try to trivialize the conflict between their personal and political reasons. Their first step is to distinguish between the political and the personal levels of action. When they encounter concrete situations as participants, they are guided, as other people are, by their personal reasons. When they stand back and think about such situations, not as participants, but as reasonable people trying to figure out what structure their state ought to have, they are guided by their political reasons. Personal reasons may be said to motivate them directly on one level, political reasons motivate them indirectly on another.

[11] Vlastos, 'Justice and Equality', 43.

Their second step is to point out how innocuous are the actions that their political reasons lead them to take. The equal respect for all points of view translates into equal rights to vote, to use public facilities, such as roads, libraries, and parks, to express private views, to run for political office, and the like. Equal respect is just respect for the rights of citizenship in a liberal state that should be accorded to all citizens regardless of whether their points of view are thought to be good, bad, or indifferent. Equal respect is perfectly compatible with having personal reasons to find morally deplorable the manner in which some citizens exercise their rights.

This way of trying to defuse the conflict between the personal and the political, and thus avoid double-mindedness, will be seen as a failure once it is realized that equal respect implies much more than the innocuous rights mentioned above. In the case of the views liberals regard as racist, for example, it includes having an equal claim to the funding of research into racial superiority and inferiority, to having racist views fairly represented in the school curriculum, to recognizing it as one important element in some conceptions of the good, to licensing TV and radio stations that advocate such views, to permitting businesses to follow personnel policies that reflect them, to having private schools, clubs, organizations, apartment buildings, and housing developments that exclude blacks, and so forth. And, of course, if equal respect is taken seriously, it must be recognized to include equal respect and public support for the advocacy of anti-Semitism, slavery, cannibalism, sadism, the repatriation of blacks, the public flogging, mutilation, and execution of criminals, and similar views, just so long as they do not break the law.

If these implications of equal respect are recognized, then the attempt to trivialize the conflict between the personal and the political reasons of liberals will also be recognized to fail. Even if the personal and political levels of actions are to be distinguished, they will still place incompatible requirements on liberals. On the political level, liberals are committed to treating their fellow citizens with equal respect, to regarding their realization of their conception of the good as being as intrinsically valuable as anyone else's, including the liberals' own, even if they are racists, sexists, specieists, homophobes, anti-Semites, and the like. On the personal level, liberals find such lives and conduct morally unacceptable. So the distinction between the personal and the political levels of action does not help to resolve the conflict liberals face.

6. *Conflict and Toleration*

Consider now the possibility of assimilating the problems to which the conflict between personal and political reasons give rise to the familiar problems involved in toleration and its limits. The policy of toleration is one of the most attractive features of liberalism. The connection between liberalism and toleration is so close as to make 'the liberal attitude' almost synonymous with 'the tolerant attitude'.

Toleration is intentionally allowing, or refraining from preventing, actions which one dislikes or believes to be morally wrong. Questions of toleration arise in circumstances which are characterized by diversity, coupled with dislike or disapproval. These circumstances serve to distinguish toleration from liberty, and from indifference, where there need be no reference to dislike. Moreover, toleration requires that the tolerator have power to intervene, but refrains from using that power.[12]

Or, put more succinctly, if less circumspectly, 'To tolerate is first to condemn and then to put up with.'[13]

The obvious question to which this account of toleration gives rise is about what is involved in putting up with what has been condemned or in intentionally allowing or refraining from preventing actions that are believed to be morally wrong. The answers to it range from interpreting toleration as passive non-interference to active support. If toleration is taken to be non-interference, then it involves my thinking that what you do is bad, and, although you could be prevented from doing it, you are allowed to do it anyway. Toleration, however, may be taken to involve not merely non-interference with actions thought to be bad, but also active support, which calls for respect and resources equal to the respect and resources for actions that are thought to be good. And, according to active toleration, this ought to be done even if the available

---

[12] Susan Mendus, 'Toleration', Lawrence E. Becker (ed.), *Encyclopedia of Ethics*, ii (New York: Garland, 1992), 1251.

[13] Maurice Cranston, 'Toleration', in P. Edwards (ed.), *The Encyclopedia of Philosophy* (New York: Macmillan, 1967), viii. 143.

resources are scarce, so that the equal distribution of resources will not only foster actions thought to be bad, but also hinder actions thought to be good.

It is clear that the conflict of liberals between their personal and political reasons is not the conflict between intolerance motivated by personal reasons and passive toleration motivated by political reasons. For their political reasons explicitly enjoin liberals not merely to refrain from acting against what they dislike, disapprove, or condemn, but to recognize 'that everyone's life matters, and no one is more important than anyone else . . . that everyone counts the same';[14] that the 'attempt to give equal weight, in essential respects, to each person's point of view . . . might even be described as the mark of an enlightened ethic'.[15] Liberals are therefore committed by their political reasons not merely to passive non-interference, but to the active support of ways of being and acting that their personal reasons lead them to regard as bad.

The conflict between the personal and the political is thus about what should enjoy active toleration, which includes equal respect and corresponding shares of scare resources. Their political reasons impose the obligation on liberals to respect all law-abiding ways of living and acting equally. Respect is to foster all these ways of being and acting not merely by not interfering with them—that would be passive toleration—but by actively supporting them through the equal distribution, which often means redistribution, of tangible and intangible resources. This support is taken by liberals to be owed, in the name of justice, even, and especially, if the available resources are scarce, as they usually are.

One consequence of the liberal commitment to active toleration is that, provided only that they do not prevent other people from living and acting as they wish, members of the Ku Klux Klan and the American Civil Liberties Union, or of the Flat Earth Society and the American Academy of Sciences, paedophiles and pediatricians, producers of simulated pornographic snuff movies and Shakespeare's plays, victims of the Holocaust and those who deny its occurrence, are entitled to equal respect and to corresponding shares of scarce resources. No wonder that liberals are double-minded when faced with the absurd implications of their political commitments.

[14] Nagel, *Equality and Partiality*, 11.   [15] Nagel, 'Equality', 112.

If liberals advocated merely passive toleration, there would be no conflict between their personal and political reasons. Their personal reasons would lead them to regard some ways of being and acting as bad, but their political reasons would prevent them from interfering with them, so long as they are law-abiding, because they realize that as they can interfere with others, so others can interfere with them. The conflict between the personal and the political arises for liberals because they advocate the active toleration of all ways of living and acting, because that involves regarding their own personal reasons as counting no more than the personal reasons of those whose lives and actions they regard as bad, and because they are led by their political reasons to favour the equal distribution of scarce resources regardless of whether they personally regard the uses to which the resources are put as good, bad, or indifferent. Since they cannot ignore the powerful motivational force of their personal reasons to reject the powerful motivational force of their political reasons, they are doomed to a permanent state of double-mindedness. This state need not prevent them from practising active toleration, but, if they do, they are bound to act in ways contrary to their personal reasons.

7. *Privileging the Political*

There are three ways in which liberals may try to cope with the conflict between their personal and political reasons, and thus to avoid double-mindedness. One is to deny that the conflict occurs; another is to resolve it in favour of their personal reasons; and the last is to resolve it in favour of their political reasons. What has been said so far ought to be sufficient to show that the conflict is real and that its denial would be mistaken. In this respect at least, the present argument is in agreement with Nagel's and those of many liberals who agree with him.

Nor is there need to say much about resolving the conflict in favour of the personal. If liberals adopted a policy of allowing their personal reasons to override their political reasons whenever there was a conflict between them, they would cease to be liberals. Liberalism, after all, is a political position, and it requires its adherents to treat everyone with equal respect. If personal reasons overrode political reasons, then only those agents would be regarded with equal respect whose ways of living and acting conformed to the personal reasons of liberals. This would make the racial, religious, sexual, and other attitudes of liberals the standards of political correctness. Although such an arrangement would be congenial to liberals, they should try harder than they in fact do to resist the temptation to favour it. For it violates their own standards of legitimacy, namely, neutrality, making the right prior to the good, or being able to justify the arrangements to those who are subject to them. If liberals were to resist this temptation, they would have to become even-handed in their attitudes towards right- and left-wing hate speech, the condemnation and the advocacy of homosexuality, the Christian celebration and the radical feminist opposition to the conventional family, fundamentalism and atheism, cigarette-smoking and pot-smoking, and so forth. It will perhaps be agreed that liberals have some way to go to achieve even-handedness in these respects.

There remains the third option: to resolve the conflict between the personal and the political in favour of the political. This is by far the most widely accepted approach. Its chief inspiration is Rawls's work. He sums up his position as providing a standpoint which is

objective and expresses our autonomy . . . it enables us to be impartial. . . . to see our place in society from the perspective of this position is to see it *sub specie aeternitatis*. . . . The perspective of eternity is not a perspective from a certain place beyond the world, nor the point of view of a transcendent being; rather it is a certain form of thought and feeling that rational persons can adopt within the world. And having done so, they can . . . bring together into one scheme all individual perspectives and arrive together at regulative principles that can be affirmed by everyone as he lives by them, each from his own standpoint. Purity of heart, if one could attain it, would be to see clearly and to act with grace and self-command from this point of view.[16]

Rawls of course does not put forward this perspective as an alternative to what has been called here the personal. Even if liberals succeed in adopting this objective and impartial outlook, they will still have specific racial, religious, sexual, and other attitudes in respect to which they will differ from others. Rawls's point must be that when their personal reasons, prompted by these attitudes,

---

[16] Rawls, *A Theory of Justice*, 587.

conflict with their political reasons, prompted by the perspective Rawls favours, then the political reasons of liberals will or ought to override their personal reasons. Their hearts will not be pure in the sense that they will only one thing,[17] it will be pure in the sense that they will subordinate their personal attitudes to what Rawls regards as a higher purpose.

This is not a trivial point. Even if the political reasons of liberals are provided by this impartial perspective, and even if they override their personal reasons, their personal reasons will not be silenced. Liberals will continue to have formative racial, religious, sexual, and other attitudes. It is just that their political reasons will not permit them to act according to the personal reasons these attitudes provide, if they come into conflict. The conflict, in other words, will not disappear; it will be resolved by favouring one of the conflicting reasons. But the defeat of the personal by the political exacts the heavy psychological cost of acting inconsistently with their own formative attitudes towards what is good, bad, and indifferent, a cost that liberals must pay.

Liberals who cope with the conflict in this way will find themselves time after time unable to act on some of their deepest judgements of what is good or bad. Their political reasons will prevent them from acting according to their racial, religious, sexual, and other attitudes. For the actions that would reflect their attitudes would strengthen what they regard as good and weaken what they regard as bad. To do either, however, would be contrary to their political reason, which requires of them to treat all attitudes with equal respect, to support them with corresponding shares of scarce resources, and to maintain institutional arrangements that favour none of them over the others.

If liberals allow their political reasons to override their personal reasons, their actions will be contrary to some of their formative attitudes, so they will lack integrity; they could not commit themselves to any of their formative attitudes without reservation, lest they show too much or too little respect for ways of living and acting they regard as good and bad, so they will never be wholehearted; their formative attitudes, the core of their moral identity, the source of much of what they value in their lives, will be

---

[17] 'Purify your hearts ye double-minded,' says James 4: 8. And Kierkegaard glosses this passage as 'purity of heart is to will one thing' Søren Kierkegaard, *Purity of Heart*, trans. Donald V. Steele (New York: Harper, 1948), 53.

defeated, and defeated again, in the civil war of their soul, so their conceptions of the good will lack coherence. By allowing the political to override the personal, they will permanently maim themselves.

8. *The Groundlessness of Nagel's View*

Nagel is a liberal who thinks that there is a good reason to bear these high costs. The case he makes for it is perhaps the most influential one available: the political ought to override the personal because morality requires it. This is because the political is moral, the personal is non-moral, and decent and reasonable agents will realize that moral considerations ought to take precedence over non-moral considerations. What makes the political moral and the personal non-moral is impartiality. The political, as liberals view it, is impartial, and that is why it is moral, whereas the personal, varying with individual agents, is partial, and so it is non-moral.

Nagel is careful in formulating his case to leave room for non-moral personal attitudes and reasons within morality. Impartial institutional arrangements ought to take into account personal attitudes and reasons, which he acknowledges to be basic features of human motivation. Nevertheless, the political and the personal will come into conflict, and when that happens, impartial political reasons ought to override partial personal reasons. As he puts it: 'My own view is that . . . moral considerations are overriding. . . . While doing the right thing is part of living well it is not the whole of it, nor even the dominant part: because the impersonal standpoint that acknowledges the claims of morality is only one aspect of a normal individual among others.' There will be times, however, 'when doing the right thing may cost more in other aspects of the good life than it contributes to the good life in its own right'.[18] The content of morality that determines what the right thing to do is derives from a

universal standpoint that does not distinguish between oneself and anyone else [and] reveals general principles of conduct that apply to oneself because they apply to everyone. There is a natural tendency to identify this higher standpoint with the true self, weighed down perhaps by

[18] Nagel, *The View from Nowhere*, 197.

individualistic baggage. There is a further tendency to accord absolute priority in the governance of life to its judgments.[19]

'As a matter of moral conviction,' Nagel writes, 'I am inclined strongly to hope, and less strongly to believe, that the correct morality will always have a preponderance of reasons on its side, even though it needn't coincide with the good life.'[20]

According to this view, the conflict between the political and the personal, between the impartial and the partial, is a particular form of the familiar conflict between morality and personal preference. The liberal point of view, implying that impartial political reasons ought to override partial personal reasons, just is the moral point of view. To reject it by allowing personal reasons to override political reasons is a violation of one central requirement of morality. The reason for paying the heavy cost of having political reasons override personal reasons consequently is that morality requires it. This makes it hard to be moral, but that is how it is.[21]

It would be natural to expect that, having described his hopes, beliefs, and moral convictions, Nagel will go on to provide reasons for them. That, however, he does not do. His account is full of deft distinctions, perspicuous clarifications, elegant turns of phrase, descriptions of what it would be like if what he hopes and believes to be true were true, but the most he provides by way of an argument for why 'the correct morality' and 'this higher standpoint' ought to override personal reasons is that the 'demand on the ordinary individual—to overcome his own needs, commitments, and attachments in favor of impersonal claims that he can also recognize . . . does not necessarily mean that it would be irrational for someone who can do so to accept such demands, or rather impose them on himself'.[22] There is, however, a very large gap between saying that ordinary individuals may not be irrational in allowing impartial political reasons to override their personal reasons and saying that their impartial political reasons ought to override their personal reasons. It is one thing to say to the woman that it would not be irrational for her to squelch her indignation with her son's racist teacher and quite another that the higher standpoint of the correct morality requires her to squelch it.

---

[19] Nagel, *The View from Nowhere*, 199.   [20] Ibid.
[21] This account is based on Nagel, ibid., ch. 10.   [22] Ibid. 203.

The amazing feature of Nagel's position is that, instead of arguments designed to close the gap, he offers again and again frank admissions that he does not have them. These admissions, listed in chronological order, are as follows:

In 'Equality' Nagel writes:

There are two types of arguments for the intrinsic value of equality. . . . I am going to explore the individualistic one, because I think that is the type of argument that I think is most likely to succeed. It would provide a moral basis for the kind of liberal egalitarianism that seems to me plausible. I do not have such an argument.[23]

In 'Moral Conflict and Political Legitimacy' Nagel advances an epistemological argument for 'a higher-order framework of moral reasoning . . . which takes us outside ourselves to a standpoint that is independent of who we are'.[24] But he says about this argument in *Equality and Partiality* that 'while I still believe the conclusion, I no longer think that [the] "epistemological" argument works'.[25]

In *The View from Nowhere* he writes: 'This book is about a single problem: how to combine the perspective of a particular person inside the world with an objective view of that same world.' In moral theory, this becomes the question of 'how to combine objective and subjective values in the control of a single life'. However, 'I believe that the methods needed to understand to ourselves do not yet exist,' and 'I do not feel equal to the problems treated in this book. They seem to me to require an order of intelligence wholly different from mine.' In discussing in the same book the specific conflict between the political and the personal, Nagel writes:

The basic moral insight that objectively no one matters more than anyone else, and that this acknowledgment should be of fundamental importance to each of us . . . creates a conflict in the self too powerful to admit an easy resolution. I doubt that an appealing reconciliation of morality, rationality, and the good life can be achieved.[26]

---

[23] Nagel, 'Equality', 108.
[24] Nagel, 'Moral Conflict and Political Legitimacy', *Philosophy and Public Affairs*, 16 (1987), 229.
[25] Nagel, *Equality and Partiality*, 163 n. 49.
[26] Nagel, *The View from Nowhere*, 3, 8, 10, 12, and 205, respectively.

In *Equality and Partiality*, he writes:

My claim is that the problem of designing institutions that do justice to the equal importance of all persons, without making unacceptable demands on individuals, has not been solved—and that is partly because . . . the problem of the right relation between the personal and impersonal standpoints within each individual has not been solved.[27]

What follows from all this is that Nagel has provided no reason to think that morality requires resolving the conflict between the political and the personal in favour of the political. The need to provide reasons for these highly controversial claims is made particularly acute by there being very strong reasons for not resolving the conflict between the political and the personal in the way liberals favour. These reasons are the great psychological costs of doing so: the loss of integrity, wholeheartedness, and coherence; the inability of agents to live and act consistently with some of their formative attitudes; and being doomed to a permanent state of double-mindedness. Liberals demand of agents, in the name of morality, to pay these costs, while being unable to provide reasons why their demand ought to be met.

9. *Conclusion: The Liberal Dilemma*

The argument has throughout proceeded within the framework of liberal assumptions. It has accepted that the moral point of view is impartial; that political arrangements ought to be similarly impartial; that when such arrangements are in place, they will be neutral, the right will have priority over the good, and they will be justifiable to those who live under them. It has also accepted that the purpose of political arrangements is to enable individual agents to live according to their conceptions of the good. The argument has been that, given these assumptions, the political and the personal will conflict and that their conflict will be acute and frequent enough to put into serious jeopardy the chances of individual agents to live according to their conceptions of the good. Liberal political arrangements, therefore, fail to serve their purpose, even if the assumptions on which liberals proceed are accepted.

This criticism of liberalism may be expressed in the form of a

---

[27] Nagel, *Equality and Partiality*, 5.

dilemma about how to resolve the conflict between the political and the personal, a conflict that liberals acknowledge will occur. If liberals resolve the conflict in favour of the personal, then they will be inconsistent because they abandon their commitment to equal respect for all law-abiding individual conceptions of the good. If they resolve the conflict in favour of the political, then they will make lives worse rather than better, because they will require of agents to act, contrary to their conceptions of the good, so as to respect equally all conceptions of the good, regardless of how good, bad, or indifferent they find them. The double-mindedness of liberals is a symptom of this dilemma.

Is there a way out? Of course there is: the assumptions about impartiality and equal respect that give rise to the dilemma should be abandoned. That, however, means abandoning the most widely accepted contemporary version of liberalism. For some, this will be a loss; for others, a gain.[28,29]

[28] For a proposal as to what should replace liberalism, see John Kekes, *A Case for Conservatism* (Ithaca, NY: Cornell University Press, 1998).

[29] This paper has benefited from the comments of Eric Fried, Jonathan Mandle, Wallace Matson, Daniel Thero, and the editor of this volume. Their help is gratefully acknowledged. It should not be supposed that they agree with its argument or conclusion.

BIBLIOGRAPHY

ACKERMAN, BRUCE, *Social Justice and the Liberal State* (New Haven: Yale University Press, 1980).

ALTHAM, J. E. J., 'Reflection and Confidence', in J. E. J. Altham and R. Harrison (eds.), *World, Mind, and Ethics: Essays on the Ethical Philosophy of Bernard Williams* (Cambridge: Cambridge University Press, 1995).

ANSCOMBE, G. E. M., 'Modern Moral Philosophy', in Anscombe, *Ethics, Religion and Politics: Collected Philosophical Papers*, iii (Oxford: Blackwell, 1981).

ARISTOTLE, *Eudemian Ethics.*

——*Nicomachean Ethics.*

AUSTIN, J. L., *Philosophical Papers*, 1st edn. (Oxford: Clarendon Press, 1961).

AYERS, MICHAEL, *Locke*, 2 vols. (London: Routledge, 1991).

BENNETT, JONATHAN, 'The Conscience of Huckleberry Finn', *Philosophy*, 49 (1974), 123–34; repr. in P. Singer (ed.), *Ethics* (Oxford: Oxford University Press, 1994).

BERGER, JOHN, *Ways of Seeing* (London: BBC Books; Harmondsworth: Penguin, 1972).

BLACKBURN, SIMON, 'Error and the Phenomenology of Value' (1985), in Blackburn, *Essays in Quasi-Realism* (Oxford: Oxford University Press, 1993).

——*Essays in Quasi-Realism* (Oxford: Oxford University Press, 1993).

——'Making Ends Meet', a Discussion of B. Williams, *Ethics and the Limits of Philosophy*, *Philosophical Books*, 27 (1986), 193–203.

——'Morals and Modals' (1987), in Blackburn, *Essays in Quasi-Realism* (Oxford: Oxford University Press, 1993).

——'Realism, Quasi, or Queasy?', in J. Haldane and C. Wright (eds.), *Reality, Representation and Projection* (New York: Oxford University Press, 1993).

——*Ruling Passions: A Theory of Practical Reasoning* (Oxford: Clarendon Press, 1998).

——*Spreading the Word: Groundings in the Philosophy of Language* (Oxford: Clarendon Press, 1984).

——'The Flight to Reality', in R. Hursthouse, G. Lawrence, and W. Quinn (eds.), *Virtues and Reasons* (Oxford: Clarendon Press, 1995).

BLUM, LAWRENCE, *Moral Perception and Particularity* (Cambridge: Cambridge University Press, 1994).

COHEN, G. A., *Karl Marx's Theory of History: A Defence* (Oxford: Oxford University Press, 1978).

—— review of A. Wood, *Karl Marx*, *Mind*, 92 (1983), 440–5.

COTTINGHAM, JOHN, *Philosophy and the Good Life: Reason and the Passions in Greek, Cartesian and Psychoanalytic Ethics* (Cambridge: Cambridge University Press, 1998).

CRAIG, EDWARD, *Knowledge and the State of Nature* (Oxford: Clarendon Press, 1990).

CRANSTON, MAURICE, 'Toleration', in P. Edwards (ed.), *The Encyclopedia of Philosophy*, vol. viii (New York: Macmillan, 1967).

DEVLIN, PATRICK, *The Enforcement of Morals* (Oxford: Oxford University Press, 1965).

DURKHEIM, E., *Moral Education* (Glencoe, Ill.: Free Press, 1961).

—— 'The Teaching of Morality in Schools', *Journal of Moral Education*, 24 (1995), 19–37.

DWORKIN, RONALD, 'In Defense of Equality', *Social Philosophy and Policy*, 1 (1983), 24–40.

—— *A Matter of Principle* (Cambridge, Mass.: Harvard University Press, 1985).

—— 'Objectivity and Truth: You'd Better Believe It', *Philosophy and Public Affairs*, 25 (1996), 87–139.

—— *Taking Rights Seriously* (Cambridge, Mass.: Harvard University Press, 1977).

EAGLETON, TERRY, *The Ideology of the Aesthetic* (Oxford: Blackwell, 1990).

ELSTER, JON, *Making Sense of Marx* (Cambridge: Cambridge University Press, 1985).

FOOT, PHILIPPA, 'Morality as a System of Hypothetical Imperatives', *Philosophical Review*, 81 (1972), 305–16.

FOUCAULT, MICHEL, 'Nietzsche, Genealogy, History', in Foucault, *Language, Counter-Memory, Practice*, ed. D. Bouchard, trans. D. Bouchard and S. Simon (Ithaca, NY: Cornell University Press, 1977).

—— *Power/Knowledge: Selected Interviews and Other Writings 1972–1977*, ed. C. Gordon, trans. C. Gordon, L. Marshall, J. Mepham, and K. Soper (Hemel Hempstead: Harvester Wheatsheaf, 1980).

FRAZER, E., HORNSBY, J., and LOVIBOND, S. (eds.), *Ethics: A Feminist Reader* (Oxford: Blackwell, 1992).

FREUD, SIGMUND, *The Standard Edition of the Complete Psychological Works of Sigmund Freud*, ed. J. Strachey, 24 vols. (London: Hogarth Press, 1955–74).

FRICKER, MIRANDA, 'Pluralism without Postmodernism', in M. Fricker and J. Hornsby (eds.), *The Cambridge Companion to Feminism in Philosophy* (Cambridge: Cambridge University Press, 2000).

GATENS, MOIRA, *Imaginary Bodies: Ethics, Power and Corporeality* (London: Routledge, 1996).

GEUSS, RAYMOND, *The Idea of a Critical Theory* (Cambridge: Cambridge University Press, 1981).

GIBBARD, ALLAN, review of Simon Blackburn, *Essays in Quasi-Realism*, *Mind*, 105 (1996), 331–3.

GILBERT, MARGARET, *On Social Facts* (London: Routledge, 1989).

GILLIGAN, C., *In a Different Voice: Psychological Theory and Women's Development* (Cambridge, Mass.: Harvard University Press, 1982).

HARE, R. M., 'Ethical Theory and Utilitarianism', in A. Sen and B. Williams (eds.), *Utilitarianism and Beyond* (Cambridge: Cambridge University Press; Paris: Éditions de la Maison des Sciences de l'Homme, 1982).

HARMAN, GILBERT, *The Nature of Morality* (Oxford: Oxford University Press, 1977).

HEGEL, G. W. F., *The Philosophy of Right*, trans. T. M. Knox (Oxford: Oxford University Press, 1967).

HOMER, *The Iliad*, trans. R. Fagles (Harmondsworth: Penguin, 1992).

HUME, DAVID, *Enquiry concerning the Principles of Morals* (1777), ed. L. A. Selby-Bigge (Oxford: Oxford University Press, 1986).

——*A Treatise of Human Nature*, ed. L. A. Selby-Bigge (Oxford: Clarendon Press, 1888).

HURLEY, SUSAN, 'Objectivity and Disagreement', in T. Honderich (ed.), *Morality and Objectivity: A Tribute to J. L. Mackie* (London: Routledge & Kegan Paul, 1985).

JAMES, SUSAN, *The Content of Social Explanation* (Cambridge: Cambridge University Press, 1984).

——'The Power of Spinoza: Feminist Conjunctions', interview with Moira Gatens and Genevieve Lloyd, *Women's Philosophy Review*, 19 (1998), 6–28.

KEKES, JOHN, *Against Liberalism* (Ithaca, NY: Cornell University Press, 1997).

——*A Case for Conservatism* (Ithaca, NY: Cornell University Press, 1998).

KIERKEGAARD, SØREN, *Purity of Heart*, trans. Donald V. Steele (New York: Harper, 1948).

KRISTEVA, JULIA, *Black Sun* (New York: Columbia University Press, 1989).

LACLOS, PIERRE CHODERLOS DE, *Les Liaisons dangereuses* (Paris: Flammarion, 1981).

LARMORE, CHARLES E., *Patterns of Moral Complexity* (Cambridge: Cambridge University Press, 1987).

LE DŒUFF, MICHÈLE, *The Philosophical Imaginary*, trans. C. Gordon (London: Athlone Press, 1989).

LOVIBOND, SABINA, *Realism and Imagination in Ethics* (Oxford: Blackwell, 1983).

——'Ethical Upbringing: From Connivance to Cognition', in S. Lovibond and S. G. Williams (eds.), *Essays for David Wiggins: Identity, Truth and Value* (Oxford: Blackwell, 1996).

LUKES, STEVEN, 'Marxism, Morality and Justice', in G. H. R. Parkinson (ed.), *Marx and Marxisms* (Cambridge: Cambridge University Press, 1982).

MACEDO, STEPHEN, *Liberal Virtues* (Oxford: Oxford University Press, 1990).

MACINTYRE, ALASDAIR, *After Virtue: A Study in Moral Theory* (London: Duckworth, 1981).

MCINTYRE, ALISON, 'Is Akratic Action Always Irrational?", in O. Flanagan and A. O. Rorty (eds.) *Identity, Character, and Morality: Essays in Moral Psychology* (Cambridge, Mass.: MIT Press, 1990).

MACKIE, J. L., *Ethics: Inventing Right and Wrong* (Harmondsworth: Penguin, 1977).

——'A Refutation of Morals', *Australasian Journal of Philosophy*, 24 (1946), 77–90.

MARX, K., 'The British Rule in India' (1853), in Marx, *Political Writings*, ii, ed. D. Fernbach (Harmondsworth: Penguin, 1973).

——*Capital*, i (Harmondsworth: Penguin, 1977).

——*Critique of the Gotha Programme*, in K. Marx and F. Engels, *Selected Works*, iii (Moscow: Progress Publishers, 1970).

——*Critique of Hegel's 'Philosophy of Right'*, ed. J. O'Malley (Cambridge: Cambridge University Press, 1970).

——'Excerpts from James Mill's *Elements of Political Economy*', in Marx, *Early Writings*, ed. L. Colletti (Harmondsworth: Penguin, 1975).

——Letter to Dr Kugelmann, in Marx, *The Civil War in France* (New York: International Publishers, 1940).

——'On the Jewish Question', in Marx, *Early Writings*, ed. L. Colletti (Harmondsworth: Penguin, 1975).

——'Towards a Critique of the Hegelian Philosophy of Right: Introduction', in Marx, *Critique of Hegel's 'Philosophy of Right'*, ed. J. O'Malley (Cambridge: Cambridge University Press, 1970).

——and F. ENGELS, *The German Ideology*, trans. W. Lough, ed. and abridged C. J. Arthur (London: Lawrence & Wishart; New York: International Publishers, 1970).

MENDUS, SUSAN, 'Toleration', in Lawrence E. Becker (ed.), *Encyclopedia of Ethics*, ii (New York: Garland, 1992).

MEYERSON, DENISE, *False Consciousness* (Oxford: Oxford University Press, 1991).

MILL, J. S., *Utilitarianism*, ed. M. Warnock (Glasgow: Collins/Fontana, 1978).

MOORE, A. W., 'Can Reflection Destroy Knowledge?', *Ratio*, new ser., 4 (1991), 97–107.

NAGEL, THOMAS, 'The Absurd', in Nagel, *Mortal Questions* (Cambridge: Cambridge University Press, 1979).

——'Equality', in Nagel, *Mortal Questions* (Cambridge: Cambridge University Press, 1979).

—— *Equality and Partiality* (New York: Oxford University Press, 1991).

—— 'Moral Conflict and Political Legitimacy', *Philosophy and Public Affairs*, 16 (1987), 215–40.

—— *The View from Nowhere* (New York: Oxford University Press, 1986).

NIELSEN, K., 'Marxism and the Moral Point of View', *American Philosophical Quarterly*, 24 (1987), 295–306.

—— and PATTEN, S. (eds.), *Marx and Morality, Canadian Journal of Philosophy*, suppl. vol. 7 (1981).

NIETZSCHE, FRIEDRICH, *Beyond Good and Evil*, trans. and ed. Walter Kaufmann (New York: Random House, 1966).

—— *Beyond Good and Evil*, trans. R. J. Hollingdale (Harmondsworth: Penguin, 1990).

—— *Daybreak*, trans. R. J. Hollingdale (Cambridge: Cambridge University Press, 1982).

—— *On the Genealogy of Morality*, trans. K. Ansell-Pearson (Cambridge: Cambridge University Press, 1994).

—— *On the Genealogy of Morals*, trans. Walter Kaufmann and R. J. Hollingdale (New York: Random House, 1967).

POLANYI, K., *The Great Transformation* (New York: Rinehart, 1944).

PRICE, A. W., *Mental Conflict* (London: Routledge, 1995).

—— 'On Criticising Values', in A. O'Hear (ed.), *Philosophy, the Good, the True and the Beautiful* (Cambridge: Cambridge University Press, 2000).

—— review of Simon Blackburn, *Essays in Quasi-Realism*, *Utilitas*, 7 (1995), 172–5.

—— 'Three Types of Projectivism', in J. Hopkins and A. Savile (eds.), *Psychoanalysis, Mind and Art: Perspectives on Richard Wollheim* (Oxford: Blackwell, 1992).

RAILTON, PETER, 'Reply to David Wiggins', in J. Haldane and C. Wright (eds.), *Reality, Representation and Projection* (New York: Oxford University Press, 1993).

RAWLS, JOHN, *Political Liberalism* (New York: Columbia University Press, 1993).

—— *A Theory of Justice* (Cambridge, Mass.: Harvard University Press, 1971).

RORTY, RICHARD, *Contingency, Irony, and Solidarity* (Cambridge: Cambridge University Press, 1989).

—— *Truth and Progress: Philosophical Papers*, iii (Cambridge: Cambridge University Press, 1998).

ROSEN, MICHAEL, *On Voluntary Servitude* (Cambridge: Polity Press, 1996).

ROUSSEAU, JEAN-JACQUES, *Du contrat social*, ed. François Bouchardy (Paris: Egloff, 1946).

RYAN, ALAN, 'Justice, Exploitation, and the End of Morality', in J. D. G. Evans (ed.), *Moral Philosophy and Contemporary Problems* (Cambridge: Cambridge University Press, 1987).

SANTAYANA, GEORGE, *Winds of Doctrine* (London: J. K. Dent, 1913).

SCANLON, THOMAS, 'Contractualism and Utilitarianism', in A. Sen and B. Williams (eds.), *Utilitarianism and Beyond* (Cambridge: Cambridge University Press; Paris: Éditions de la Maison des Sciences de l'Homme, 1982).

—— 'The Significance of Choice', in Sterling M. McMurrin (ed.), *The Tanner Lectures on Human Values*, viii (Salt Lake City: University of Utah Press, 1988).

SCHEFFLER, SAMUEL, *Human Morality* (New York: Oxford University Press, 1992).

SCHIFFER, STEPHEN, 'A Paradox of Desire', *American Philosophical Quarterly*, 13 (1976), 195–203.

SCHNEEWIND, J. B., *Sidgwick's Ethics and Victorian Moral Philosophy* (Oxford: Oxford University Press, 1977).

SHAND, ALEXANDER, *The Foundations of Character, Being a Study of the Tendencies of the Emotions and Sentiments* (London: Macmillan, 1920).

SHER, GEORGE, *Beyond Neutrality* (New York: Cambridge University Press, 1997).

SIDGWICK, HENRY, *The Methods of Ethics*, 7th edn. (London: Macmillan, 1967).

SKILLEN, A. J., 'The Ethical Neutrality of Science and the Method of Abstraction: The Case of Political Economy', *Philosophical Forum*, 11 (1980), 215–33.

—— *Ruling Illusions* (Hassocks: Harvester Press, 1977; Aldershot: Gregg Revivals, 1993).

—— 'Workers' Interests and the Proletarian Ethic: Conflicting Strains in Marxian Thought', in K. Nielsen and S. Patten (eds.), *Marx and Morality, Canadian Journal of Philosophy*, suppl. vol. 7 (1981), 155–70.

STRAWSON, P. F., *Freedom and Resentment and Other Essays* (London: Methuen, 1974).

—— 'Perception and its Objects', in G. F. Macdonald (ed.), *Perception and Identity* (London: Macmillan, 1979).

—— *Skepticism and Naturalism: Some Varieties* (London: Methuen, 1987).

THOMPSON, JOHN B., *Studies in the Theory of Ideology* (Cambridge: Polity Press, 1984).

VELLEMAN, DAVID, 'The Guise of the Good', *Noûs*, 26 (1992), 3–26.

VLASTOS, GREGORY, 'Justice and Equality', in Richard B. Brandt (ed.), *Social Justice* (Englewood Cliffs, NJ: Prentice-Hall, 1962).

WALDRON, J., 'When Justice Replaces Affection: The Need for Rights', in Waldron, *Liberal Rights* (Cambridge: Cambridge University Press, 1993).

WALZER, MICHAEL, *Thick and Thin* (Notre Dame, Ind.: University of Notre Dame Press, 1994).

WHITFORD, MARGARET, *Luce Irigaray: Philosophy in the Feminine* (London: Routledge, 1991).

WIGGINS, DAVID, *Needs, Values, Truth*, 2nd edn. (Oxford: Blackwell, 1991).

—— 'Truth, Invention, and the Meaning of Life', *Proceedings of the British Academy*, 62 (1976), 331–78; rev. in Wiggins, *Needs, Values, Truth*, 3rd edn. (Oxford: Clarendon Press, 1998).

WILLIAMS, BERNARD, 'Deciding to Believe', in Williams, *Problems of the Self* (Cambridge: Cambridge University Press, 1973).

—— 'Do Not Disturb', review of Martha Nussbaum, *The Therapy of Desire, London Review of Books*, 16/20 (20 Oct. 1994), 25–6.

—— *Ethics and the Limits of Philosophy* (London: Fontana, 1985).

—— 'Philosophy as a Humanistic Discipline', Third Royal Institute of Philosophy Annual Lecture, *Philosophy*, 75 (2000).

—— 'The Point of View of the Universe: Sidgwick and the Ambitions of Ethics', in Williams, *Making Sense of Humanity* (Cambridge: Cambridge University Press, 1995).

—— 'Replies', in J. Altham and R. Harrison (eds.), *World, Mind, and Ethics: Essays on the Ethical Philosophy of Bernard Williams* (Cambridge: Cambridge University Press, 1995).

—— *Shame and Necessity* (Berkeley: University of California Press, 1993).

—— 'Truth in Ethics', *Ratio*, 8 (1995), 227–42.

—— 'Who Needs Ethical Knowledge?', in A. Phillips Griffiths (ed.), *Ethics*, Royal Institute of Philosophy suppl. 35 (1993), 213–22.

WOLLHEIM, RICHARD, 'Correspondence, Projective Properties, and Expression in the Arts', in Wollheim, *The Mind and its Depths* (Cambridge, Mass.: Harvard University Press, 1993).

—— *Painting as an Art* (London: Thames & Hudson, 1987).

—— *The Thread of Life* (Cambridge: Cambridge University Press, 1984).

WOOD, A., *Karl Marx* (London: Routledge & Kegan Paul, 1981).

—— 'Marx against Morality', in P. Singer (ed.), *A Companion to Ethics* (Oxford: Blackwell, 1991).

WRIGHT, CRISPIN, review of Simon Blackburn, *Spreading the Word, Mind*, 94 (1985), 310–19.

INDEX